The Brevard Rosenwald School

CONTRIBUTIONS TO SOUTHERN APPALACHIAN STUDIES

1. *Memoirs of Grassy Creek:*
Growing Up in the Mountains on the Virginia–North Carolina Line.
Zetta Barker Hamby. 1997

2. *The Pond Mountain Chronicle:*
Self-Portrait of a Southern Appalachian Community.
Leland R. Cooper and Mary Lee Cooper. 1997

3. *Traditional Musicians of the Central Blue Ridge:*
Old Time, Early Country, Folk and
Bluegrass Label Recording Artists, with Discographies.
Marty McGee. 2000

4. *W.R. Trivett, Appalachian Pictureman:*
Photographs of a Bygone Time.
Ralph E. Lentz. 2001

5. *The People of the New River:*
Oral Histories from the Ashe, Alleghany and
Watauga Counties of North Carolina.
Leland R. Cooper and Mary Lee Cooper. 2001

6. *John Fox, Jr., Appalachian Author.*
Bill York. 2003

7. *The Thistle and the Brier:*
Historical Links and Cultural Parallels Between Scotland and Appalachia.
Richard Blaustein. 2003

8. *Tales from Sacred Wind:*
Coming of Age in Appalachia. The Cratis Williams Chronicles.
Cratis D. Williams. 2003

9. *Willard Gayheart, Appalachian Artist.*
Willard Gayheart and Donia S. Eley. 2003

10. *The Forest City Lynching of 1900:*
Populism, Racism, and White Supremacy in Rutherford County, North Carolina.
J. Timothy Cole. 2003

11. *The Brevard Rosenwald School:*
Black Edcuation and Community Building
in a Southern Appalachian Town, 1920–1966
Betty Jamerson Reed. 2004

The Brevard Rosenwald School

Black Education and Community Building in a Southern Appalachian Town, 1920–1966

BETTY JAMERSON REED

CONTRIBUTIONS TO SOUTHERN APPALACHIAN STUDIES, 11

McFarland & Company, Inc., Publishers
Jefferson, North Carolina, and London

LIBRARY OF CONGRESS CATALOGUING-IN-PUBLICATION DATA

Reed, Betty Jamerson, 1937–
    The Brevard Rosenwald School : Black education and community building in a southern Appalachian town, 1920–1966 / Betty Jamerson Reed.
        p.   cm.—(Contributions to southern Appalachian studies ; 11)
    Includes bibliographical references and index.

    ISBN-13: 978-0-7864-1743-8
    (softcover : 50# alkaline paper) ∞

    1. Brevard Rosenwald School (Brevard, N.C.)—History. 2. African Americans—Education—North Carolina—Brevard. I. Title. II. Series.
LC2852.B73R44   2004
371.829'96073—dc22   2004001523

British Library cataloguing data are available

©2004 Betty Jamerson Reed. All rights reserved

No part of this book may be reproduced or transmitted in any form or by any means, electronic or mechanical, including photocopying or recording, or by any information storage and retrieval system, without permission in writing from the publisher.

On the cover: *(Top)* Rosenwald School; *(bottom)* Brevard Colored School

Manufactured in the United States of America

McFarland & Company, Inc., Publishers
   Box 611, Jefferson, North Carolina 28640
      www.mcfarlandpub.com

This work is gratefully dedicated to the citizens of
Brevard's Rosenwald community
for their unflinching pursuit of justice
and for their tireless struggle to claim
their rights as citizens.
In the five years that I have researched
the school's history, many have become
my friends and my true neighbors.

Acknowledgments

THIS IS NOT MY STORY, but my life has been enriched as I collected the saga of the "black experience" in Brevard and Transylvania County, North Carolina. I am grateful to the folks in Brevard's African American community for sharing their rich history with me. I was a pest in their midst, constantly begging, prodding for more information, but they were endlessly patient. For those who graciously allowed me to copy personal photos, I am deeply indebted.

My attempt to weave together the various facets of this tale has been intense, but the insight that I have gleaned from this remarkable community has made me a wiser person. The warm reception that I found in the homes of Selena Robinson, Nathaniel Hall, Samuel Howell, James Gardin, Bernetha Owens, Annie Marie Hailey, and Brenda Hunt was inspiring. With laughter and pathos, they freely shared their knowledge of life in the community during the twentieth century.

Howard and Juanita Spanogle became my professional consultants and made pertinent suggestions. Juanita photographed the places and personalities within the community. Howard contributed his literary skill and educational experience. Their expertise helped me tremendously.

Agnes Wilson and Nathaniel Hall read the original document to ensure accuracy. My special thanks also go to Lois and William Wynn, Kay Howell, Robbie Gardin, Jesse and Dorothy Mock, Ethel Mills, Frederick Gordon, Samuel Raper, Diane Gardin, Stella Trapp, Alice Robinson, Vincent Gordon, Glenda Sansosti, Heidi Buchanan, Lisa Sheffield, Barbara Freeman, Jan Osborne, Kris Blair, Daniel Owens, Carolyn Ives, Cliff and Nancy Brookshire, N.A. Miller, Lori Jacques, LaRue Betsill, Roberta Ashley, Pat Austin, Jenny Hunter, and Joyce Owens. Their encouragement and the information they provided were extremely valuable.

Thanks also to Paul Pickett for boosting my spirits. Staffs at the archival collections at Winston-Salem State University, North Carolina State Archives, Fisk University Special Collections, Transylvania County Archives, and Transylvania Public Library tracked down obscure bits of information.

Any worthwhile project requires help from God as well as encouragement of family, of friends, and of colleagues. A strong measure of gratitude goes to my family, whose assistance was invaluable. My son David took photographs and used his considerable technical knowledge to assist me. Support and interest offered by Floyd and Vanessa as well as by Sara-Ann and Caleb spurred my efforts. My husband Bill kept my goals realistic and offered comments about the manuscript.

Contents

Acknowledgments	ix
Introduction	1
1. Sociological Foundations	5
2. Ideological Foundations	19
3. Educational Transformation	34
4. Pedagogical Traditions	60
5. Achievement of Integration	100
6. Adjustment to Integration	120
7. Patterns of Success	136
8. Revitalization of Community	160
9. Contributions to Education	172
Appendix A: Timeline	185
Appendix B: Methodology	195
Appendix C: Documents	200
Appendix D: Transylvania County School Superintendents, 1877–2003	211
Selected Bibliography	213
Index	223

Introduction

IN 1910, IN THE NOW QUAINT town of Brevard, North Carolina, a rural school opened its doors to welcome eager and not-so-eager learners. That school, which became the Brevard Rosenwald School, welcomed only African American students, as dictated by the segregation prevalent in western North Carolina in the early twentieth century. Though it existed because of segregation, the school became a positive force. Nostalgia can dull the pain of the past and rewrite history, but documentation details the school's vitality and impact, which still affects today's educators.

Officially, the Rosenwald School opened its doors as an educational institution in 1920, an expansion of the Brevard #2 Colored School that had opened in 1910. Unofficially, both began in the late 1800s. Parents united to provide an education for their children, organizing assemblies in churches, log cabins and frame buildings. (Judson Corn identified schools for colored children in Districts 1, 2, and 3 in 1897.)

In a 1919 letter to state school administrator N.C. Newbold, Principal G.W. Thompson asked if money from the Rosenwald Fund would be available to improve the school building. The fund was part of an effort by Julius Rosenwald, then the president of Sears, Roebuck and Company, to help improve educational facilities for blacks. Communities receiving support from the Rosenwald Fund were required to make their own monetary contributions and to maintain the structures, and the schools were incorporated into the local school systems. In this way Rosenwald hoped to foster a better relationship between the black and white communities, uniting them in a common cause. Hundreds of small schools and other community buildings were built across North Carolina and elsewhere using money from the Rosenwald Fund.

Expansion of the Brevard #2 School began in 1920; minutes from meetings at the time mention plans for new rooms, two cloakrooms, and new desks for the teacher and students. The outside of the building was cleaned and painted, and the name was changed to Brevard #2 Rosenwald School. It would provide a segregated education for black children until it burned down in 1941. Rosenwald students met in churches until 1948, when a new building was completed. Token integration began in 1962 in Transylvania County, but de facto segregation — and the Rosenwald School — would linger for several more years. The school closed its doors after the 1965 school year; in 1967 it reopened as an education center for the school district.

The Brevard Rosenwald School in Western North Carolina was a microcosm of the community it served. Teachers and their pupils lived on the same streets, shopped in the same stores, and worshipped at the same churches. They also viewed one another's laundry flapping in the breeze. There was, however, a limited intimacy in their relationships.

Always, the teachers performed as professionals, leaders who were training learners. Their pupils knew that the standards at home endorsed the standards at school. In almost every instance, parents totally supported the teachers' decisions. Teachers and parents served on the same committees, confronted similar social and economic problems, rubbed elbows with family members at the same places of business, responded to the same sermons, and sought one another's advice about the right course of action in daily situations.

Informal opportunities to learn allowed a casual, almost automatic, intake of knowledge. Families read together from the Bible and quizzed one another around the fire. Eager children hiked miles to earn merit badges in scouting. Ministers appealed to the youth of their congregations to seek learning as a way to honor God and as an avenue to ascertain the greater truth. Routine interaction guaranteed that educators received support for their efforts from the total community.

The Brevard Rosenwald School, a small community institution of the past, can serve as an example to modern communities trying to deal with today's educational issues. Every resident of the neighborhood took an interest in the school as the hub of the community. The school staff kept the public aware of resources needed to improve the quality of instruction, and the public willingly sacrificed personal resources to provide enriching experiences for their children.

Now, lessons of history are honored by their use as topics of dialogue and as sources of qualitative and quantitative data. A 2002 Community Development Block Grant for the area surrounding the Brevard Rosenwald School helped reawaken interest in the school's history. While the past enlightens the present, the present often reveals the contributions of the past. By studying the school's history, both teachers and parents can discover the importance of the community. Then, parents yearned for the best for their children, the same as they do now, but the proximity of neighbors, sharing similar experiences and conditions, nurtured concern for one another when difficulties arose. The impact of the Brevard Rosenwald School continues only as long as people hear the historical voices, those of teachers, parents, and students.

This study allows people to speak about their history, most particularly from 1920 to 1966. It brings to life a record of their stories, narratives that capture educational goals, pursuits, and accomplishments. There can be no returning to the past, but the present can provide a different context for attitudes and achievements worth keeping. Individuals can never escape the influence of parents and teachers, any more than they can ignore the influence of the past on the present. By considering past problems—whether social, economic, or educational—and strategies used to solve those problems, the present generation can empower itself to act with wisdom. The history of the Rosenwald School in Brevard can teach valuable lessons about the past and help inform the future.

The journey back to the Brevard Rosenwald School took me on assorted paths: interviews with teachers and a 100-year-old principal, conversations with alumni, e-mails to professional historians, study of Transylvania County Board of Education minutes, research at specialized libraries in Winston-Salem and Raleigh as well as at Fisk University in Nashville, investigation of local newspaper morgues, documentation via obituaries and cemeteries in the Brevard area, searches on the Internet, questionnaires circulated through the mail, analysis of theses and dissertations, survey of the history of education for Negroes, and constant application of the tenets of collecting oral histories as practiced by scholars at Western Carolina University.

But more dramatic is how the journey began. I learned to listen. Five men kidnapped my mind by "telling tales out of school." It began when I substituted for an adult education class at the Pisgah Forest Ranger Center near Brevard. Only five male students were present, two blacks and three whites. Like the teenagers I had taught for four decades, all five declared that it was not a good day to do "book work." Encouraging a focus on oral communication skills, I suggested that they tell stories about their school experiences. All were interesting, and I hastily scribbled notes about each one.

However, James Gardin's and Samuel Howell's memories of their children being bused from Brevard to Hendersonville angered me. The unfairness of that experience made me furious. When the two men were unable to answer all my questions, they suggested that I call Mrs. Ethel K. Mills, who turned out to be nearly 100 years old then. Soon after the class was over,

I stopped at the home of Mrs. Mills, who invited me into her house to talk about the Brevard Rosenwald School. An almost instantaneous bonding occurred. She was so easy to talk to. Although advanced in years, her mind was clear and her ability to relate her experiences at the school was unimpaired.

The more I listened, the more interested I became in pursuing the story of the Brevard Rosenwald School. That resulted in an increasing passion to find those voices that would bring the school to life. Up to that point, my acquaintance with the Rosenwald heritage consisted solely of recognizing Rosenwald Lane as the site of Transylvania County's central public education offices, the Eugene M. Morris Education Center. A chance substitute teaching experience had aroused my curiosity to such an extent that I shelved other projects and focused intensely on researching that small Rosenwald School.

Although the bulk of research for this history extends from the early 1920s to 1966, the saga of the Rosenwald School includes all previous efforts to provide learning experiences for African American children in Transylvania County. Schools for blacks existed as early as the nineteenth century. In 1910, the Brevard Colored School was built. Nine years later Principal G. W. Thompson requested funds for improving that building. The money came from the community, from public agencies, and from the Rosenwald Fund. In the early 1940s, the razing of the school by a fire provided additional challenges for public education of African American children. Later, with the Civil Rights movement, came the demise of the Brevard Rosenwald School, but the influence of that institution continues.

For me, the journey was a road less traveled. But it soon became a road well traveled with great satisfaction, one with more paths as I discover additional references to the school's history. Now I view the gaps in the story of the Brevard Rosenwald School as an indication that there is still more to recall, especially more ways to benefit from the hard-won victories of a determined community of learners.

Chapter 1

Sociological Foundations

BEFORE SUBURBAN SPRAWL dominated the landscape, a suburb existed in the small mountain town of Brevard, North Carolina. Called "Colored Town" by residents, the neighborhood was home to a thriving community of African Americans. Within its confines, supportive family interaction, bustling economic activity, and lively community involvement existed. Of greater importance, the education of children was a tri-institutional effort — a trinity of home, church, and school united to enlighten the community's children and youth.

The hub of the community was the school, and residents viewed education as a pathway to a more promising future for their children and grandchildren. Racial discrimination was the norm. Nevertheless, sheltered in the cocoon of their section of town, life was amazingly good. As a result, the vigor of Brevard's African American community intensified the origin, the development, and the expansion of Brevard Rosenwald School. Voices of the past echo memories that help reconstruct the full impact of the neighborhood.

Historically, the community was an extended one, embracing the acres surrounding the school building but extending to more remote neighborhoods, known as Pinnacle, Frog Bottom, Glade Creek, and French Broad. Gertrude Gash, whose 107th birthday celebration in July 2002 was a major event in Transylvania County, fondly recalled spending many hours of her childhood playing with her cousins and "buddies" uptown in Brevard though she lived at Glade Creek, about ten miles from the center of town. Her children, after completing the scholastic program at nearby Glade Creek School, traveled to Brevard to take advantage of additional years of academic study available there (interview, June 25, 2002).

Students whose homes were located in the Pinnacle area, which is near the present site of the Brevard Music Center, walked to school by way of Probart Street. Pupils residing in Frog Bottom, between the courthouse and the Brevard College campus, trekked across town and then hiked up a steep wooded area to reach the school. Traveling from Glade Creek and French Broad required motorized transportation: cars, trucks, or buses. An occasional ride to Brevard from Glade Creek via train cost ten cents, according to Gash (interview).

As in all towns, schools and churches provided the community with opportunities for both learning and worship. Businesses in the neighborhood also contributed to genial interaction of citizens in the black community. Local stores provided products to purchase for daily needs as well as nonsegregated locations for friendly social exchanges. There, business translated into vigor, energy, and vitality. Stories about the past pervade the memories of the neighborhood's citizens. They associate local streets with specific traditions and share tales about men and women who built the school and the community.

Local place names bring color to recollections of the past. Greasy Corner is located at the juncture of Carver, Oakdale, and Mills Avenue. Traditionally a center of social and business activity, Greasy Corner served as a gathering point during the days of rampant segregation, which reserved public meeting places exclusively for white citizens. Scholar Nathaniel Hall explained that the name was derived from its proximity to the Transylvania Tanning Company, from which emanated the smells of stacks of decaying animal hides awaiting treatment. The unpleasant aroma of tannic acid was a necessary by-product of a thriving industry, which provided a livelihood for many black families.

During warm summer evenings groups congregated at Greasy Corner to visit with one another, to play games, to relax outdoors, and to catch up on news about those who had moved away. Children played tag, hopscotch, or hide-and-seek. Sometimes there would be "exhibition" boxing. One man challenged another to prove his skill. Mostly it was to entertain the crowd, but onlookers served as officials of the bout and kept matches from getting out of hand (Transylvania County: *Across the Woodland*, 1997). Resident Eversta Smith believes her Uncle Isaac Bailey, also known as "Battling Bailey," and Vernon Mills, two men who were accomplished boxers, met at Greasy Corner for a chance to demonstrate their boxing expertise (interview, October 22, 2002). Thomas Gardin, who later boxed while serving in the United States Army, was an amateur who developed his skill at "the Corner" (interview, November 25, 2002).

The proximity of Greasy Corner to the nearby tannery brought a lot of white folks through the community because the tannery's work force was integrated. There are tales of white boys who revved their motors as a warning that they were coming, then raced down the hill at top speed, dispersing the crowd. One white fellow, high on weekend whiskey, bragged about throwing cherry bombs into the crowd, according to an article in the *Transylvania Times*. Young hunters, greedy for ready cash, walked through Greasy Corner in hopes of selling a fresh kill of rabbit, squirrel, or possum. The scene abounded with activity, both desirable and undesirable.

Georgia Hill, a nearby section, was populated with residents who had moved from Georgia to Brevard.

Keith Howell visits Georgia Hill. (Courtesy Kay Howell.)

Another area on the opposite side of Bethel Baptist Church, on Mills Avenue, became known as Goose Hollow. Folks sitting on their porches in good weather yelled back and forth to one another. Smith and others credit Homer Price, Smith's uncle, with saying, "You all sound like a bunch of cackling geese." After Price's comment, Goose Hollow became that section's nickname.

Price's service in the Armed Forces provided him with a background for regaling neighborhood children with tales of faraway places. "He had us convinced that he had traveled all over the world," Agnes Wilson said, "but I think he was just a good storyteller" (interview, December 13, 2002).

Sometimes a team of boys from Goose Hollow challenged another team from Greasy Corner to a ball game (Michael Owens, interview, February 29, 2000). A friendly sense of rivalry existed among the groups.

These houses and the streets held the minds and the spirits crucial to the development of the Brevard Rosenwald School. Snapshots of those intangibles can be seen by examining the activity that permeated Brevard, especially in the interaction of blacks located there. The area's past is marked by vitality, vigor and imagination, which has carried over into the present.

Interest in the neighborhood and in the Rosenwald School has been renewed with the Rosenwald Revitalization Project, begun in 2001. The educational achievements of a united group of staff and parents, who strove for over forty years to make the Rosenwald School a success, have been reaffirmed by examination in the present. A sign marking Rosenwald Lane is the only physical reminder of that past.

The black community in Transylvania County was active not only in education, but also in the local economy. The presence of ready workers was a major capital asset. Black businessmen catered to the economic opportunities offered by the needs of their neighbors, but a few served both the white and the black communities. School children stopped by a favorite store for a lunchtime snack or an after-school treat. Occasionally, a student ran an errand to a local business for the school principal.

African American entrepreneurs in the area achieved lasting reputations; among them were James P. Aiken, operator of a barber shop, a café and a bakery; James Johnstone, operator of a movie theater; J.F.W. "Jip" Mills, a grocery store owner; Victor Betsill, a barber shop proprietor; Annie Bell Killian, a grocery retailer; Charles Lloyd, a mail clerk; Callie Mills and Evon Kelley, owners of beauty shops; Edward Killian, a notary public, a bondsman, and a taxi driver; Julius Whiteside, a railway fireman; and Etta Aiken Hall and Lela Benjamin Dudley, midwives (*Across the Woodland*, p. 44, 1997).

Former resident Lewis Whiteside, in a speech presented at Bethel Church during the Martin Luther King, Jr., birthday celebration and published in the February 21, 2002, issue of *The Transylvania Times*, documented additional African American businesses: Sherman Crite, Jr.'s grocery and janitorial service; Grady Elliott's café; Hill's Parlor, owned by Ms. Mattie Pierce and Ms. Dorothy Pierce Hill; and Whiteside Café, owned at various times by Roy Whiteside, Ed and Ophelia Hutchison, and Sam and Winona Whiteside. He also mentioned William Henry Hutchison's barbershop, Grady Elliott's garbage service and the garbage service of Cleo Mackey. Rental property was managed by the Reverend and Mrs. J.F.W. Mills, the Avery Benjamin family, the Leroy Brown family, and the Leroy Whiteside family. Contracting services were operated by Avery Benjamin and by Fred Mills, who were also rock masons.

Boarding houses made it easier for people to move into the community. Annie Marie Hailey reported that her grandparents, the Condry Sharps, ran a Carver Street boarding house used by teachers, principals, and workers for whom Brevard's hotels were off limits. Eliza Cunningham operated another successful boarding house on Carver Street (interview, August 21, 2002).

After school Betty Hunt High met her friends at the local store and played the piccolo (juke box) there. Thomas Gardin described Mattie Pierce and Dottie Hill's store as a gathering place where customers quenched their thirst or munched on sandwiches (interview). Gardin also remembered purchasing snacks at the front of Victor Betsill's barbershop. "There was a limit to where black people could gather. We could congregate up to the bridge or trestle — that's about where Marva Lytle's house is. We played touch football or stickball. We'd find a stick and look for a stray tennis ball," he said.

"We had fun in our part of town.... In town we could go to the movies, upstairs, but not to the Co-Ed. If we bought a sandwich at downtown cafés, we used the back doors. Got 'em and went. No way to use the library, but there was no problem with the banks. Only one back then, the Transylvania Trust. You knew where to go, and you didn't go where you couldn't" (interview).

The establishment of tanning and lumbering enterprises lured blacks to Transylvania County, but always they struggled to overcome the hardships of poverty. Though limited in their opportunities by the strictures of segregation, they conducted a frenzied search for ways to eke out a living. Businesses required a work force to labor in distinctively unpleasant jobs that poor whites were unwilling to perform. Frequently black laborers filled these positions.

Other opportunities emerged in the early twentieth century. In 1902, J. Frances Hayes established the Brevard Tannin Company at Pisgah Forest. An integrated work force labored there. Approximately a decade later Louis Carr erected a sawmill that utilized a 75-mile-long logging railroad. The Carr Lumber Company was a large operation (Phillips and Thompson, 1998). Also, a cotton mill and two whiskey distilleries employed an integrated work force (Hall, 1984). Tales relate that the latter had competition from bootleggers. Young boys enjoyed gathering at the courthouse to watch while revenue officers disposed of gallons of white lightning by emptying barrels of the illegal whiskey down the drain (Kilgore, 1998).

Early in the twentieth century Joseph Simpson Silversteen established businesses in Transylvania County. First came the Toxaway Tanning Company in 1901. Approximately a decade later he created the Gloucester Lumber Company and the Rosman Tanning Extract Company. In 1916, he opened the Transylvania Tanning Company, located in the heart of the black neighborhood in Brevard. Today a smokestack towers above the area, but time has dimmed the memory of a once thriving business. It exists simply as a compass point. One young person, whose home provides a view of the 180-foot tall smokestack, assured visitors that it had something to do with an old school building. The smokestack is the only surviving relic of a once prosperous business.

The Transylvania Tanning and Extract Company was the focal point of industrial activity until the Depression, when hard times made it necessary to shut down for days at a time. The company's owner paid in scrip, which was redeemable at the company store. Cash rarely exchanged hands.

Silversteen hired African Americans to work in all his businesses, but individuals remembered the tanning company most vividly. Hides of animals were made pliable by using tannic acid extracted from hemlock, chestnut, and oak. The proximity of lush forests with vast timber resources and

Although the Transylvania Tanning Company no longer exists, its smokestack remains. (Photograph by Juanita Spanogle.)

the presence of a railroad that facilitated delivery of coal made the location ideal for a tannery.

Luther Gray's memories of the tannery date to his childhood. He played with his black playmates in the area around the tannery, and at 14 he began working there. At first, Gray unloaded supplies. Eventually he worked in all departments. He was adept in the Roller Room, which had huge machines stretching along long walls. A *Transylvania Times* reporter also recorded Gary Carden's memory of working there "in the inner circle of hell" on eight-hour shifts with only half-day shifts on Saturdays.

Thomas Gardin worked at the tannery during the 1950s. "Yes, law, was it hard! I cut hides. Not many whites worked there when I started," he said. "All that's left is that smokestack. My granddaddy Will Gardin used to fire the furnace over there" (interview).

Silversteen industries provided essential employment for the breadwinners of the black community, but the better jobs were reserved for white workers. Nevertheless, the location of the Transylvania Tanning Company increased the economic vitality of the black community.

Although black citizens

of Transylvania County were kept "in their place" by the practice of segregation during the first 50 years of the twentieth century, their interaction with the white community was frequently positive. However, Hall (1984) documents conflicts. Henry Sharp was lynched for alleged rape, and Philip Mills was electrocuted for murder. These conflicts still occur; in 1985, there was a controversial murder case. As of 2003, black citizen Stanley Sanders still awaits his punishment on death row, though there are questions about the evidence. Did someone plant jewelry as evidence? Why were witnesses ignored during the trial? Was there a cover-up to protect a police contact? (Dorothy Mock, interview, February 23, 2003).

Hall also documents the 1948 denial of voting privileges to a group of black citizens, including the principal and a teacher of a colored school. After a successful suit against Fred Shuford, chairman of the board of elections, and Dillard Pittillo, registrar of the Second Precinct, the county finally registered black citizens as voters. As Rosenwald alumna Selena Robinson said, the black people of Transylvania County always had to wage battle to win their rights (interview, December 6, 2002). That same year, 1948, through the efforts of Bessie Rosemond, a chapter of the National Association for the Advancement of Colored People was established in Transylvania County. During that era, the community remained calm. In fact, there was a low rate of criminal involvement by African Americans — a fact that Hall attributes to the strength of community churches (Hall, 1984).

Men who took advantage of work opportunities in Brevard often had school-age children who needed to be educated. Black residents of Transylvania County had established small community schools, often in makeshift buildings, since the latter half of the nineteenth century. School superintendents date back to 1877, but their early involvement in African American education is sketchy. The November 4, 1896, issue of the *French Broad Hustler* announced an election to vote on a school tax in 39 counties in North Carolina.

The front-page article summarized the institutions supported fully or in part by the state: district public schools for both races, city public schools for both races, a university, a college, and a Normal and Industrial School for members of the white race. The College of Agriculture and Mechanic Arts for the colored race existed in seven cities in the state. Also, the newspaper cited institutions for the deaf and for the blind and an orphanage for the colored race.

The typical school term for district public schools was identified as lasting 65 days. Evidently, by the 1896 decision of *Plessy v. Ferguson*, the provision of schools for the colored race had been established in North Carolina. Transylvania County's present black community and documents in the county's archives indicate the existence of schools for black children as the norm prior to the advent of the twentieth century. The records provide evidence of efforts to educate black children before a school building was built for that purpose. This tradition of community involvement in education would continue with the construction of the Rosenwald School.

As individuals share memories of their Rosenwald School days, colorful vignettes surface. Older citizens recount stories that are historical heirlooms. Some are about parents, such as Pete Owens, who added "s" to his surname and who sent his children to the school. Descendants of Pete and Dora Owens live in the modern Rosenwald community and clearly recall their school experiences.

Their ancestor, Pete Owens, entered the community through a back door. Ninety-two-year-old Bernetha Owens said that her father-in-law was riding a horse in the Rosman area and fell off. A white man found him, took him to his own home, and cared for him. He could tell his rescuer only that his name was Pete (interview, August 22, 2002). Regional documents complement the family's history of Pete Owens; he was adopted by the parents of a Baptist minister, Dr. Jesse C. Owen, who loved Pete, a black man, as much as his other siblings. Jesse said that the saddest day of his life was when his mother told him that Pete was not his blood brother (D. H. Orr, *The Heritage of Transylvania County*, 1995). Pete Owens' children and grandchildren attended the segregated schools of Transylvania County.

James P. Aiken (1861–1909), a man who was very prominent in the early history of the community, successfully ran a number of businesses and took an active role in overseeing a school for black children. According to Selena Robinson, Aiken was the son of a slave, Jane Rhodes Aiken, and her white owner. The Aiken family provided financial support for the establishment of his business (interview, October 10, 2002). Aiken, who sold gingerbread and cider, became a well-respected businessman in Brevard.

Another respected member of the black community during the early twentieth century was Robert Gudger Smith. The son of a former slave, he was born on October 19, 1890, on the John Thrash Farm, which later became the Everett Farm. As was typical of the times, he worked at a variety of jobs, including laying the rails for the railroad track, paving Brevard's streets, laying the first sewer lines, and butchering. Smith butchered for 22 years, and he also worked for the local tannery.

One of Smith's passions was playing baseball. He played for the Brevard Sluggers in 1929, the Brevard Blues in 1946, and the Brevard Giants in 1948. Smith described the kind of ball he played as a youngster as "one-eyed cat ball." The batter hit the ball, ran to one base in the middle of the field, and then back to home.

Both Smith and his wife, Sara "Mary" Erwin, were gifted in their knowledge of the healing power of plants. Mrs. Smith, who died in 1980, used onion poultices and bone-set tea to cure a variety of ailments. Often she helped nurse sick folk. Also, she was a laundress for the local hospital and for Brevard College students. Mr. Smith, who died in 1993, lived to be 102 (*The Heritage of Transylvania County*, 1995). Known affectionately as "Poppa" and "Big Mama," the Smiths were representative of the caring, hard working, and knowledgeable members of Brevard's African American community, who zealously supported the local school.

While business successes reflect the strength and the individuality of community members, the school itself was built thanks to the concerted effort of a caring faculty and determined parents. Both the staff and the parents remember that building Brevard Rosenwald School required more than lumber and a spot of land. Rather, the true foundation lay in the attitudes of the community, and in the distinct milestone of the idea of equal access to education.

Historical figures, organizations, and events of Brevard's West End laid the foundation for Brevard Rosenwald School. The history of the school is inextricably linked with the history of the community. Living in a town that provided steady employment freed parents to focus on the benefits of educating their children and to develop a keen interest in supporting their school.

Brevard Rosenwald School was part of the ongoing effort to achieve meaningful education for blacks, which began long before the doors of the Rosenwald School opened. From slavery to the Civil War to the era of freedom, the thirst for knowledge was always present, and was the foundation for educational efforts to come.

Like thousands of other towns, Brevard met the expectations of Southern society before, during and after the Civil War. That historical context helps citizens today realize that the Rosenwald School did not appear magically on the Brevard landscape. Prevalent conditions of neglect, apparent since the Civil War, continued and intensified in the twentieth century.

Even though the patterns of educational neglect are well known, it is important to replay how neglect marred generation after generation. The patterns scarred the mindset of Transylvania County citizens. Sometimes, though, the marks were hidden in a rural community. The neglect galvanized the community, intensifying the momentum that led to the establishment of Brevard Rosenwald School.

Stories of neglect emerge the same way stories of success emerge, in documents and oral traditions that record the truth behind the struggles of Brevard Rosenwald School. Truth cannot be swept away by the tides of prejudice, nor can it be buried by silence.

The driving force of fear impacted the efforts to educate African Americans, but there were also other forces: paternalism, religious fervor, economic concerns, humanitarianism, and academic and political zeal as well as philanthropy. Despite the power of negative forces in the mountain area of Brevard, eventually the positive forces found their way to the schools of that community.

Throughout the five decades of its formal existence in the twentieth century, both staff and students of Brevard Rosenwald School knew there was a reason for older books, for lower wages, and for fewer supplies. The tangibles reminded them daily that separate was definitely not equal, and that ruling whites were unwilling to relinquish their status as a favored people.

Though slavery was a thing of the past, deep-seated cultural influences led to continuing neglect. But the African American desire for education also has deep roots. In Brevard, that spirit created a spirit of power, of determination, and of commitment. There was a long tradition of underground schooling, fed by antislavery literature (Woods, 1995). Slaves learned to read and to write but often in a clandestine manner.

The efforts to educate slaves were the foundation of a desire for schooling in the Brevard community and elsewhere. In blatant defiance of South Carolina's attempt to impede slave education, the daughters of State Supreme Court Judge John Fouchereau Grimke taught their household slaves by firelight in a locked room. Slaves such as author Frederick Douglass and Thomas H. Jones of Wilmington, North Carolina, defiantly sought additional learning. Jones had his own forbidden spelling book, and Douglass bribed a young white boy to give him lessons (Bullock, 1967; Gordon, 1971). The thirst for learning drove African Americans to risk punishment rather than to remain ignorant. It is a thirst that endured in Brevard during the twentieth century.

Denying an education to blacks was part of a long tradition, one that must be recognized to understand the pressures that the Rosenwald community had to overcome in Brevard. Once abolition pamphlets were distributed in the South, slave owners experienced apprehension. What would happen if slaves learned to read? During the first half of the 1900s, the question changed, though the forces behind it were the same: What would happen if young African Americans in Brevard read as well as young white children in Brevard?

Restrictions on education were a hard tradition to overcome. Journalist Frederick Douglass, whose writing talents were challenged as "too sophisticated" after writing *Narrative of the Life of Frederick Douglass* (1845), received instruction from his female owner. If masters did not educate slaves, family members and overseers sometimes taught blacks and their children (Franklin and Moss, 1994). Recognizing the early restrictions makes it easier to understand why people challenged the educational limitations that led to the establishment and to the growth of Rosenwald School.

In the twentieth century, economic necessity made it easier for business leaders to accept the value of an educational effort in Brevard, especially one emphasizing basic learning skills like the Rosenwald School. Therefore the school benefited not only the black community, but the entire Brevard community.

The school always had to overcome challenges, and the obstacles were unbelievable. Teachers and parents had to seek acceptance of theory, and to overcome the obstacles presented by limited finances and the region's geography. In addition to fighting for the toleration of literacy, they had to overcome the prevailing doubt as to the intellectual prowess of African Americans.

Fortunately, one man's success story challenged those traditional assumptions. As an experiment to determine whether a black man possessed the intelligence to earn a college degree, John Chavis of North Carolina was enrolled at Princeton from 1779 to 1781. His experience proved the Negro was quite capable of acquiring a college education. He succeeded and became a leading teacher in the South from 1808 until the mid-1830s (Batey, 1954). Chavis, however, was allowed to teach only white and free black students. A charismatic teacher, Chavis taught students from prominent North Carolina families who became successful in professions such as politics, law, medicine, religion, and education.

The efforts of philanthropists like Julius Rosenwald greatly improved public education, but black education during the days of segregation was not equal to that of white education. Rosenwald, the president of Sears, Roebuck and Company, established a fund that helped finance the building of hundreds of schools for blacks across North Carolina. His efforts were among the first to try and improve facilities for public education for African Americans. It took more than a building with a distinguished name on it to achieve equal opportunities for blacks in Brevard. The gap between black and white education became more and more obvious as educational doors opened in rural communities and in urban centers. Less was invested economically in the black pupil, and their teachers were generally paid less.

In her study of the Caswell County Training School (1996), Emory University professor and historian Vanessa Siddle Walker cites the following discrepancies as presented in 1935 to North Carolina's governor by a commission composed of 50 whites and 50 blacks:

> In a great many instances the school buildings now in use for the colored children are in a poor state of repair. Generally many are poorly lighted and heated, and in many instances are too small to give adequate accommodations to the pupils.... In many of the classrooms, the furniture is antiquated, the blackboards are insufficient in size and badly abused.... Very few rural colored schools are equipped with modern

single desks. Little or no provision is made for teaching health and sanitation. Laboratories for science and vocational subjects are few and inadequate [p. 2].

This was the assessment of North Carolina, the state that had exceeded all others in the use of Rosenwald funds to provide adequate buildings for black children. Discrepancies existed in all southern states in the pupil–teacher ratio, in the length of the school day, in the provision of supplemental services, and in the expenditure per pupil in average daily attendance.

Walker (1996) further cites a blatant lack of equality in school facilities and resources:

> At the end of the Rosenwald building program in 1932, the per pupil value of school property was less than one-fifth that of the property of white schools. In North Carolina in 1945-46 the value of school property per pupil enrolled was $217 for white students and $70 for black children. In 1951, ... blacks comprised about 30 percent of North Carolina's population. They possessed only about 14.3 percent of its school facilities. As late as 1954 ... discrepancies still remained between black and white education [p. 2].

Walker argues that most studies of segregated education emphasize inferior aspects of that schooling. It is as though a "national memory" of segregated schools has created a harsh judgment demanding that nothing good could have occurred in all-black schools. Walker's 1996 study responds to this assessment, which she considers limited. The history of Brevard Rosenwald School reveals how silence and the failure to recognize building needs contributed to the struggles of segregated schools. Education was possible only through the efforts of teachers and students to overcome the limitations of inferior resources.

Institutional neglect was a constant hurdle at Brevard Rosenwald School as elsewhere. A study of the minutes of the Transylvania County School Board reveals little reference to the Rosenwald School, and the 1954 report from the field study group of George Peabody College for Teachers pinpoints only one recommendation specific to the Rosenwald School — the need to add a combination auditorium-playroom. Such silence speaks eloquently. The community was left to its own ingenuity to enrich the educational experiences of its children.

Obviously the concept of equalization did not apply to Negro schools. As late as 1924, only two graded high schools for Negroes existed in western North Carolina. One was located in Asheville, and the other, in Hendersonville. Two hundred and seventeen students attended the Asheville school, but only nineteen students sought a high school education in Hendersonville.

In 1933-34, ten secondary schools for Negroes were operating in the 24 counties of western North Carolina. Staffing was inadequate, and the salaries of Negro teachers with the same qualifications as white teachers were considerably lower. The situation continued until 1943-44, when equalization of salaries for white and Negro teachers was realized. In counties where the meager student population made operating a black high school impractical, school officials transported black students to other counties if students wanted to earn a high school diploma (Van Noppen and Van Noppen, 1973).

The history of black education in Brevard reveals many telling facts and statistics. Teachers and students confronted attitudes that blocked references to their world, as evident by the all-white resources used in schools. Little existed in educational texts to affirm the identity of African Americans, and such was the case for almost a century. Outside school, Rosenwald students daily confronted attitudes and efforts restricting their educational development. Menial labor as their just employment was the result of decades of brainwashing by advocates of white supremacy.

Appalachia was committed to separate but unequal educational opportunities. Negro status was low, and racial tensions could escalate dramatically. White supremacy was the philosophy of the times. Walker (1996) chronicles the restrictions imposed on black access to trains, to buses, and to restaurants. Selena Robinson, a slave's granddaughter who fought for school integration in Transylvania County, referred to restrictions placed on water fountains. She grew up thinking a black person could be arrested for drinking from the public fountain in front of the courthouse in Brevard (interview, July 16, 1999).

Little hope existed for rural Negro residents to become well educated. Terms in their schools were usually shorter than those of white public schools. However, according to Hugh V. Brown (1964), North Carolina's school term improved remarkably from 1900 to 1936. Rural white schools averaged 73.3 days in 1900, and rural black schools averaged 65.5. By 1935-36, the white school term had increased to an average of 160.1 days, and for the rural black school, 159 days. Inequities persisted in other areas as well. Although money was disbursed from state capitals to counties based on total enrollment, only a small portion was used for educational needs of Negroes (Harlan, 1958). The mistreatment is startling.

As late as the 1950s and the 1960s, blacks throughout Transylvania County experienced the problem of taxation without representation as they struggled for equality after the life-changing 1954 Supreme Court decision in *Brown v. Board of Education*. They were denied entrance into public high schools even though their taxes helped support those schools.

In spite of legislative barriers and social unrest, students, teachers and parents in Brevard worked towards quality in education, taking matters into their own hands. Students walked to school. They bought books at the dime store to supplement worn-out texts. Teachers dressed well, worked industriously and patrolled the halls confidently. They prodded young learners to take new steps on the road to education. The destination was always upward and onward — another school, a future degree, and a better job.

Efforts towards a quality education at Brevard Rosenwald School were continuous throughout its history, and those efforts survived a fire and inattentive administrators. The dreams of an education came true because of the combined efforts of home, church, and school. The spirit of progress led to tangible results, reflecting values that the community has maintained from one century to the next.

Chapter 2

Ideological Foundations

THE BREVARD ROSENWALD SCHOOL emerged within a larger historical framework that shaped educational decisions in the Southeast. The school benefited from a movement that swept into Appalachia and eventually into western North Carolina because of the influence of the respected black leader, William Edward Burghardt Du Bois, and of the visionary white entrepreneur, Julius Rosenwald. Du Bois provided the ideology, and Rosenwald provided the finances.

The two-pronged approach, the theory of Du Bois and the pragmatism of Rosenwald, laid a lasting foundation. Great ideas stir the imagination, but money equips educators with the means to initiate those ideas. Du Bois spoke as the intellectual leader of African Americans. He was the renaissance man for his people. Rosenwald acted as the utilitarian businessman. He knew how to make money, but he also knew how to use money to build centers of learning for people aspiring to enter the capitalistic society on an equal level.

Rosenwald left his name indelibly on an institution that became the headquarters for directing education in Brevard and Transylvania County. While Du Bois' name seems more distant, his ideas were part of the daily substance of activities at the Brevard Rosenwald School. In one sense, Du Bois' influence is more potent because his ideas helped shape the experiences of both staff and students at the school.

From the 1920s through the 1940s, black educators taking courses for teacher improvement would have been exposed to the ideas of Du Bois. His ideas parallel the efforts and the goals of education at Brevard Rosenwald School. The history of education at Brevard Rosenwald School mirror the priorities of Du Bois.

Philanthropist Julius Rosenwald sponsored the construction of over 5,000 schools for African Americans in the South. (Courtesy Fisk University — Special Collections.)

Ideological influence for the Brevard school is apparent in a 1938 Du Bois speech during the graduation exercises at Fisk University in Nashville. Du Bois, who had co-founded the National Association for the Advancement of Colored People in 1909, presented "The Revelation of Saint Orgne the Damned." The title, announced prior to the event, had motivated curious professors to search encyclopedias for "Saint Orgne" but to no avail, because Du Bois had created the name as an anagram for Negro. In his address, the educator probed facets of a personal philosophy of life as experienced by African Americans in the United States during the early part of the twentieth century. Contemplating the experiences of the fictitious Saint Orgne, Du Bois described the vital role of the elementary school:

> The ... essential difficulty with Negro education lies in the elementary school; lies in the fact that the number of Negroes in the United States today who have learned thoroughly to read, write, and count is small.... The reason that we cannot do thorough college work and cannot keep high university standards is that the students ... are fundamentally weak in mastery of those essential tools to human learning. Not even the dumbest college professor can spoil the education of the man who as a child has learned to read, write, and cipher....
> The trouble lies primarily ... in the elementary schools of the South; in schools with short terms; with teachers inadequate both as to numbers and training; with quarters ill-suited physically and morally to the work in hand; with colored principals chosen not for executive ability but for their agility in avoiding race problems; and with white superintendents who try to see how large a statistical showing can be made without expenditure of funds, thought, or effort.... This is the fault of a nation which does not thoroughly believe in the education of Negroes.... But the fault does not end there.
> The fault lies with the Negroes themselves ... for not being willing

and eager and untiring in their effort to establish the elementary school ... and not pause ... until every Negro child ... is getting at least nine months a year, five hours a day, five days in the week, in a modern school room, with the best trained teachers, under principals selected for training and executive ability, and serving with their teachers ... and with the school under the control of those whose children are educated there [Aptheker, 1973 (Du Bois, as republished), pp. 107–108].

As implied by his speech, Du Bois advocated high standards for schools. He wanted talented black students to aspire to lives enriched by the great thinkers of western civilization. He reasoned that black students' course of study should not be limited to mastering servile skills for productive farming or for efficient housekeeping. Black people should not be automatically assigned, solely on the basis of race, to denigrating work harvesting fields and serving tables. Instead, an education that stressed academic accomplishment could enable blacks to find satisfaction in intellectual achievement. Such exposure offered the prospect of living a better life. Brevard Rosenwald alumni, especially those who completed professional training, were beneficiaries of an educational tradition that allowed them to reach that goal.

The first and most important step in education took place at elementary schools like Brevard Rosenwald School. Du Bois spoke decisively about the importance of the elementary school. He was alarmed that public apathy hindered improvement in grade school classrooms. He believed that proper training at that level would accompany students through life. They would be adequately equipped to continue seeking knowledge. Du Bois adamantly insisted that black students be trained to use their brains, not simply their brawn. He knew, as the Rosenwald faculty proved, that capable and committed elementary educators establish the foundation for lifelong learning. In Brevard, dedicated black teachers exposed their students to the challenges of literature, science, history, and mathematics. Reflecting the values of Du Bois, they sought to ignite an interest in academics and to arouse the power of thinking. Indeed, black educators in Brevard challenged the stereotypes. They turned back the presumptions of racism.

Du Bois objected to the philosophy of industrial education, a biased educational philosophy that for many whites validated the idea that Negroes were unequal. Rather, he advocated education that would elevate members of the black race out of a state of defilement into a state of equality. He believed that teachers should realize that students' character deserved more attention than their need to be financially successful.

W.E.B. Du Bois boldly emphasized that African Americans deserved an education of the same caliber as that offered to whites. If white people needed college training, then certainly black people needed the same to achieve a higher stature in life. An outspoken proponent of classical education, Du

Bois believed that schools should emphasize literature, languages, history, science, and mathematics in the classroom. Black students should be challenged to think and to appreciate the accomplishments of thinkers, whether Aristotle or Shakespeare. He knew that a double standard for learning was unacceptable. Du Bois proclaimed ideas that foreshadowed the goals of civil rights activists in the 1960s, when integration finally occurred in Transylvania County.

Repeatedly Du Bois stressed the importance of recognizing that all men are created equal. He wanted this conviction to be uppermost in the minds of black people. Certainly that idea prevailed as generation after generation benefited from a Rosenwald education. As Du Bois proposed, both staff and students found purpose and meaning in clinging to the ideal. When establishing the officially named Rosenwald School in the 1920s, the goal was to resuscitate a building. A place with walls and rooms was simply a cry for equal educational opportunity. Later, after experiencing the benefits of a new stone building, the Rosenwald community lifted its horizons. By the 1950s, it became clear that the only way to achieve equality was to experience education at the same facilities, with the same resources, and in the same classrooms as white children.

The influence of both Du Bois and Rosenwald is clear. Targeting the education of blacks, Du Bois pinpointed six tangential issues: personnel, leadership, training, resources, finances, and community involvement. The striking connection to the Brevard experiment is that the Brevard Rosenwald School utilized each of these concepts to achieve its success. Du Bois stressed the importance of the community's endorsement of education as a pursuit that impacts the quality of life. His ideas clearly suggest that powerful educational support builds strong foundations so students may enrich their intellectual development. In comparison, the Rosenwald Fund, which was created more than two decades before Du Bois' address, utilized motivating forces that coincided with the issues Du Bois urged blacks to face.

Before federal funds were allocated to support black education, schools for Negroes existed in the South, including small towns and rural areas. Communities pooled their resources to provide opportunities for their children to learn to read perceptively and to write fluently. Such skills would, it was believed, enable those who were educated to build a good life and to help others to do so. Parents who had limited formal experience with school urged their offspring to grasp every opportunity to acquire an education.

The concept of Rosenwald schools originated in Chicago, and it took about ten years until the tangible results were apparent in Transylvania County. In 1912, Julius Rosenwald, a Chicago entrepreneur with a vision for improving race relations, provided money to stimulate school construction in the South. According to Virgie Alcorn (1986), Rosenwald established a building fund in 1912 at Booker T. Washington's Tuskegee Institute to provide for "offshoot" schools of Tuskegee. The Rosenwald Fund, officially created in 1917, underwrote the construction of more than 5,000 buildings for black schools in the southern states. The fund paid for 813 Rosenwald structures—not all were schools—in North Carolina, more than in any other state (Hanchett, 1987).

An urgent need for assistance in replacing and renovating educational facilities existed in North Carolina, where school buildings for blacks were noticeably inferior. Throughout the state, white schools were typically valued at $1,643, as compared to $483 for black schools. In practical terms the figures meant African American children were forced to labor on their lessons in overcrowded, substandard classrooms. A black school in Greene County, North Carolina, measured 18 by 26 feet, had no ceiling and was in need of repair. With 85 pupils enrolled, space was extremely limited. Students had to be sent outdoors frequently, even in harsh weather (Leloudis, 1996). Teaching in such environments, which were also prevalent in western North Carolina, often seemed to be a waste of time.

The Rosenwald Fund was a godsend for rural black communities, from Brevard to the east coast. N.C. Newbold, director of the Division of Negro Education in North Carolina's Department of Public Instruction, found the black population jubilant at the prospect of receiving Rosenwald funds. In response to the policy of matching funds, historian James L. Leloudis of the University of North Carolina documents the effort of the rural Aberdeen community in Moore County, where day laborers, who possessed less than $500 worth of property and owned no homes, banded together to raise $425 in hopes of influencing Newbold to build their school without delay (1996). Similar sacrifices occurred in Transylvania County though no records confirm the fund-raising methods. In North Carolina, black communities, in collaboration with their white neighbors, sought to secure matching funds—often in the form of labor, land, and building materials—to become eligible for aid from the Rosenwald Fund.

In Transylvania County, the Rosenwald School stood in a heavily wooded area beyond the extreme end of West Main Street in Brevard. The school was accessible by a steep, rugged trail. From the early 1920s until the school's closing in 1966, the school provided seven to eight years of education on the elementary level. According to retired Principal Ethel K. Mills and former students, there were years in the middle to late 1930s when the Brevard Rosenwald School provided training beyond the eighth grade. Documents at the North Carolina State Archives in Raleigh support the existence of high school classes for black students in Brevard prior to 1948. The school grew from a minimal wooden building into an educational institution.

Money was the only thing strong enough to counteract continual efforts to prevent blacks from acquiring an education. And that required lots of money. Wealthy men, such as William H. Baldwin, Jr., a railroad tycoon and an employee of thousands of Negroes, advocated industrial education for practical jobs. He believed that the pragmatic education of blacks would enhance the strength of the nation.

Pioneering philanthropists, such as George Peabody, Anna T. Jeanes, John D. Rockefeller, and John Slater, contributed generously to the cause of education. They channeled millions of dollars to rural schools and southern blacks.

While these names have stature, Julius Rosenwald was the magnanimous man who changed the possibilities for blacks in Brevard. He contributed such abundant amounts of money that effectively managing the finances required the establishment of the Julius Rosenwald Fund, which had a committee to review requests and to make executive decisions. That his name is still revered in Brevard is just one testament to his impact. Historian Henry Allen Bullock (1970) wrote, "The work of the Rosenwald Fund has permeated the educational experiences of the African American more deeply than that of any other fund" (p. 138). That generosity adds to the importance of Brevard Rosenwald School as a microcosm of African American education in a small rural community.

Rosenwald's participation generates important questions: How lasting is one man's contributions? What kind of foresight generates philanthropy? How did his vision influence a community? How was the "matching vision" multiplied in the growth of the school and within the classrooms of the school?

The Rosenwald project could not have occurred at a better time, both for the region and for Transylvania County. The loss of a steady immigrant labor force during World War I prompted northern industries to tap the South for African American workers. The circumstances led to what became known as the Great Migration. The promise of high wages, respect, and the absence of Jim Crow practices enticed thousands of blacks to leave North Carolina and the South. Between 1914 and 1920 approximately 500,000 black laborers relocated to the North. Within the next decade that number almost doubled. By 1916, severe labor shortages existed in North Carolina. The increase in day-labor salaries to $1.25 did not curb the exodus. Consequently, North Carolinians and other southerners concluded that the lives of Negroes must be improved to retain their valuable labor force.

The most direct way to achieve this change was by improving educational opportunities for the black population. The inequity of school facilities was a frequently cited motive for leaving the state. Although legislative reformers did not consider ending segregation, the need for better schools had captured their attention (Leloudis, 1996). The key to keeping the Negro in the

South was better schools. The Brevard Rosenwald School typifies the appeal of that need.

In 1925, Rosenwald, upon viewing the results of the Great Migration first hand in the city of Chicago, explained that by helping the Negro, he would also be helping the white man. His motivation, according to an account in *Collier's National Weekly*, was to make the world a better place for his grandchildren. By constructing rural schoolhouses to provide an uplifting environment, he hoped black children would be motivated to become productive citizens who valued their rural communities (Leloudis, 1996). By providing a means to battle ignorance, Rosenwald aspired to improve the lives of both African Americans and their white counterparts.

Rosenwald, the school's namesake, was born in 1862 in Springfield, Illinois, close to the home of Abraham Lincoln, the Great Emancipator. His parents emigrated from Germany as a reaction against growing militarism, and settled in Springfield, where they operated a clothing goods store. At 17 and without completing high school, Julius Rosenwald left home and relocated in New York City to work for relatives in the wholesale clothing business. Soon he had amassed enough capital to open his own store and to begin manufacturing summer clothing for men (Dalin, 1998). His thriftiness and enterprising spirit brought success at an early age.

In 1885, Rosenwald moved his factory to Chicago. A decade later, with capital provided partially by his brother-in-law, he invested in a small mail-order company that had purchased clothing from his business. His former customer was Sears, Roebuck and Company (Dalin, 1998). For the remainder of his life, Rosenwald served as an officer of the company. He became the president in 1910 and the chairman in 1925. Rosenwald's chief contribution to the company was its policy of guaranteeing money back if customers were not satisfied. Such a concept spurred the widespread purchase of Sears' products in rural America and resulted in an amazingly successful business. Julius Rosenwald, the man chiefly responsible for the company's effective marketing, was astounded at his sudden ascent to the ranks of the nation's wealthiest citizens (Brown, 1996).

By 1910, the giant corporation's gross sales exceeded $50 million, and Rosenwald's investment had grown from $37,500 to a breathtaking $150 million. That figure stands as an immense contrast with the limited finances of families in the Brevard Rosenwald community that his gift helped.

The Sears magnate was a trailblazer not only in the corporate world but also in philanthropy. Influenced by Emil Hirsch, the rabbi of Chicago's Sinai Congregation, Rosenwald placed great importance on the doctrine of helping others to help themselves. Consequently, he provided money only to communities that raised amounts equal to or greater than his own contribution. His requirement of matching funds, which formed a vital component of his school building program, was quite a novelty at the time. The practice created a partnership with the community (Dalin, 1998). Descendants of Brevard's African Americans, whose contributions exceeded those of Rosenwald for the project, can be justifiably proud of their ancestors' efforts and of their willingness to make extreme sacrifices to provide educational opportunities for their children.

To become a reality, the Brevard school had to meet precisely designated standards. In a folder labeled Rosenwald Fund in Box 2, General Correspondence of the Director, September 1915–August 1916 in the Division of Negro Education in the Department of Pubic Instruction Archives, the criteria established by Rosenwald for the construction of rural schools are given and included these stipulations: Money provided is to be used in a manner that encourages the local Board of Education and members of the community to supplement the construction of rural schoolhouses; the construction of any school should receive prior approval from the state, county, and local school officers; the people should raise an amount equal to or greater than the money provided by Rosenwald funds; plans for the building should be approved by Tuskegee Institute; no construction may begin until the local funds have materialized in the form of land, labor, material, or cash.

Apparently Rosenwald's intention was to foster a coming together of the white and black segments of rural communities to accomplish the provision of adequate schools for young children and to strengthen the idea that what was good for one race had a positive outcome for the other. Decades after the Brevard Rosenwald School closed, the positive effects for both blacks and whites endure.

The school epitomized the partnership between Rosenwald and African American communities. In *A School in Every County* (1995), Jeffrey Sosland records the following statement made by Rosenwald in 1911: "As an American and as a Jew, I appeal to all high-minded men and women to join in a relentless crusade against race prejudice, indulgence in which will result in the blotting out of the highest ideals of our proud nation" (title page). Upon his death in 1932, Rosenwald was called "one of the greatest friends of the Negro race since Abraham Lincoln" (Sosland, 1995, p. 11). For the past century, African Americans in Transylvania County have enjoyed this friendship.

In North Carolina, Governor O. Max Gardner made the following tribute:

> The death of Mr. Julius Rosenwald brings together in a feeling of sorrow the thoughtful leaders of all races. This man knew how to make money. What is more important, he knew how to spend it wisely. It was his privilege in life to turn the currents of commerce into channels of philanthropy. His generosity knew neither creed nor color. North Carolina will remember him forever as one who promoted the welfare of

2. Ideological Foundations 27

Negro schools and the Negro race generally. In serving the Negro and lifting him to a happier and more complete life, Mr. Rosenwald was indeed a true friend of the South. Let us contemplate his life with pride and thankfulness [Office of State Superintendent of Public Instruction, 1932].

The widespread effect of Rosenwald's philanthropy, which changed life for African Americans in Brevard, is definitely impressive simply from an economic standpoint. In the February 24, 1998, edition of the *Wall Street Journal*, economist Herbert Stein indicated that the present purchasing power of Rosenwald contributions would be $650 million. Robert M. Solow, Massachusetts Institute of Technology professor of economics and Nobel laureate in economics, has developed a method for measuring the dollar value of Rosenwald's contribution in modern sums. By Solow's accounting, dollars donated by Rosenwald from 1910 until 1932 equal roughly two billion dollars when considering both purchasing power and earning power. After the matching fund policy is taken into account, an additional three to five billion may be added. More than half of the money went directly to communities of desperately poor blacks (Sosland, 1995).

Via his financial commitment, Rosenwald empowered "black America with the basic tools of education and vocational skills to move from the stagnation and poverty of the post–Civil War period toward the Civil Rights era" (Sosland, 1995, p. 12). By providing the means for African Americans to organize themselves, Rosenwald's techniques created a progressive agenda that supported efforts for equality through the Civil Rights era and into the twenty-first century. All of these claims ring true in the history of Brevard, and they continue to resound this century in the town's revitalization block grant project.

In 1927, the William E. Harmon Awards presented Julius Rosenwald a gold medal for Distinguished Achievement in Race Relations (Office of the Superintendent of Public Instruction, 1932). According to grandson and biographer Peter Ascoli, Rosenwald was proud to become the recipient of this award. However, because his wife was ill, he was unable to accept the award in person (www.networkchicago.com/chicagostories/rosenwald.htm, 10/03/02). The attitude that earned such an award for this high school dropout is evident in statements from a speech he made in 1911 at Hampton, one of the nation's first black institutions:

> Race prejudice is merely destructive. It offers nothing but a hopeless warfare and a blank pessimism ... two nations cannot live side by side at dagger's point with one another and maintain a healthy state of progress in either. Perpetual feud destroys what is best and most helpful in both.... No man can in any way render greater service to mankind

than by devoting his energy toward removal of this mighty obstacle. The destruction of ... prejudice is the beginning of the higher civilization [Sosland, 1995, p. 13].

What caused this gentleman to invest so heavily in elevating educational opportunities for the Negro race? According to Rosenwald himself, in 1910 his friend and business associate, Dr. Paul Sachs, gave him two books that influenced him more than anything he had ever read. One was a biography of William H. Baldwin, Jr., a railroad executive who influenced the founding of the Urban League. The second was Booker T. Washington's autobiography, *Up from Slavery*. Baldwin, who urged that greater attention should be given to educating blacks, contended that the fate of Negroes was vitally linked to the future progress of the nation-at-large. Washington's belief in hard work and personal initiative strongly impressed Rosenwald. As a result, Rosenwald sought out and developed a friendship and lasting partnership with the founder of Tuskegee Institute. These two books galvanized Rosenwald to actively provide for the improvement of black education. Herbert Stein (1998) also attributes Rosenwald's motivation to the Jewish emphasis on charity and on acts of "loving-kindness" to help the needy.

Washington personally urged that Rosenwald consider providing for the construction of elementary schools for African American children. The idea apparently appealed to Rosenwald. Incorporating the concept of challenge grants into his plan, he contributed to a building program that resulted in the construction of more than 5,000 new schools in the segregated South.

Washington insisted that a pressing need existed for the construction of elementary schools in the South (Woods, 1995). Rosenwald acted on that recommendation, thus empowering the philosophical views of both Washington and Du Bois.

The ideology of Du Bois contrasted sharply with that of Booker T. Washington. Du Bois advocated paying attention to political and civil rights, issues that he felt Washington ignored. Also, Du Bois denounced industrial education as insulting to the African American intellect because it pigeonholed learners into a path leading to dead-end jobs. He believed that a school that offered only training that enabled students to obtain jobs undesirable to whites was not offering equal educational options. An irony exists in Du Bois' opposition to Booker T. Washington, because Washington prodded Rosenwald to invest in education by building elementary schools for blacks in the Southeast.

The Brevard Rosenwald School benefited from the input of both Rosenwald and Du Bois. While Rosenwald shaped the physical structure, Du Bois indirectly molded the intellectual framework that led to a nurturing curriculum and to effective teaching within the building.

In addition to understanding the source of the funding and of the aca-

2. Ideological Foundations 29

demic focus of the Brevard Rosenwald School, it is essential to consider the need — why blacks were without an adequate school. The education system in Brevard, like elsewhere in the South, mirrored race relations in the community. Separate schools for African American children and for Caucasian children existed until the late 1950s and beyond. Race became an inherent issue in the schooling of America's children, for poor white children had access to more extensive resources than did black children.

Although the Brevard Rosenwald School had been established in 1920, its purpose was the same as that pondered by Du Bois in his 1938 speech: to provide an opportunity for intense academic experiences from the beginning of the child's schooling to the completion of that schooling.

The black community, in its efforts to ensure that its children not remain ignorant, encountered burdens that in part led to the movement for school integration. African Americans, who lived in a poverty intensified by the legacy of slavery and by the propaganda of white supremacy, had limited means for educating black students, but the conditions that they lived under solidified the desire to acquire equal educational opportunities.

The Brevard Rosenwald mindset was also greatly influenced by the school's geographical location. It was located in Brevard in western North Carolina, an elevated region of foothills with the Blue Ridge Mountains on the east and the Great Smokies and Unakas on the west. A high plateau located between the Blue Ridge range and the Unakas has altitudes ranging from 3,500 to 4,000 feet. In another range is Mt. Mitchell — at least 80 miles north of Brevard and a place few students ever saw — with an even higher altitude of 6,684 feet. Transverse ranges cross the tableland. These ranges include Black, New Found, Pisgah, Balsam, Nantahala, and others that surround Brevard. Extending over 20 miles, the Black Mountain range is covered with dense forests.

The region of Western North Carolina measures 250 miles in length and up to 150 miles in width. It comprises one fifth of the land area of North Carolina, but as late as 1973 it contained only one seventh of the state's population. Its scenic beauty, pleasant climate, pure air and water, and abundance of wildlife attracted bold pioneers. However, the idyllic environment rarely made life easier for the Rosenwald community, and it certainly separated both the young and the old from educational opportunities.

In the early history of Transylvania County, most blacks were enslaved. A brief look at their background illustrates why their response to educational opportunity is so remarkable and so inspiring. Transylvania County, known as "the land of waterfalls," is a forested region and site of the French Broad and Davidson rivers. Within its remote and rural boundaries in the southern part of the western region, bordering on South Carolina, some residents were slaveholders. The Board of Tax Listings for May 5, 1862, recorded

447 slaves and three free Negroes. Their homes were scattered throughout the county. The valuation of the slaves was registered as $199,335 for taxation purposes. State tax on this "property" amounted to $358.67, and the county received $448.34. Thirty-two slaveholders owned at least five slaves. Nine individuals owned at least 13. The average number held was six. In 1863, the list named 586 slaves and two free Negroes. From the Civil War onward, the records show there was a black presence in Transylvania County, and their children were in need of an education.

The history of Transylvania County schools is part of the saga of education for black children in western North Carolina, the Appalachian region of the state. Studying the region's history clarifies the struggles of the black community, and shows why there was such a need for the Brevard Rosenwald School. According to John C. Inscoe in *Mountain Masters: Slavery and the Sectional Crisis in Western North Carolina* (1996), slaves equaled fewer than ten percent of the antebellum Appalachian population in the Carolina mountains. Among the total white population, fewer than ten percent were slaveholders. Owners of slaves in the region were chiefly businessmen; agricultural enterprises, traditional utilizers of slave labor, were not always a viable means for accruing wealth in western North Carolina. No slaveholder from Transylvania County is included in one list of western North Carolina's 50 largest slaveholders (Inscoe, 1996).

It is easy to imagine the struggle of the small and isolated population of blacks. Long on desire but short on finances, the outpowered minority needed outside help. And beyond the financial limitations, they had geographical hurdles to jump. By 1880, the Negro population of Transylvania County was 517, and the white population was 4,822 (Van Noppen and Van Noppen, 1973). The black population in mountainous Transylvania County remained small in the twentieth century, and that fact made provision of schools for black children especially difficult. As a result, the Brevard Rosenwald School in Transylvania County experienced problems typically associated with separate schools for a small population. Facilities were simple, and resources were meager.

Though the African American educational experience was marked by hardships and struggles, it is relevant to present and future school concerns. At Brevard, as at other Rosenwald schools, instructors focused on traditional educational approaches, such as phonics, reading, spelling, vocabulary, and mathematics, as opposed to whole language, new mathematics, and multiculturalism that became popular trends in the decades following the closing of the Brevard Rosenwald School. African Americans, as did other citizens of the Appalachian region, regarded education as a means that would make it possible for their children to build a better life.

The black population of Transylvania County found the bridge to a better life at the Brevard Rosenwald School. There were poor facilities, a dearth of materials, and little support from the school board. In addition, bus transportation was rarely provided. But there was spirit and ambition to transform the ordinary experience into an extraordinary experience even though there was a less-than-ideal environment.

The difficult conditions and the imposing geographical circumstances make the results of the contributions by Du Bois and Rosenwald more remarkable. However, other national attitudes interfered with the potential their efforts provided.

While the influence of Du Bois, the thinker, and Rosenwald, the entrepreneur, was positive, other forces combined to undermine the educational potential for black children in Transylvania County. Some of these negative forces were given formal recognition in a courtroom. The words "separate but equal" swept into Transylvania County with the power of an ongoing blight, one that lasted for 70 years.

While Brevard is separated geographically from the metropolitan centers of North Carolina, the history of education in the small town is integrally linked to courts in distant states. Ironically, the origins of "separate but equal" education for blacks originated as policy in a court decision about transportation, not education. A pernicious policy, the concept of "separate but equal" was established by *Plessy v. Ferguson* (1896) and achieved only separateness. Homer A. Plessy, himself only one-eighth black, boarded a car designated for "whites only" on a train in New Orleans, Louisiana. He was arrested for violating segregation laws, and Judge John H. Ferguson found him guilty. Believing his constitutional rights had been violated, Plessy sought a ruling against the railroad. The United States Supreme Court ruled that separate but equal facilities were acceptable and rejected his claim.

More than a century later, the opinion of the one dissenting vote stands out as a noteworthy analysis, one that is now supported by the law of the land. Prophetically, Justice John Harlan wrote:

> Our Constitution is color-blind, and neither knows nor tolerates classes among citizens. In respect of civil rights, all citizens are equal before the law.... In my opinion, the judgment this day rendered will, in time, prove to be quite as pernicious as the decision made by this tribunal in the *Dred Scott* case.... The present decision ... will not only stimulate aggressions, more or less brutal and irritating, upon the admitted rights of colored citizens, but will encourage the belief that it is possible, by means of state enactments, to defeat the beneficent purposes which the people of the United States had in view when they adopted the recent amendments of the Constitution [*Plessy v Ferguson*,163 U.S. 537, p. 6].

The need for a Rosenwald school continued because of the effect of this court ruling. Once established, the concept of "separate but equal" extended to other aspects of living, even sanctioning the Jim Crow laws, which permitted treatment of blacks as second-class citizens during Reconstruction and for almost 100 years afterward. The concept rigidly regulated practices for educational institutions (Emmerich, 1998). The name Jim Crow was taken from a yes-man comic character developed in 1832 by Thomas "Daddy" Rice, a white actor. Jim Crow obnoxiously portrayed the black people's way of life. By the beginning of the twentieth century, the Jim Crow caricature furthered segregation in American institutions. There were segregated schools, restaurants, and water fountains. Restrooms were designated as colored or white. In a South Carolina factory, blacks and whites were restricted from looking out the same window. In Florida, there were "white" and "black" textbooks. In a North Carolina hospital for the mentally ill, an 1877 policy prohibited the intermingling of black and white mental patients (Haley, 1987).

In small rural communities such as Brevard, the concept extended to social customs:

> Blacks were expected to tip their hats when they walked past whites, but whites did not have to remove their hats even when they entered a black family's home. Whites were to be called "sir" and "ma'am" by blacks, who ... were called by their first names by whites. People with white skin were to be given a wide berth on the sidewalk [Williams, 1988, p. 10].

The *Plessy v. Ferguson* decision barred blacks in Brevard, as well as in other communities, from equal educational opportunities. After its formal inception in the early 1920s, the Rosenwald experiment opened an alternative avenue of acquiring a formal education for several decades. Money from the Rosenwald Fund assisted in improving the physical condition of the segregated black school in Brevard, North Carolina.

The 1966 closure of the Brevard Rosenwald School occurred as the result of another court decision that outlawed discrimination. It meant the demise of an influential name in Brevard, but the school itself illustrates the black experience in a rural community in Western North Carolina. Educational changes also portray local civil rights conflicts in a historical setting. In this context, it is important to examine the role of government — local, state, and federal — in the school's operations to provide an increased awareness of the hardships imposed on Negro education in Transylvania County.

Pioneers of education, such as Du Bois, and of philanthropy, such as Rosenwald, turned back the tide of neglect in Transylvania County. Their philosophical inspiration spoke to local pioneers, mainly black educators and black parents. The message of national leaders aroused the educational vision and commitment of local leaders. Du Bois and Rosenwald made substantive contributions during their lifetimes. In Brevard, a measureless consequence of their effort endures. In that town, black educators and black parents have worked for decades to reap the benefits of the motivating vision that resulted in the Brevard Rosenwald School.

Chapter 3

Educational Transformation

Though small and isolated from the mainstream activity of Brevard, Rosenwald School immediately transformed itself into the center of education for blacks. Its influence outweighed the size of the building. Proof of that influence lives in the memories of the principal, of the staff, and of the alumni. Their voices vibrate with the conviction that their Rosenwald experience was a positive one. To them, the small school takes on towering proportions because their measurements focus on what happened within classes and outside classes, both the official learning and the unofficial socializing. Their descriptions resound with judgments about what individuals taught and how they taught, and they also reenact the daily process that evolved into the Rosenwald strategy in Brevard.

One individual witnessed the metamorphosis for five decades. Ethel Kennedy Mills began teaching there in 1923, three years after the Rosenwald grant to improve the building that stood at the top of the hill in west Brevard. Later she became interim principal of her beloved Brevard Rosenwald School. Of course, in the minds of the community she was the "official" principal. Even after integration in 1966, Mills continued her work as an educator.

As a result, she speaks authoritatively as the resident historian, the individual who pictures the past and has a clear understanding of the present. She sees things through the perspective of the educator, one who always places the needs of students foremost. Rather than advancing her own career, she supported improvements that advanced the cause of education so children could learn in classrooms.

Mills, born in Franklin, North Carolina, brought the heritage of her father, the Reverend James Thomas Kennedy, who built both a church and a school for African Americans in Macon County, to the Brevard community.

3. Educational Transformation

In Asheville, the Reverend Kennedy and educator J.H. Michael developed a strong friendship. Mr. Michael suggested that Kennedy's daughter Ethel would excel at teaching. As a result, at the age of 15 Ethel Kennedy began a career that lasted 51 years. "I often think about that. If Mr. Michael hadn't seen that potential in me, what would I have done? My sister became a cook, a good cook, but I have always loved teaching" (interview, June 17, 1999).

First the expanded building brought about a centralization in the physical location of learning. Long-term Principal Mills identified three Negro schools—Glade Creek, Everett Farm, and Rosenwald—that were operating when she arrived on the scene. Soon, major changes began to develop. As a result, the newly named Rosenwald school dominated the educational experience for black children. Mills' testimony verifies that the three schools for black children eventually consolidated into one school at the Rosenwald site.

The changes, though, occurred slowly. However, they happened methodically as Brevard Rosenwald School marched forward from educational disorder to educational security, from a rather haphazard approach to a formally regulated approach. Both the curriculum and the social life enriched the opportunities of the students and the community.

It was a transformation that evolved gradually. First came the improvements in the building. That made it possible to achieve organization of classes. Later came the improvements in the faculty, both in numbers and in formal training. That made it possible to institute programs that enriched lives socially as well as academically.

Because of its meager enrollment, the Everett Farm School was eventually shut down. The shutdown forced its young students to attend Glade Creek School. Social practices meant that school attendance was not the highest priority, often due to the economic circumstances of African American families. Mills explained that school closed for three weeks each fall to allow children to aid in gathering the harvest. "People don't remember that school closed for three to four weeks so the children could stay out to pick corn, to pile fodder, and to do other farm chores" (interview, June 6, 1999).

It took two more decades before the Glade School students switched to the Rosenwald School. According to the *Transylvania Times* issue of August 26, 1948, Glade Creek closed its doors on September 1, 1948, and transported the students to the new Brevard Rosenwald School. The front-page article announces:

> It is a significant fact that two new school buildings in Brevard will be open for use for the first time. The new Brevard Elementary School ... will house the classes of the sixth, seventh and eighth grades. The other new building, Rosenwald School for colored children, will also be ready for occupancy on Wednesday and will house all of the colored

students of the county. Since the completion of this building, it was deemed wise to consolidate Glade Creek School with Rosenwald.

The next paragraph in the news article calls for a meeting of all white principals and teachers at the Brevard High School auditorium in preparation for the opening of school. The Rosenwald School faculty was not invited.

Before the changes the new building permitted, the faculty had created an atmosphere that satisfied both students and parents. Though the strategy was definitely informal, the daily operation of the school led to positive psychological results. Individuals who attended classes in the old school building, which burned in 1941, remembered mostly happy times.

Eyewitnesses still attest to that happiness. Eighty years later, while seated on her front porch and basking in the sunshine, Bernetha Mills Owens, who had recently celebrated her ninety-second birthday, recalled that G.W. Thompson, an early principal who was a tall, dark-complexioned man, walked through the sewing room frequently with a friendly smile for all the students (interview, August 27, 2002).

Another alumna, Eversta Bailey Smith, credits basketball for providing her true motivation to attend school. She vividly recalls her demanding coach, Ethel Coleman, and her principal Javan Jones, another sports lover. "Basketball was one reason I liked to go to school," Smith said. "We had green and white uniforms. We was hard to beat. Tryon beat us one time, but the next time we set 'em down. We beat the stew out of them. We got to go to lots of places in the school bus. Prof Jones really liked sports."

Smith also voiced judgments about teachers' personalities in the classroom. She described Wilkie Johnstone as sweet but tough. She remembered Synetha Glenn as being very young and Ethel Mills as a terror if a student misbehaved. "Mrs. Mills was tough on us. She would point that hand, and you'd better be good. If you cut up in church, well, on Monday she would tear into us, but it made us good kids," Smith said. "There weren't any drugs in that school." Other than sports, Smith's key interests were the weekly spelling bees and special programs planned for the parents (interview).

Alumni also credit the strategy at the Rosenwald school as one reason they have enjoyed a life of participation. Selena Robinson, an outstanding community leader whose 14 children became Rosenwald students, was well prepared for the demands of life by her Rosenwald education. During a conversation in her home, where one wall is decorated with plaques and awards honoring her achievements and community service while another wall honors

Opposite: Now the Eugene M. Morris Education Center, this building was the Rosenwald School from 1948 until 1966. (Front and back views.) (Photograph by Juanita Spanogle.)

her family heritage, she spoke highly of the good times and wonderful teachers at Rosenwald. Robinson also recalled the fun of sharing lunches.

> I sometimes took a jar of pinto beans and a hunk of cornbread. If I had a nickel and another child had a nickel, we could walk to Mr. "Jip" Mills' Store.... You could get a scoop of peanut butter for a nickel and a nickel's worth of crackers. That was a fine lunch [interview, March 26, 2000].

Nathaniel Hall, retired educator and author of a book delineating the history of the Negro in Transylvania County, also affirmed happy memories of school days. Other alumni speak vividly about their experiences at the Brevard institution.

Reesie Madison, while wearing a Stanford University sweatshirt celebrating her grandson's alma mater, recited her children's accomplishments, which sounded like a compilation for a *Who's Who* publication. Madison recalled the teachers and activities of her student days with great respect. Though the teaching strategy at Brevard Rosenwald School may not have met textbook standards, it worked wonders in the minds of students in the classrooms.

While it is uplifting to recognize the happiness children experienced, it is also essential to face the hardships they endured. As children, they sometimes did not recognize the pain of poverty. Mills described children as oblivious to the lack of "things." As long as teachers enthusiastically presented new activities, little children were "as happy as larks." One reason is that the faculty instilled them with the natural desire to learn new skills and to discover unknown facts.

One tragedy in the school's history, the 1941 fire, was so extensive that it could not be overlooked. The fire altered the school's strategy, and it forced major adjustments in life at Brevard Rosenwald School. This occurred during World War II, when many communities had to reach new heights of self-reliance to meet daily needs. The students and faculty of Brevard Rosenwald School had to rely on those internal resources for years longer than should have been necessary.

Dorothy Pierce Hill described the fire that destroyed the original building and the sense of despair that pervaded her spirit when she confronted the realization that the site of her early educational experiences had been destroyed. Charred particles whirled through the neighborhood for days, a silent reminder that the school was gone.

Sadness also involved personal loss. Winona Whiteside, who resided on West Main Street in Brevard until her death in December 2002, found that memories of school days flooded her mind with ease. She shared the joy of carrying lunch to school in a bucket, but she also shared the unhappy expe-

3. Educational Transformation

The Brevard Rosenwald School was destroyed by fire on March 12, 1941. (Courtesy the Transylvania County Archives.)

rience of having a friend die. Her sadness at recalling the death of a classmate, Maude Killian, was apparent. She described Maude's school desk as being draped in black and white crepe paper on the morning after her death (interview, March 7, 2000). With an energy and an outlook that belies their age, former students spoke with animation about the fulfilling experiences at Rosenwald. However, they also recalled some of the school's problems.

The tragic fire required an innovative shift in the educational strategy. During the interim before the new building was ready for occupancy, from 1941 to 1948, students attended classes in community churches. Grades one, two, and three met in the wooden annex of the Bethel "A" Church with Ethel K. Mills. Grades three, four, and five met in the basement of the Mills Chapel A.M.E. Zion church with Synetha G. Benjamin, and the upper grades met at Bethel Baptist Church on Carver Street with Wilkie C. Johnstone and John P. Sartor as the instructors. It was a plan required by necessity but shaped to guarantee that education would continue for black students in Brevard.

While schools were becoming more formal elsewhere, Rosenwald students shifted to a make-do system. They learned that a strategy of cooperation was essential. Annie Marie Hailey recalls that her classmates in the Methodist church basement began volunteering early in the morning to round up kindling and drag wood to start the next day's fire. "Oh, yes," Hailey said, "those boys knew they could leave school early to search for wood so they started early to get their names in the pot. The teacher would decide after lunch, and they could tramp around the woods picking up fallen limbs" (interview, October 3, 2002).

Daniel Owens, a resident of West Main Street not far from the reconstructed Rosenwald building, attended school at the temporary sites from 1941 to 1948. Because he was six when the temporary sites opened, he was in the new Rosenwald School for only one year. The temporary classrooms caused uncomfortable moments for him. On one occasion he was tardy when he arrived at the Annex. Instead of walking in to join his class, he remained outside until recess brought the others out to play. "I guess I was shy. I just stayed on the steps till recess" (interview, February 29, 2000). After his elementary and junior high years, he traveled to Hendersonville's Ninth Avenue School.

For others, the move to another physical location for classes did not dim the learning strategy. Betty Hunt High, a retired librarian living in the Raleigh area, recalled happy days in the church school sites and a relentless war on ignorance (interview, February 25, 2000). Alice Glaze Robinson found comfort in her classes at the Bethel "A" Church annex (interview, October 25, 2002). Students willingly helped one another. As year followed year in the "temporary" headquarters, they accepted the church school sites as normal. Somehow teachers instilled a more important concept: learning was a permanent experience and definitely more important than dwelling on years of inconvenience.

That sense of cooperation prevailed to make the Brevard Rosenwald School an institution that survived the Depression, World War II, and a destructive fire. However, from the Civil War era to the first half of the twentieth century, a lack of cooperation in Transylvania County had delayed the opportunity for blacks to receive an academically targeted education.

Though the establishment of Brevard Rosenwald School seems rather smooth when viewed as an accomplished fact, the school faced an endless struggle both before and after its doors opened. Confrontation with racist historical attitudes was a constant threat, one requiring resourcefulness and innovation to make education successful. History documents African American efforts to become an educated people.

Because historical patterns set the bar of meaningful educational opportunities at a higher and higher mark, each generation found it difficult to vault to the new pinnacle. Every decade blacks reached for attainment: the privilege of attending school and gaining knowledge.

Feeling that enforced servitude had robbed them of an education, the former slaves, upon becoming freed men, sought literacy with intensity. Harriet Beecher Stowe commented on their educational goals in 1879: "They rushed not to the grog-shop but to the schoolroom — they cried for the spelling-book as bread and pleaded for teachers as a necessity of life" (Anderson, 1988, p. 5).

Following the Civil War, North Carolina's Constitutional Convention of 1868, composed of Northerners, Negroes, Radicals, and Conservatives, adopted this resolution: "The interest and happiness of the two races would be best promoted by the establishment of separate schools" (Van Noppen and Van Noppen, 1973, p. 123). The concept "in the best interest of both races" permitted strong rationalization for segregated schools. The General Assembly, in the School Law of 1869, subsequently established taxation to finance public schools and specified that such schools would be free for all children between six and twenty-one years of age (Van Noppen and Van Noppen, 1973).

The 1868 resolution was the beginning of a barrage of roadblocks making the road to education almost impassable. Less than a decade later, additional legislation hindered equal educational opportunities for Negroes. North Carolina's Constitutional Convention of 1875 stipulated strict limitations on the rights of black citizens. The convention prohibited both integration of schools and interracial marriages. Local school control was placed in the hands of whites (Haley, 1987). The number of defeats for educational equality increased dramatically with such legislation.

The absence of financial undergirding became an obvious hindrance. Eliminating funds from taxes severely restricted educational opportunities for both whites and blacks. Education was dependent on local provision of funds and buildings, on availability of willing teachers, and on parental support. Mountain counties were especially poor, for money was a scarce commodity and their school systems were often considered failures (Van Noppen and Van Noppen, 1973). In the mountain region, education was regarded as a luxury, a non-necessity.

In the western counties, the small Negro population made it difficult to house a separate school in each district. Also, feelings of inferiority and prejudice hindered the advancement of learning. Whites enjoyed a measure of status if their African American neighbors could be categorized as their subordinates.

Gradually minimal inroads of awareness nudged the public to do something, however small. Sporadic support of African American education appeared early in the twentieth century in Transylvania County. A letter in a 1907 issue of the *Sylvan Valley News*, cited by Sue Dempsey Brewer (1992), indicates white support of education for black families in the county. The editor identifies a request from the Rev. I.Z. Phillips, a "colored teacher" at the Davidson River School, to publish a letter:

> You will please allow me space in your paper to say that I find the white people of this county like the good white people of Rutherford. They are not the Negro's enemy as many of us suppose but always ready to help the Negro who will help himself.
>
> When the committee of my school decided to cut off a month and repair the building, Mr. T.T. Patton advised me to raise the money among

ourselves to pay off the indebtedness, and he would head the list with a dollar. So I raised enough with the assistance of our white friends to pay off the indebtedness, run over five months instead of three, and got a $30 library for the school.

The names of the friends to Negro education are as follows: Brevard Tannin Company, $2; T.T., T.E. Jr., and J.S. Patton, Geo. Gillespie and E.E. Bishop, $1 each; F.H. Patton, I.M. Shepard, J.B. Bailey, G.W. Wilson, Miss Bessie Clark, Mrs. G.L. Wilson, Drs. Wm. and A.E. Lyday, W.L. Talley, W.K. Osborne, Jno. C. Deaver, Rev. W.H. Davis, N.W. Galloway, W.H. Smith, Perry Townsend, Rev. R.G. Tuttle, Ed Patton, 50 cents each; E.B. Hamilton, E.O. Shipman, E.A. Allison, C.A. Shuford, Walter Orr, W.F. Whitmire, C.M. and Van Gallimore, J.J. Patton, Geneva and W.H. Allison, R.L. Nicholson, M.A. Cooper, R.L. Gash, Mrs. S.M. Mackey, Ed Poor, Thomas and Jefferson Wilson, G.F. Chapell, 25 cents each.

Allow me to thank you again for what you have done toward making the Negro a better citizen for the state and race. Signed, I.Z. Phillips [p. 78].

In essence, the letter is a thank you note, but it also serves as a documented account of the funds received. In addition, it provides evidence that Negro education was a community concern in Transylvania County and that the school term ranged from three to five months. Also, it identifies those who helped in this instance. A suggestion of servility on the part of Phillips exists in the tone and content of the letter.

In Transylvania County, as was common in most rural areas, each community worked to achieve education only for families within township borders. Residents established small schools in rural neighborhoods. Both African American and white communities sought ways to improve learning opportunities for their students. Negro parents, faced with social restrictions resulting from the scourge of segregation, pursued all available avenues for educating their children. Parents viewed education as a weapon to counteract social forces pushing black students to the brink of failure. The positive impact combined the small-school strategy with the neighborhood location. Both the size and the place contributed to the vitality of the Brevard Rosenwald School as a center for African American activity in Brevard.

Schools for blacks appeared soon after the Civil War. Historical records document a series of efforts, each working to transform the quality and the availability of education for blacks. Efforts in the 1800s established the roots of opportunity that led eventually to the designated Rosenwald School. The long-term strategy eventually made it possible to concentrate on short-term strategies in the classrooms during the 1900s.

In *The Negroes of Transylvania County: 1861–1961*, Hall (1984) documents the construction of a one-room frame schoolhouse near Brevard at Shady Grove, a school that operated from 1862 to 1901 with Ben Herrin, a resident of Arden, North Carolina, serving as the first teacher.

3. Educational Transformation

Hall also identifies the establishment of another school for Negro children, one that was destroyed by fire in 1866. The school, initiated by the French Broad Church, was the forerunner of the Glade Creek School. It operated on a three-month term for approximately 15 years with Henderson County resident Jim Killian serving as the instructor. The school then moved from the church to a one-room building at the stockyards and later became an annex to Glade Creek Church. There it provided up to seven grades of instruction. In 1938, the Glade Creek Colored School was described as a one-story frame building with a metal roof. Its floor area was 1300 square feet. The school had an estimated replacement cost of $1,700, with an estimated sound or insurable value of $1,200. The 1938 insurance in force for Glade Creek School amounted to $1,000.

At age 107, Gertrude Gash recalled attending school at Glade Creek, as did her mother. "My favorite teacher was Mr. Allen. I've got a picture of him in my trunk. He used a great long hickory. I was his pet," she said (interview). In later years, Gash's son Eural, who was known as a strong student, graduated from the Brevard Rosenwald School, but her daughter hated school and left home on the pretext of attending school only to play around the bridge until time to return home. "I never could understand why she didn't want to go to school," said Gash (interview).

After seventh grade the Glade Creek children, under the sponsorship of Spurgeon and Gertie Hemphill, attended schools in Brevard until the 1948 consolidation with the Brevard Rosenwald School (Hall, 1984). At that time the Glade Creek School was closed, and all students from that community were bused into town.

Another school, a two-room building, was constructed on land provided by Randall W. Everett and his wife, to shorten travel time and distance for students attending the Glade Creek School. Its first teacher was Annie Gash (Hall, 1984). Ethel Mills, who was a teacher at the Everett Farm School for several years, recalled that the school closed in the 1930s because the student population was too small to merit keeping the school open (interview, June 9, 1999). A 1938 Aetna insurance estimate placed a value of $700 on the school building on the Everett farm.

Further references to black education are evident in the school board minutes and a few other public documents from 1880 to 1966. Although two colored teachers are referenced in 1880, no "colored school" was formally recognized in a list recorded in the Transylvania County School Board minutes dated 1901–1902. However, documents from records maintained by Judson Corn in 1897 identify three schools and the families that supported them as well as the members of the school committees. In the section dated 1904–1906, the list includes a Boyd colored school. Three years later, a June 2, 1909, report refers to two colored schools: the Boyd Colored School and the

Brevard Colored School. The former had one teacher, hired at a salary of $25 per month, and the latter was a three-teacher school with one teacher hired for $30 per month and the other two hired for $25 per month. The salary scale indicates white teachers received the same salaries, but at least three of them were paid $45, and two, $40. The same account estimated that school funds for the academic year to commence on July 1, 1909, amounted to $5,600.

Transylvania County's Deed Book 26, page 427, documents that a deed was registered on May 4, 1909, in which land was transferred by Robert A. and Adeline Garrett to J.F.W. Mills, Jones Mills, and Lee Kilgore as trustees for the Brevard Colored Industrial School. The deed identified the area, known as Indian Mounds, and the transaction was completed for $10 and other valuable considerations. In the May 28, 1909 issue of the *Sylvan Valley News*, an article about the Colored Industrial School presents this account:

> It has always been the policy of this paper to give publicity to the colored people only when they do something meritorious and deserve it. The move making for a colored industrial school in Brevard we look upon as of this class.
>
> The aim of the promoters of this enterprise here is to teach the colored girls to cook, wash, iron, sew and keep house properly so that when there is a call for a cook or laundress, people wanting help can apply to the school and find those who know their duties and can be relied on to perform them properly. The boys will be taught farming, garden work and the use of tools of various kinds so they will be better able to secure work at good wages.
>
> Those having this enterprise in hand (prominent among whom is Jim Aiken — and what Jim undertakes generally goes) have secured three and a half acres of land in the western section of town ... [if] W. Main Street is extended ... [it] will reach it — and want the assistance of white people to help them build a schoolhouse. They have already carried on a successful school for the past two years and feel that they have merited the confidence and support of all good people. They have done well, and we believe they deserve encouragement.

As early as 1877, the black community had opened a school for its children. In 1909, the *Sylvan Valley News* editor, a respected member of the white community, encouraged his neighbors to support the construction of the new Brevard Colored Industrial School building. The editor, who lauded the success of the institution's predecessor during the two previous years, recommended support of the new industrial school.

The October 22, 1909, edition of the local paper announced the arrival of J.H. Johnstone, M.D., from Knoxville, Tennessee. Along with his family, Johnstone had moved into the former residence of James P. "Jim" Aiken on

Oak Lawn Avenue. His mission was to erect a colored industrial school in the west part of Brevard. The building was already under construction.

Editor J.J. Miner added another article about the Colored Industrial School. He wondered why there was no shortage of money. According to the article, Miner had attempted to uncover the source of the funds by talking to the colored people, but he learned only that the community had sponsored neither festivals nor church sales as fund-raising projects. Members of the colored community united in their refusal to reveal the source of the money. Miner's investigative reporting had stumbled on an immoveable obstacle: the silence of the black community.

Startled by the three-story building being erected atop a beautiful wooded knoll, Miner indicated that its dimensions were 40 × 50 feet. The school had been elevated to tap into the town's water supply, but the building was also to have its own water supply. When completed, the building was used as a center of instruction for young girls. Another building was planned for the boys, with the expectation of teaching them a number of industries, including brick making. The school was slated to open January 1, 1910. Both schools were forerunners of the Brevard Rosenwald School.

Records of January 3, 1910, refer to both the Brevard and the Boyd colored schools. The school board designated that $775 be paid on the Loan Fund to the State Treasurer and that school districts be charged various amounts, but the two colored districts were not included. The board allotted Davidson River School an additional room and extensive repairs. It solicited bids for the construction of a schoolhouse for the colored children of Brevard. The contract was awarded to T.C. Holtzclaw and his son, R.W. Holtzclaw. The contract, signed by Superintendent T.C. Henderson, is dated April 8, 1910. The $999 terms designate the construction details:

> The said parties of the first part ... agree to furnish all material and build for the said party of the second part for Brevard school district #2, colored race, a new school house.... The said house to consist of two rooms ... separated by ... folding partition doors, the said doors to begin not over four feet from either wall ... and to construct ... a porch ... and two cloakrooms ... and a flue.... Which flue shall rest on the ground and extend at least five feet above where it passes through the roof of the building.... The said house is to be placed on good brick or stone pillars ... and to be covered with ordinary Cortright shingles. All the material ... is to be #2 except the siding which is to be #1. All the windows in the building are to be checkrailed except those in the cloakrooms.... The workmanship on the said building is to be as good as the workmanship done on the building at Davidson River [school board minutes, January 3, 1910].

In the board's minutes, dated June 6, 1910, surplus desks at the Rosman

School were to be transferred to the Davidson River School. The board would pay one half the cost of the desks, and the district of Brevard would pay the other half. In the same meeting, it was decided that the old school benches at Davidson River would be transferred to the school at Colored District #1 of the Boyd Township. In addition, the board appropriated funds to support a four months' school term. The board agreed to approach the commissioners to levy five cents on each $100 valuation of property and 15 cents for each taxable poll to create a school fund, which would make the county eligible for funds from the state.

Other records indicate that public recognition of the educational needs of the African American population in Brevard and Transylvania County dates at least to 1904–1906. Transylvania County Superintendent Judson Corn's papers show that three schools for colored children were operating in 1897 and imply that the schools were well established.

The county maintained separate schools for the two races. Teacher salaries were within the same range, although a few white teachers received $15 to $20 more each month. Buildings for both the white and the black communities were the school board's concern. Contractors were expected to construct schools of the same quality for both groups. In regard to furniture, the more out-of-date benches were to be used at the Boyd colored school. Until 1910, the transfer of used benches is the only documented designation of blatant discrimination other than the use of separate facilities.

Two years later, the schoolhouse in Colored District #1 was slated for an additional room. The school board accepted the bid of L.C. Orr, who agreed to furnish all materials and labor for the construction of a one-room frame school building as well as for repairs on the old building. James Y. Joyner, State Superintendent of Public Instruction, prepared the specifications, and the architectural firm of Barrett and Thompson drew the plans. The work was to be completed by October 1, 1912, for $500.

Defective work or improper materials were not to be tolerated. Specifications for the Boyd #1 Colored School House included a 20 × 28 room with a 12-foot high ceiling, a well braced roof, six windows, 10 × 14, 30 lights hung with weights, an 8 × 10 cloak room, and an 8 × 8 porch with steps. Pillars were to be built with good stone and were not to be more than seven feet apart. They were to be of good size and well placed in the ground. Specifications indicated sills must be at least ten inches off the ground and the construction of a brick flue must extend at least five feet above the roof. This indicates that the construction was the result of careful planning, and the involvement of the state superintendent indicates an expansion of Raleigh's interest in mountain community needs. The decisions may also show that there was a responsible school board in Transylvania County.

Subtle details disclose that the need for transformation existed at the

3. Educational Transformation

higher administrative levels as well as in building provisions. The next reference to the education of black children is recorded in the minutes of December 3, 1917, but a reference in the monthly report of N.C. Newbold, director of the Division of Negro Education, indicated that he had visited Superintendent T.C. Henderson on February 19 and 20, 1915. He spoke only to the white teachers during a two-day workshop that addressed the need for including industrial subjects in elementary schools and in high schools. Newbold had also visited the Brevard Institute, a school for whites that offered high school classes in industrial subjects such as cooking, sewing, agriculture, printing, and manual training. Though Newbold, who was in charge of Negro education for the state, could have communicated with black schools, his report makes reference only to situations involving whites.

At the same time, documents record less-than-ideal options for black students. The December 1917 board of education minutes refer to classes for black children in a private home for a term of four months. The use of a private home may indicate that the building constructed by the Holtzclaws was no longer large enough for the number of students. Wilkie C. Johnstone, a black educational leader, delivered a bill for $10 for four months rent of her house for the Brevard Colored School. Originally from the Humid community in Cleveland County, Johnstone accompanied her husband James H. Johnstone to Transylvania County to establish an industrial school for young blacks. A 1902 graduate of Lincoln Academy at Kings Mountain, North Carolina, she had been assigned by Emily Pruden to Brevard to assist in starting a school (Hall, 1984).

Minimal changes at black facilities continued. On January 7, 1918, the school board ordered that P.E. McGuire be paid the sum of $4 from the Glade Creek School apportionment for painting the school roof and $4.40 for replacing bricks. Forty cents was to be placed in the Glade Creek account. At the same meeting, the Board considered the Rosenwald Fund, which was financing school construction throughout North Carolina. Action was postponed pending further study.

However, the Transylvania folder in Box 4, General Correspondence of the Director, Division of Negro Education of the Department of Public Instruction, at the North Carolina State Archives, contains a handwritten letter, dated September 21, 1919, and signed by G.W. Thompson, who identifies himself as the principal of Brevard's Colored School. In the letter directed to N.C. Newbold, Thompson wrote:

> I am again in the work as principal of the col. school at the above name place. I wrote you over a year ago to visit our school. Your answer was that you would at your earliest. On your way to the County Supt. Conference in Asheville on last year you was called back home [due] to the

illness of your child and wired me that you could not come. I accepted that and looked for you at another date.

You did come a time when the school session wasn't on hand, viewed the place and talked to some of the col. men as well as the Supt. of the County. You proposed to send us a sum of money from the state in which we did realized the intention by a nice large ell to our old building worth about 7 or 8 hundred dollars. And besides the County Supt. says you have promised us very soon $900 more. When will we get it?

Our work is very good this fall. I would of liked to met you when you was here. We sure highly appreciate what you have done. Will this money come from the Rosenwald Fund next time? You are the Agent. Our Convention is going to meet at Hendersonville N.C. this week, and we want to raise all we can and put into this school if possible. We need a county supervisor, a col. man or woman to work under you like in Spartanburg County, Spartanburg, S.C. and other counties.

Could we get one? Or do you have anything to do with that affair? We need more rooms since the compulsory law has been enforced. We hope you will work fast to see to it that we will get the money very soon. I believe you are a race man showing help for the colored as well as for the whites.

Let me hear from you soon.

Nine days later Newbold responded to Professor G.W. Thompson in a typewritten letter:

> I think it would be possible for us to secure some assistance to employ a Jeanes' Supervisor for Transylvania County if your County Superintendent and Board of Education desire to employ such a worker and could make an appropriation from county funds to pay a large part of the salary.
>
> You evidently have a misunderstanding about assistance previously promised on your building. In view of the fact that all districts are being consolidated in the Brevard Schools, I have thought it possible to get $900 from the Rosenwald Fund to aid in the construction of the building and also paint and furnish it.
>
> Your Superintendent sent me some applications some time ago that were forwarded to the Rosenwald Committee and have been returned to Mr. Mitchell for some corrections. I think there will be no trouble about getting this money when the plans have been fully agreed upon. If you get this money and will add the Industrial room, the two cloak rooms and complete the building by making some changes in the windows of your old building, paint and furnish it, I think I might be able to visit you when all the work has been done.

The communication sheds light on the origins of the Rosenwald School. Also, internal transactions in the 1920s brought changes to the education of blacks in Transylvania County. In additional records, dated March 1, 1920,

3. Educational Transformation

the superintendent instructed that $70 be taken from the Building and Furniture Fund for the Brevard #2 Colored School, and that Brevard #2 School — Colored is not indicated — should have the bill for the piano.

On March 26, 1920, the board verified the need for renovation and/or repair on the Brevard Colored School. With a loan from the state, two additional rooms had been built and a bit of repair done. New furniture, including desks, had been purchased. The board minutes mentioned that "said school and the said school district" are poor and therefore unable to meet their part of the expense. The superintendent was instructed to contact Newbold to see if he would be willing to sponsor a loan for the district.

On April 5, 1920, the board approached the state for a loan through A.S. Brower, as evident in records in Box 87 of Special Collections, Department of Public Instruction, Office of the Superintendent. Correspondence from the Julius Rosenwald Fund, preserved at the North Carolina state archives, contains notes from W.F. Credle, director of the Rosenwald Fund in Nashville, Tennessee. In a May 5, 1920, letter, P.C. McGuire is ordered to complete the work at Brevard #2 Colored School "at once."

Later there is reference to the $500 Newbold addition Then, on July 6, 1920, the school is referred to as the Rosenwald School. In the minutes of July 6, 1920, Allard Allison is expected to submit a bid to the school board for the job of painting all the outside walls on the Rosenwald School House.

The painting job constitutes the first reference to a Rosenwald school in Brevard. The stage was set for the beginning of the transformation of black education in Transylvania County. Two months later, on September 8, 1920, Allard Allison of Penrose was awarded the contract for a painting, caulking, and puttying job on the Rosenwald Colored School. N.C. Newbold, who handled distribution of Rosenwald Funds in the state, suggested a color scheme.

The Rosenwald Committee was specific about the paint, available from the General Refining Company of Cleveland, Ohio, used at sites receiving Rosenwald money. The board acknowledged its responsibility to supply the paint and putty to Mr. Allison. The next board reference to the school occurs in minutes of 1925 when C.C. McGuire was ordered to complete the Brevard #2 school "at once."

In addition to building problems, transportation and staffing challenges plagued black schools, as apparent in a document at the NC State Archives in Box 18 of the series Operational Budgets, 1919–45. On February 20, 1923, A.F. Mitchell, Superintendent of Transylvania County Public Schools, wrote the following letter to Mr. A.S. Brower, director of Teacher Certification at the State Department of Public Instruction in Raleigh:

> With reference to the Glade Creek school, ... there are in Boyd #1 colored district two school buildings. One [is] on one side of the French

Broad River, and another on the other. The reason for this is that during high water it was impossible for the children at the Everette place on one side of the French Broad to reach the school on the other side at the Glade Creek school proper.

At the Glade Creek school proper, there are two teachers maintaining an average daily attendance of approximately 40 or more. On the other hand, at the Everette school, part of the Boyd #1 district, the average maintained at that school ranges around 15 or 16....

Is it going to be possible for us to get an appropriation for all three teachers even though the average daily attendance cannot be as I see it for this year 65?

Brower's response to Superintendent Mitchell was, "I think that matter ... may be easily handled by not treating them [Glade Creek and Everette Farm Schools] as two separate schools, which, of course, they really are." Similar attendance problems existed in the small white schools of Transylvania County.

More documents establish the importance of the Rosenwald initiative in Brevard. A report in Box 8 of Special Subjects File, Rosenwald Fund at the State Archives entitled "Rosenwald School Buildings in North Carolina from the Beginning until July 1, 1930," contains a table indicating that funds were allotted for a Type 3 school located in Brevard in Transylvania County for the budget year 1920-21 (p. 16). A Type 3 school indicated that three teachers worked in the building. A document at Fisk University in the Rosenwald Archives, Special Collections, includes this notation: "Built under Tuskegee." No year was indicated. Rosenwald money was managed from Tuskegee Institute until 1920. After that the distribution of funds originated from Nashville, Tennessee. The same document indicates that the total cost of the Brevard school amounted to $4,850. Of that sum, the Negroes of Transylvania County contributed $1,195; the whites, none, and public funds, $2,755. The Rosenwald contribution was $900. The Negroes raised an amount greater than that donated by the Rosenwald Fund, and the Rosenwald contribution was slightly more than 20 percent of the total cost.

In an insurance document dated 1938, the Brevard Colored School is depicted as a one-story frame building with a wood and metal roof having a floor area of 4,300 square feet. Its estimated replacement value was $5,600 with an insurable value of $4,000. In 1938, the insurance covered damage up to $2,000.

In the 1933 school board minutes, committeemen for three colored schools are named. At Glade Creek School, the committeemen were Charlie Smith, Preach [Pritchard] Gash, and Ambro Camp. At Everett School, the committeemen were Lewis Smith, James Hutchison, and Gurley Orr. At Brevard #3, the Rosenwald School, the committeemen were Arthur Hefner, J.F.W. Mills, and A.B. Benjamin.

3. Educational Transformation

In Transylvania County's Operating Budget for 1940-41, a budget of $107,041.14 was submitted. Of that amount, white elementary school teachers received $46,981.20 in salary, with a total of $3,296 going to the four colored teachers. White high school teachers were allotted $12,128, and the only colored high school teacher received $888. White principals received $3,928. No colored principal was identified. Out of a total of 74 positions, African Americans filled only five slots. John Pulaska Sartor taught grades eight through ten; Wilkie (Mrs. J.H.) Johnstone, grades six and seven; Ethelwyn K. Mills, grades three through five; Synetha F. Glenn, grades one and two. Mrs. Gertie Hemphill taught grades one through seven at Glade Creek School. After seventh grade, if transportation could be arranged, the Glade Creek students attended Rosenwald. Often Spurgeon Hemphill devised ways to transport those students, according to Mills.

In striking contrast, a total of $1,067 was provided for instructional supplies for white teachers and $40 for supplies for colored teachers. The figures were out of proportion with the number of students accommodated. No money was allotted for the black schools for travel or for teaching home economics or agriculture, but those services existed for the white schools. Only $129 was spent on fuel, water, and power and janitors' supplies at the black schools while $3,179.72 was used at the white schools. No telephones were in the schools for black students, nor were any janitors hired for the black schools. Total maintenance of the school for whites was $4,175. For the colored, the total came to $675. Insurance on buildings and equipment was $1,150 for white schools and $100 for black schools. Contract transportation for whites cost $2,624; for blacks, $192. No library services existed at the black schools, but $40 was spent on textbook replacement. A total of $300 was designated for "health" at white schools, and $50 at black schools.

The remainder of $8,579.89 was used for auxiliary services for the white schools. Fifteen white and two colored schools existed. Enrollment for white high schools was 465, and only 26 black students were receiving credit for high school courses. There were 1,653 white elementary students and 124 colored. The differential explains the need for spending the bulk of the money in the white schools, but integrated schools would have been more economical. However, integration was not considered an option.

To compound the insults and restrictions of financial impediments, the school collided with an unexpected snag. A fire destroyed the original Rosenwald School on the night of March 12, 1941. Young Cleo Mackey was driving home from work late that evening when he spotted the fire and raised the alarm. Upon hearing about the matter, Fred and Ethel Mills walked up the hill to investigate. Ethel Mills remembers that a brigade of volunteers carried buckets of water from nearby homes in a futile attempt to douse the flames. Firemen were there fighting the blaze, but the situation was beyond control.

Nearby in the white community on Probart Street, Dottie Vaniman was alarmed by the fire. "It lit up my bedroom like midday. What a waste! Shingles were flying off and burning in the neighborhood," she said. "For days debris from that fire was floating around the community" (interview, June 25, 2002). Patricia Austin, who also lived on Probart Street, watched the flames billowing above the skyline as the school was consumed (interview, December 4, 2002).

Upon entering her bedroom as she was retiring for the evening, young Dorothy Pierce saw through the window that the sky was "all lit up." She rushed to the living room to tell her parents and their boarder, Principal Sartor, that the school was on fire. They rushed to the scene, but saving the building was hopeless. She has no recollection of any firefighters being there. "Of course," she said, "there was no hydrant." The roof caved in shortly after her arrival. "The top just fell in," Hill recalled. "We all stood around the flames teasing one another about wearing our nightclothes."

The next day she reported to Superintendent J.B. Jones' office for work. Shortly after arriving, she heard him answer the telephone. Then he shouted, "What? That nigger school burned?" She assumed that no one thought the superintendent needed to be disturbed about the catastrophe (interview, February 13, 2000).

Ethel Mills, adding another item of interest, recalled that Sartor was "very torn up" about the loss, partially because that day he had visited the superintendent to express the need for a new building. "I never saw a man so all to pieces. Now I never heard anyone else mention it, but he was upset," Mills said. "No one ever accused him of burning the school." He feared, according to Mills, that the public would suspect him of arson (interview, July 16, 1999).

Others believed that unsafe wiring caused the fire. Electrical lines had reportedly been extended from Johnstone's house to the school. Dorothy Pierce Hill suggested that the oiled floors of the building contributed to its being destroyed so quickly. She believes that the coal stored underneath the building fueled the intensity of the flames (interview, February 12, 2000). In his end-of-the-year principal's report, Sartor wrote across the section to be completed about the state of the building—"Destroyed by fire March 12, 1941."

Decades afterward, members of the black community recall the tragic event. Selena Robinson and her brother, Nathaniel Hall, said that black citizens regarded the school as a pivotal center and that a sense of grief over its loss permeated the neighborhood (interview, February 14, 2000). "One day there was a school, and the next day there was nothing but ashes," Sherman Crite, Jr., said (interview, November 21, 2002).

Reesie Madison explained that the fire occurred when she was in the tenth grade and scheduled to graduate at the end of the term. She remembered that the school term ended in April and that a service was held at Bethel "A" Church for the graduates. The graduating girls, who wore white dresses, recognized that a celebration took place, but they also felt a sense of regret — like an air of gloom (interview, February 22, 2000).

During the school board meeting of March 31, 1941 — 19 days after the fire — Superintendent Jones was authorized to replace the Rosenwald School with a "semi-fireproof building with walls of rock or brick and a central heating system." Four years later on August 4, 1945, Jones was told to investigate the possibility of purchasing property from the English estate for the construction of the Rosenwald School. Page 146 of Deed Record Book 92 documents a transaction made on July 22, 1947, to acquire property from Wilkie C. Johnstone as a site for the Rosenwald Colored School for $1,500.

On October 7, 1946, five years after the fire, a resolution was entered into the school board minutes:

> Whereas, it is necessary, in order to maintain the constitutional six months' school term in the Transylvania County Administrative Unit to erect [sic] new school buildings, and remodel and enlarge existing school buildings and acquire necessary land and equipment therefor [sic] in said Transylvania County Administrative Unit; now, therefore, BE IT RESOLVED by the Board of Education of Transylvania County: ... adequate school buildings are not now available in Transylvania County ... for the operation of the constitutional six mon [sic] school term.... That it is necessary ... to erect [sic] new school buildings, and ... enlarge existing school buildings and acquire necessary land and equipment ... as follows:
>
> *Erect new school buildings at the*:
> Rosenwald School at Brevard
>
> *Remodel and enlarge existing school buildings at the following schools:*
> Brevard Primary and Grammar Schools,
> Rosman Elementary School
>
> *Remodel the existing*:
> Brevard High School building
>
> *Enlarge the existing:*
> Pisgah Forest School building
>
> ...As no funds are available ...it is necessary that the Board of Commissioners ... authorize and issue bonds ... in order that said school improvements may be provided.

In a joint meeting with the board of commissioners on April 17, 1947, it was determined that with the use of insurance money and other available funds work on the Rosenwald building should begin immediately. That decision was made more than six years after fire razed the building. At the same time the two governing bodies determined that the white Brevard Elementary School should have ten rooms and possibly a cafeteria constructed and that the remainder of the county be served in order of need.

Principal Mills explained that Harry H. Straus, founder and first president of the Ecusta Paper Company, became concerned about the lack of a traditional school building for black students. She recalled that Straus elected to pay corporate taxes, waiving the county's agreement to cancel those taxes as part of its efforts to entice the company to locate in Brevard. According to Mills, Straus agreed to pay corporate taxes provided the Rosenwald School were rebuilt. His intervention brought the need to the forefront after years of delay. Straus' civic responsibility triggered the action to erect a black elementary school. "There was plenty of rock available at Pisgah Forest, and laborers were ready and willing to start the job. I always thought the school should have been named for Straus. He made the sacrifice," Mills said (interview, March 28, 2000).

While the students of Rosenwald School were meeting in churches, Mills became curious about the ownership of a nearby section of land. After investigating court records, she learned that the committeemen held a deed for the industrial school. Then Mills met with Superintendent Jones to explore a faster means to fund the school's construction. "That land was so steep I knew it wouldn't be good for children. There would be no playground. It was even dangerous, and the exchange [of the land for money] helped get the school built," she said (interview, October 27, 2002).

After acquiring two additional parcels of land on October 7, 1946, movement for the long overdue construction of an elementary school building for black children was set in motion. In 1948, the community was told that the building was complete, but that there was no furniture. Though the building had been constructed, the transformation of black education still lacked essentials. The job was only partially complete, as those who would inhabit the school soon discovered. However, neither administrators nor the school board had to function without appropriate equipment and furniture.

James Outlaw emotionally described carrying the furniture from the three churches across the fields to the new building. "I remember the black PTA said the only thing we need is furniture. All the young men took desks we had been using in church annexes and walked through the field to transport desks to the new building" (interview, February 10, 2000). Dorothy Pierce Hill, by then a parent of Rosenwald students, recalled that the school board announced they would be able to hire cooks for the new building, but that no funds were available for equipping the kitchen. She and other parents purchased a refrigerator, a stove, and a stainless steel sink from Asheville Showcase for the school. Hill described the purchase:

I went with the committee to Asheville Showcase. We got a stove, a refrigerator, and a stainless steel sink. When they closed the school, I think they threw those things away. And we bought a piano from Dunham and paid for it monthly. I think it got thrown away [interview, February 17, 2000].

Mills affirms that the kitchen at the Brevard Rosenwald School was probably better equipped than that of any other school in the county. She attributed that achievement to a supportive PTA. "If we couldn't get it from the Board, the PTA got it for us. Some of the parents had little 'entertainments' to raise money. I talked to the manager at Asheville Showcase. I can't remember his name, but he said, 'Take whatever you need for those children, and you can make payments.' We did, and we never missed a payment. We bought wonderful equipment" (interview, March 28, 2000). With the cooperation of the school board and of the community, the doors of the new Brevard Rosenwald School were opened. The final phase of Rosenwald education had begun.

Erecting the long-delayed building helped teachers and students jump one major hurdle, but another major obstacle prevented students from receiving a complete public school education. African Americans were not permitted to attend any high school within the county borders.

According to the June 20, 1949, minutes, the Transylvania County Board of Education agreed to pay Henderson County $300 for allowing Transylvania County students to attend their high school for Negroes. A bus was purchased to transport the young people. On June 21, 1949, school board minutes indicate that Negro high school students were transported to adjoining Henderson County to attend the Ninth Avenue School, an all-black institution.

Minutes of the Hendersonville City Board of Education for June 27, 1949, record Superintendent A.D. Kornegay's report that he had been approached by Transylvania County Superintendent Jones, who was acting on the advice of the state board of education. Jones requested permission to allow Brevard's Negro high school students to enroll in the Hendersonville Negro High School. Kornegay, who recommended the arrangement, pointed out that an additional teacher would be allotted to the black high school and that transportation would be provided by the Transylvania County Board of Education. The arrangement was beneficial for the Henderson County school system. The Hendersonville City Board passed a motion that Superintendent Kornegay work out an additional financial agreement with Superintendent Jones.

This inter-county agreement proved to be a problematic decision. Although state records indicate attempts to provide secondary education in Brevard, for decades Negro youths had been forced to leave home to attend

Mr. "Jip" Mills' store provided a school bus stop for students traveling to Ninth Avenue School in Hendersonville. (Photograph by Juanita Spanogle.)

high school. Poverty, which characterized the economic condition of African American families, often prevented such a move. Students in those families simply forfeited their dreams of graduating from high school.

The decision to bus students to Hendersonville's Ninth Avenue School emphasized the inequitable educational opportunities for Negroes in Transylvania County. Daniel Owens, an alumnus of both Rosenwald School and Ninth Avenue School, recalled that his brother, George Eliot Owens, Jr., was hired to drive the bus (interview, February 29, 2000).

Samuel Howell and James Gardin, parents of Rosenwald students, lament the inadequate education that resulted after students exited the bus at the Ninth Avenue School. Some of them spent the day roaming the streets of Hendersonville. The truants returned to the school only for the homeward ride on the school bus. "Sometimes they would find a room where they could gamble ... or watch men gamble," Howell said (interview, June 9, 1999). Thomas Gardin, who admits he found little joy in high school, elected to skip class and attend movies in Hendersonville in a segregated balcony area. "I would walk down to Main Street and watch a movie. It didn't cost more than a quarter, and the time was just right to get back to Ninth Avenue in time to catch the school bus home," Gardin said (interview).

In response to a questionnaire, Brenda Elliott, a Blue Ridge Community College instructor whose father, Grady Elliott, provided an advanced education for all five of his children, reacted to being victimized by racial discrimination:

> Had the schools not been integrated in the mid-1960s, I would have had three options for continuing my education. I would have had to (1) be bussed to a black high school in another county, (2) move to my grandparents' in another town to attend high school or (3) attend a private high school in another town. People talk about bussing their children to another part of town and complain.
>
> My two younger brothers traveled about 45 miles daily to and from school. My older brother moved 75 miles away to live with our grandparents to attend high school. My older sister attended an all girls' private high school 30 miles away.... My older sister and brother ... had to leave home four years before they should have. I was denied getting to know them during that time.
>
> This was discrimination. A white family would not have put up with this situation. We had no choice.

Elliott's sister, Lois Wynn, reported that she had attended the private Allen School in Asheville and that her brother lived with their grandparents in Cleveland County so he could attend Green Bethel High School at Boiling Springs (interview, March 24, 2002). Other students expressed a feeling of being uprooted to attend school in the adjoining county. They suffered an initial sense of being outcasts in an unfamiliar environment.

In 1953, State Senator Robert T. Gash, responding to a request by a group of parents from the black community, sought facts about the possibility of building a Negro high school in Transylvania County (interview, March 9, 2000). The action was in response to the Fisher bill in the state legislature. Representative Ralph Fisher, a Brevard native, had proposed the construction of a Negro high school in Transylvania County at the Rosenwald site. On April 17, 1953, School Board members E.M. Medford, J.F. Zachary, F.S. Best, Homer McCall, and Harry Morgan, along with Superintendent Jones, adopted the following statement in response to Gash's query:

> We would like for it to be understood clearly that we favor the establishment of a Rosenwald High School at Brevard if and when the number of pupils is large enough to justify it and funds are available for constructing and equipping [sic] the building. The Rosenwald Elementary building consists of seven rooms, including the library. Five rooms are now filled with pupils, leaving only one room actually not in use, one being used for the library. With normal growth this room will be filled with elementary pupils within one or two years. Even if this room is not filled [sic], it would be impossible to put the high school pupils in the present Rosenwald building next year.

> If we establish a colored high school at Rosenwald ... we are sure that Supreme Court decisions will require facilities equal to Brevard High School. Therefore rooms would be necessary for teaching home economics, bookkeeping, shorthand, typewriting, and vocational agriculture as well as science laboratories, in addition to rooms for teachers of academic subjects. It would be necessary to purchase a site and construct a new high school building. The initial cost would be no less than $200,000.
>
> At the present, there are 36 pupils in the high school grades. After allowing for normal growth, the number of pupils available would make the cost per pupil fantastic. The state allots only one teacher for 30 pupils. Therefore, it would be necessary for the county to pay the salaries of several teachers to maintain a standard school with vocational subjects. This would postpone indefinitely construction of any other new buildings in the county.
>
> Our Negro high school pupils are now transported to Hendersonville in a new bus to a new high school building housing a standard high school with modern equipment. The distance is 21 miles, which is not as far as a considerable number of our white children in this county travel. The time required for the Negro pupils to reach Hendersonville is even less than the mileage would indicate for after their bus leaves Glade Creek there are no stops for picking up other children whereas the white high school pupils are picking up other children until they reach the city limits, some traveling as much as 30 miles. This causes some of the white children to leave home before daylight in the winter months.
>
> In a modern high school like Hendersonville, the Negroes have many opportunities which they could not enjoy in a very small high school. They have more competition and better opportunities from an academic, social, and athletic standpoint. For example, some of our boys are outstanding on the Hendersonville football team.
>
> It is our opinion that we are doing the best thing possible for the Negro high school children under existing circumstances. The Board of Education will be ready to act as soon as circumstances warrant a local high school for them [attachment to school board minutes, April 28, 1953].

The desire of the Negro community to expand Rosenwald into a high school was based in part on frustration derived from being forced to leave home in order to obtain a true high school education. Students attended boarding schools in Asheville, Concord, and other locations, including some in South Carolina. At times ten or eleven years of training had been incorporated into the old Rosenwald School curriculum, but alumna Dorothy Pierce Hill called its high school program a "myth," because she received no credit for her final two years when she enrolled at Asheville's Allen School (interview, February 17, 2000).

Nathaniel Hall moved to Washington, D.C., to live with a cousin to attend high school (interview, July 16, 1999). Cornelius Hunt graduated from Central High School in Louisville, Kentucky. Thomas Kilgore, Jr., earned his high school diploma at Stephens Lee High School in Asheville. LaRue Betsill graduated from Lincoln Academy in King's Mountain, North Carolina.

The black youth of Brevard had to exert a purposeful effort to earn a high school diploma. Though the memories of happiness remain, the inequities of history made their educational journeys a struggle. It took more than a building with a famous name and more than a new stone structure to overcome the restrictions placed upon black students in Transylvania County.

Chapter 4

Pedagogical Traditions

WHILE THE TRADITION OF SLAVERY and of segregation shaped Brevard Rosenwald School, other traditions emerged as more powerful in the classroom. The traditions at the Brevard school left many students with a positive memory of educational priorities and achievements. The small-school setting also presented obstacles on the road to education. Both staff and students had to deal with inadequate facilities, cast-off equipment, and outdated textbooks. Students at the Rosenwald School never let these hindrances take away their dignity, bolstered as they were by a traditionally tight-knit community that had long valued education as a source of personal development.

Consistent themes recur in the history of Brevard Rosenwald School. Some are comparable to those outlined in W.E.B. Du Bois' speech at Fisk University in 1938: personnel, training, finances, resources, community involvement, and leadership. In addition, careful analysis of students' responses to questions regarding their education reveals resentment, distinct attitudes about the curriculum and school traditions, and the satisfaction of success stories. Former Rosenwald students also reflected on diverse teaching styles that were part of the school's tradition.

Brevard Rosenwald School personalities left lasting impressions on students. Teachers who commanded respect in the pre-fire days, before 1941, included Synetha Glenn Benjamin, Ethel K. Mills, Gertie M. Hemphill and Wilkie C. Johnstone. The women were accomplished professionals who sought opportunities to improve their teaching skills. Alumni still describe Mills as an effective no-nonsense teacher. The Reverend Frederick Gordon portrayed her as one who "always dealt justly with everyone" (interview, February 9, 2000). Gertrude Gash's granddaughter, Doris Gardin Jeter, dreaded

Mills' strictness. Benjamin was described as "not so tough," a teacher who was always willing to do for children. Wilkie C. Johnstone was very committed to the school; her daughter, Coragreene Johnstone, a graduate, returned for a brief time to teach at her alma mater (interview, July 16, 1999).

Principals also made memorable impressions on students. In reference to "Prof" John Pulaska Sartor, the principal during the 1940s, Reesie Madison recalled that he was "a nice person who was interested in me going to a Columbia, South Carolina, school.... He encouraged us to get more education" (interview). Of "Prof" C.E. Burney, principal during the 1930s, Dorothy P. Hill reminisces, "He was nice to me.... He always smelled so clean ... like Lifebuoy soap ... said he wanted me to go to college (interview, February 17, 2000).

Allie Belle Mackey remembered Burney as a very tall man, someone whose presence was instantly noticed. Another individual felt that Principal Burney was a harsh disciplinarian, lacking in "proper" diction. On one occasion, he was described as striking a young woman across her breast with alarming force. He punished her in front of the class because she was unwilling to go outside to play. When student Nathaniel Hall voiced his displeasure at what he considered physical abuse, he was ordered out of the school. His sister Selena accompanied him home. At a School Committee meeting, Hall yielded to his mother's wishes and apologized, saying "We were both wrong," but Hall continues to feel strongly that such action was inappropriate (interview, February 14, 2000).

Teacher Wilkie C. Johnstone became a legend at the Brevard Rosenwald School. (Courtesy Wanda Johnstone Foster.)

A number of male teachers and principals joined the Rosenwald staff for short periods of time. Said Mills:

> I don't know where they found all those men, but I know why. At that time North Carolina paid a higher salary than South Carolina so money brought them.... Teachers from out-of-state liked our higher salaries. It was easy just to reach over and pull one in. Some were very, very good.
>
> I don't remember all the principals. Sessoms went to Washington when he left. He was from South Carolina. Javan Jones was from South Carolina. Now, was he principal? Sessoms was an elderly man. Well, I don't know if he was elderly or not, but he had white hair. He was a nice person to work with. He got me to do secretarial work, and ... it was against him. They didn't ask questions. He was gone when I found out. They assumed I was doing his work. They didn't ask if I was doing the report or copying. I was copying. He wasn't pleased with his writing. They let him go. I had helped with filing final reports.
>
> I learned things I didn't know ... had to do attendance each month. One guy had messed things up.... He had doctored that thing from A to Z. Soon J.B. Jones asked me to help. It took both of us to take the attendance record and check it and make it right. I was surprised that that happened. We were told to do things the right way ... to tell the truth [interview, March 23, 2000].

Mills viewed discipline as an essential part of the learning environment. Her philosophy embraced corporal punishment as an effective deterrent to misbehavior if it were used only rarely. She believed that sometimes a gentle tap sent a message of authority. "I would spank a little, just a little. I generally listened and used other punishments. I never liked the idea of spanking another's child. I didn't want any child to be afraid. I remember a comic drawing in a paper of an old darky who said, 'You can't beat the devil out of a child, but you sure can beat him in.' A better way than a spanking is to talk to a child. Soften your voice, and let the child know how to conduct himself," Mills said (interview, March 1, 2001).

Discipline was a routine part of the Rosenwald tradition. However, there were moments when violence was a threat. On one occasion, Mills heard a commotion between a student and the principal. I could hear the principal saying, "Put that down. Now put that down." That prompted her to look into the matter. "I felt concerned and when I stepped out, I could see that the student had a baseball bat ready to attack the principal who had picked up a broom to defend himself. The boy was a quiet one who usually kept to himself, but that time I could feel his anger," Mills said. "Oh, he could be hateful, and he had shown a streak of meanness a time or two, but never with me. He kind of kept to himself, but he would sometimes flare up. I said, 'Just put that down. We don't settle things that way.' Well, he did finally put it down and went on home. He moved away" (interview, September 22, 2002).

Teachers taught Rosenwald students to set high goals for their learning. The pressure to master academic material depended to a large extent on the standards established by the various teachers. Hall reflected on his extensive training in geography: "Miss Wharton taught enough geography to last us till graduate school. We made our own maps, maps of North Carolina, the United States, the world" (interview, February 14, 2000). Hall described Ben Herrin as "a principal as tough as Joe Lewis" (interview, July 16, 1999).

Agnes Wilson attended kindergarten in the home of Agnes Hunt, an active educator who was principal of another black school in the county. Wilson described Hunt as a "precious" teacher (interview, February 8, 1999). The county hired Hunt to provide training for black teachers and interested adult residents of the community. She also offered evening classes for individuals wishing to acquire teacher certification (Selena Robinson, interview, July 16, 1999). The classes were part of an emerging effort to emphasize teacher training.

Wilson remembers Gertie M. Hemphill as a teacher gifted in using interesting illustrations. "It was from her that I learned that teaching didn't have to be boring. We could have fun and still learn. I respected her, but she let us have fun." Wilson related a story in reference to behavior management. One little classmate had a habit of fibbing, and everyone knew she was doing just that — fibbing. "Well, Mrs. Hemphill wanted her to break the habit. She said, 'When you tell fibs, hair will grow on your body. If you continue, your appearance may change and you will look like a monkey.'" According to Wilson, students, in the unkind way of children, called the little girl "Monkey." When the child's mother learned about her daughter's difficulty, the parent reinforced Hemphill's lesson by dealing directly with her child's tendency to lie. Wilson said that the student's fibbing was quickly curbed (interview, February 8, 2000). Respect for Hemphill and evidence of her effectiveness as a teacher and principal pervade the comments of her former students. In 1963, students at the Ninth Avenue School in Hendersonville dedicated *The Tiger*, their yearbook, to her and to Mary Agnes Jones. The dedication praised the teachers for the "good they have exerted in young lives" that "goes on and on."

Teachers emphasized specific subjects in their classrooms. Julia Smith, a retired teacher who resides in Wilmington, North Carolina, said that, as a recent graduate of Winston-Salem State College, she took her fresh knowledge of teaching methods to Rosenwald in 1948, where she taught for approximately ten years. She highlighted music: "I had them do an operetta. They had never heard of one before. Most of their teachers had been there for years and years, and I was young and wanted to do different things. I did my thing, and they did theirs. We got along. I can get along with the devil" (interview, March 24, 2000).

Annie Marie Hailey recalled "Cabbage Patch Magic," an exciting operetta showcasing 50 or more children, dressed in paper costumes like tulips and cabbage heads. At the end, characters bowed down so that it looked like a garden on the stage. The operetta featured lots of dancing (interview, August 21, 2002). Smith's programs were usually musical so that many students could participate.

Lois Elliott Wynn described Smith as a "jewel" in the community. Wynn, who studied piano with her, recalled that Smith was strict about posture and finger positions on the keys. "She would rap on my fingers if I didn't do it right. That hurt, but my mama said, 'You want to learn to do it right, don't you?' And I did want to do it right" (interview, March 24, 2002).

Hailey thought that Wilkie Johnstone was "very strict." Hailey remembers that Johnstone's lessons were outlined on the chalkboard and that she pointed to each line with a yardstick as she taught. "She was not hard to get along with if you wanted to learn. She made it easy for you to learn," Hailey said. "We each tried to outdo each other to please her. Everybody tried to make the highest score on the Friday spelling test to get her praise. I loved her classes" (interview, March 24, 2002).

F. Douglas Cantey shares Hailey's appreciation for Wilkie Johnstone. "There was one teacher I was very fond of: Mrs. Johnstone, my seventh and eighth grade teacher. She was very positive," he said. "In looking back, I think she did a lot to make me realize I had some potential. I also had a great deal of respect for Mrs. Gertie Hemphill. She taught me in the early grades. She was such a nice woman. She emphasized art and other forms of literature. I think she did a lot to take the rough edges off me" (interview, December 18, 2002).

Sherry Edington said that Mary B. Kilgore was dramatic in the classroom. "She taught us how to accent certain syllables in poetry with our voices, like "The Land of Counterpane" by Robert Lewis Stevenson. I remember how she waved her hands in the air to give us directions. That has stuck with me. The Reverend Duncan taught us 'The Gettysburg Address.' We had to memorize it. And did we have fun at recess. We played ball and a lot of ring games, like Little Sally Walker with everybody sitting in a circle. And kickball—we had a time playing kickball. My sister Mavis and my brother Paul went to Rosenwald too. We all had fun playing games" (interview, August 29, 2002).

Recalling another teacher specialization, Frederick L. Gordon, Rosenwald student from 1956 until 1961, said:

> Mrs. Benjamin taught third and fourth grade. She was the scientist of the school. She kept animals that had been "pickled" and made sure we learned to spell. She had her own way of doing it. James Baten's music

Rosenwald students performed at teacher Mary B. Kilgore's anniversary party. Left to right: Gwyn Norman, Gwyn Mooney, Sonya Kilgore, Gwyn Robinson, Nadine Young, Ella Whitmire, Althea Mills, Pam Kilgore, Valeria Crite, Lynnette Wynn, and Vickie Johnstone. (Courtesy Patricia Austin.)

> impacted us a lot. Mary Kilgore taught seventh grade. She was the literature person, particularly poetry. We learned a lot of poetry. She opened doors to the arts. She worked as the librarian. Robert Duncan was a preacher and a teacher. He taught seventh and eighth grade. He was a mathematician and the disciplinarian of the school. Paul Hunter came before Baten to teach music. He was a vocal singer and worked with Scouts and PE [interview, February 9, 2000].

Although the staff and the community appreciated the leadership of the Transylvania County Superintendent of Public Instruction and of the County Board of Education, the administration's presence was distant. County leaders responded mainly to official duties. However, both Julia Smith and Paul Hunter indicated that the board of education provided for the school. "Nothing was really missing. We got what we needed from the main office," Hunter said (interview, March 24, 2000).

Smith was more critical of the teaching conditions. "All the schools were in bad shape when it came to materials, books, facilities.... Integration made things better for blacks and whites.... The board of education provided the best they could," Smith reported (interview, March 24, 2000).

Mills, who was remembered as a strong leader, asserted that each Rosenwald principal provided the leadership for his or her tenure with little interference from the white community (interview, June 9, 1999). Mills' tenure illustrates how she built the tradition of effective leadership. Lillie M. Jones, who believes that educational leaders should remain teachers and pursue lifelong learning, explained that Mills modeled those qualities while exhibiting a strong advocacy for children (interview, November 26, 1999). Decades after completing her administrative career, Mills reiterated her long-standing conviction: "I'm for the schools, but I'm for the children first" (interview, June 17,1999).

Mills acted upon her philosophy. She felt it was her responsibility to find ways to assist children in need. She paid for haircuts and clothing, sometimes compromising her honesty to provide school lunches for deprived students. Alumna Ida Hemphill Ellens, the primary caregiver for her nine-month old sister, vividly remembers Mills. Hemphill's father worked at the tannery to earn a living, but he was unable to groom her hair and sew clothes for his daughter. Mills could tell that the girl needed more attention than Mr. Hemphill could provide. "Mrs. Mills paid for me to have my hair done every two weeks. Ora Mills fixed my hair in her house just across the street from the school. We didn't have money to pay, but Mrs. Mills insisted" (interview, June 18, 2001). Decades later Ellens and Lewis Whiteside have assisted Mills during her senior years. Each asserts that her kindness during their early years and beyond outweighs any support they can give Mills.

Reflecting the traditional regard for all school workers, faculty and students also respected the support staff. Over and over again faculty and alumni became nostalgic about time spent in the cafeteria when students ate together. Reliving lunchtime in the basement cafeteria of the new Rosenwald School building, former students raved about loving treatment and enjoyable food. Workers such as Trilby Elliott, Marie Davenport, Johnsie Lee Mills, and Ada Smith served delicious and nutritious meals. Alumni claimed they still crave those meals of macaroni and cheese, grilled cheese sandwiches, and hot soup. Several recited foods for specific weekdays, such as Friday's menu of fish, hot homemade rolls, and Jell-O. Robbie Outlaw Gardin, a woman who knows how to turn out tasty dishes, complimented the food served during her school days and expressed amazement that such good meals were so cheap. "Flora Bailey could make the best soup and green beans and gingerbread. Lunch was just five cents" (interview, August 25, 2002). She added that cafeteria personnel were always looking out for the welfare of the children.

Cafeteria workers planned special menus around classroom units of study — all part of the tradition of celebrations. For example, a former Rosenwald alumna recalled huge chocolate cakes cut in long strips and cherry pies served on two February birthdays, for Abraham Lincoln and for George Washington. She concluded that the cooks were depicting the tallness of Abe Lincoln with his hat, and the honesty of George Washington when answering the famous question about the cherry tree (interview, February 10, 2000).

Frederick Gordon praised the cafeteria crew's culinary skill. "They were the best cooks in the county. Those women dreamed about cooking" (interview, February 9, 2000). Alice Glaze Robinson spoke of being pleasantly bombarded by tantalizing aromas as she descended the stairwell to the basement. She also claims love radiated from the faces of the women serving the food. "Even in line waiting to be served we felt like family" (interview, February 24, 2000). Others remembered that the cafeteria workers laughed and joked as students went through the line. Recalled one: "It was as though they had the job of mothering the whole school" (interview, February 10, 2000).

Mills explained the dilemma of a superintendent who was invited to have lunch with the Rosenwald School family. "Jones was a nice fellow — tall but a little stooped. Part of his jury duty was to visit the schools." He had been interested in examining the cafeteria books and the menus, and he asked for information about preparing turkey. "Do you boil the turkey?" he inquired. After explaining that her staff roasted turkey an entire day before serving it on the next, Principal Mills suggested that he join them for a turkey lunch. He refused because of a prior commitment, but later the she met him at the town newsstand. Superintendent Jones, who expressed regret that he had not joined her for a famous turkey dinner, said, "I could have kicked myself. I ate at Brevard Elementary, and they served pinto beans." With her wise look, Mills declared: "Some white people don't think we know A from bull feet. They think blacks are dumb enough to try to throw an elephant, but it's pure, unadulterated ignorance.... They've had no experience with Negroes.... I don't measure people by me.... Who are we to judge? I can be just as crazy as anybody" (interview, October 1, 1999).

Previously, in the original wooden building, students brought lunches to school in buckets or in jars. The staff brewed tea on the potbellied heater (Winona Whiteside, interview, March 5, 2000). During the no-school-building era of the 1940s, Daniel Owens carried sandwiches to school, but he explained that it was possible to go home for lunch if students lived nearby (interview, February 29, 2000). Agnes Wilson said that every Wednesday at the annex was "soup day." Boys and girls took a bowl and a mug to school. Active grade mothers brought soup, hot chocolate, and homemade cookies. "We missed that when we moved to the new building," Wilson said (interview, February 8, 2000).

Betty Hunt High recalled that during the "annex days" each student carried a bowl and a folding cup to school. Water was available in a bucket, and children used their own cups for drinking. At lunchtime, the Reverend Freeman Daugherty often brought a big pot of hearty soup from what was known as the "Green Fly" cafeteria at the tannery where he worked. High wonders who arranged for the soup. She proposes that it could have been the school board, the parents, or the staff at the tannery — or it may have been a personal act of kindness by the Reverend Daugherty. It was a treasured memory (interview).

Annie Marie Hailey confirmed that hot lunches were not a daily event. However, each week parents provided hot soup. At times the cook at the Green Fly cafeteria made a big pot of soup with carrots, okra, and corn. Someone delivered it to feed the children at each facility. Hailey's great-grandmother, Mrs. Sharp, fed her grandchildren at home. She provided lunch for Hailey and for her brothers. "She would often have buttermilk and cornbread, but one of my brothers wanted biscuits and jelly and sweet milk, and she was good to fix what he wanted" (interview, August 21, 2002).

Another staff member who impacted the lives of the students was janitor Randall Gash, a kind man with a ready greeting for each child. He always said, "Good morning. How are you?" The Reverend Gordon recalled that he moved around doing his work in an unobtrusive manner. However, Gash sometimes placed a hand on a child's shoulder and said, "Now, maybe you shouldn't be doing that" (interview, February 9, 2000). Oral history cites his positive influence as a gentleman who loved children.

Teachers did not automatically step into a classroom and achieve success. They made a continual effort to improve themselves as teachers, which is one reason that they left such lasting, positive impressions. Though the methods and the certification procedures were simpler than today, Rosenwald School teachers persevered to meet training standards. It was a behind-the-scenes tradition that facilitated the more obvious achievements of the school.

Although their task was to train the student, teachers also needed training. Principal Mills recalled attending summer institutes to learn new teaching techniques and to acquire certification. Both white and black teachers took courses in the same setting. It was necessary to pass a state test to be certified, and Mills recalled that most of the teacher-students had to retake the test two or three times. When Mills returned for her third attempt, the superintendent of Buncombe County Schools, a white woman, said, "I am sure you will pass it this time." And Mills did, but she still treasures superintendent Ethel Terrell's encouraging remarks (interview, June 9, 1999). Mills described the constant shove from the state to mandate additional training: "You had to keep taking classes, or you'd lose your job. They had you by the tail, and they'd keep twisting it" (October 27, 2002).

4. Pedagogical Traditions

Teachers remember their professional development experiences. Paul Hunter, a young bachelor teacher at the time, referring to opportunities for improving teaching expertise, said, "After I finished college, I went to Western Carolina to take classes and get renewal. It helped us out. I think it was nine hours that we needed for renewal" (interview, March 24, 2000). James R. Baten attended Western Carolina University, where in 1965 he became the first African American to earn a master's degree from that institution.

Summer institutes designed to upgrade teacher certification were held in almost every county in North Carolina as early as the 1920s. In the reports of Dr. G.E. Davis, Rosenwald building supervisor for the state, those possibilities for teachers are outlined. In one report found in Box 8 of the Special Subjects File, Rosenwald Fund, at the state archives, Davis recorded that he visited a state summer school in Asheville, North Carolina, on June 12, 1925. He commented that there were about 70 participants and that each seemed to be doing good work.

Nathaniel Hall and Selena Robinson recalled that not every Rosenwald teacher had attended college. However, Robinson affirmed, "They were all good teachers. They wanted us to learn" (interview, July 16, 1999).

J.H. Michael, a Buncombe County educator who had graduated from the Tuskegee Institute in Alabama and from Branch Normal of Pine Bluff, Arkansas, was director of summer institutes, a program in Asheville sponsored by Winston-Salem State College, for more than 20 years. In 1938, World Geography (with an enrollment of 26), Mental Hygiene (with 29), and Rural Education (with three) comprised the summer offerings for one session. B.A. Bianchi assisted with that institute, and Ethel K. Mills earned six semester hours credit.

While attending summer institutes at Hill Street School in Asheville, the then Ethel Kennedy met Wilkie Johnstone, who persuaded her to join the teaching staff in Brevard. "The teachers from Brevard and I enjoyed one another's company. We had a lot in common, and I thought it would be fun to teach with them" Mills said (interview, June 9, 1999).

Other institutes attended by the Brevard faculty were held in Winston-Salem. Documents at the Winston-Salem State University archives contain the names of Rosenwald teachers, the subjects they studied, and, in some instances, their grades. Instructors provided by Winston-Salem Teachers College were well qualified. For example, instructor Roberta O. Peddy, after earning her high school diploma at Berry O'Kelly Training School in Method, North Carolina, and her bachelor of science degree at Winston-Salem Teachers College, received a master's degree from the University of Michigan in Ann Arbor in 1935. In summer institutes Peddy taught a variety of classes, such as Principles of Guidance, Methods of Teaching Social Studies, and Improvement of Reading. Peddy's pursuit of learning enhanced her ability to train teachers.

Irma Swepson began teaching at the Brevard Rosenwald School in the 1922-23 school year. She taught a combination class that included part of the 4th grade and all of the 5th grade students. Her salary was $55 per month. (Courtesy Irma M. Fletcher.)

In a Principles of Guidance class for the summer session ending on July 15, 1936, Ethel R. Mills received two semester hours of credit and a final mark of 88. In the second session, Mills earned a 90 and two semester hours in Principles of Elementary School Education. Two years later Mills received a grade of 87 in Mental Hygiene under the instruction of J.H. Michael. During the second session, she earned a grade of 92 in Tests and Measurements with Thomas J. Brown as her instructor and a 95 from Peddy in Rural Education. Mills' pursuit of excellence and efforts to improve her teaching skills were representative of many aspiring Negro teachers.

Teacher Synetha Glenn also attended the institute. She earned a 90 in General Mathematics and a 92 in the Study of Negro Life and History. Wilkie Johnstone is also listed as a student in the files on summer schools in Winston-Salem State University archives. During the 1938 summer institutes at Winston-Salem Teachers College, demonstration schools were offered, consisting of a non-graded class in a single room. The purpose, according to Dean B.A. Bianchi, was to assist rural teachers by demonstrating techniques for improving instruction in multilevel classes, which was the norm for most rural black schools. The program provided another option for teachers.

Mills remembered that some summer school instructors came from Tuskegee. She related this account about one of them: "One man from Tuskegee wanted us to believe in ourselves. He said, 'Any time you doubt you can do something, throw yourself on the floor, spin around three times, jump up, and say dammit, I can do anything.' And he did it. He threw himself down, spun around, jumped up and said, 'Dammit, I can do anything.' Well, you know that changed the attitude of the class. He gave us something to think about, and it was funny seeing him on the floor spinning around. We got more interested and thought more about our potential" (interview, August 19, 2002).

4. Pedagogical Traditions

The Rosenwald School staff learned to catalogue library books. Mills and other members of the staff took training sessions to develop skill in handling library issues. "A Benjamin girl, who lives in a rock house up the hill, showed us how, and the teachers did it. We were so slow, but it was easy to do. We got that library done" (interview, March 28, 2000).

For a short time during the late 1920s and early 1930s, Coragreene Johnstone returned to Rosenwald to teach. Winona Whiteside, an octogenarian who was enrolled in her class in 1929, remembered Johnstone as an excellent teacher (interview, March 5, 2000). From Johnstone's instruction, minister and civil rights activist Thomas Kilgore acquired a lifelong interest in English literature and in poetry (Kilgore, 1998). Johnstone, who earned her doctorate at the University of Michigan, became a university professor (Nathaniel Hall, interview, July 16, 1999). Other students were inspired by her example, and some pursued graduate degrees.

In the 1960s, James R. Baten, who taught the fifth and sixth grades at Rosenwald School, became the first African American to earn a master's degree at Western Carolina University. "The folks there were always asking if some group sponsored me. Going was my idea. I went because I wanted a master's degree. There was one man, a really nice fellow, who would take me out of the line and handle my registration personally " (interview, October 21, 1999). Baten left Brevard in 1966 when the Rosenwald School was integrated.

Former students of the Brevard Rosenwald School testify that there was always homework to do. It was a traditional part of their training, and they were expected to get it done. Students from each phase of Rosenwald history affirmed this tradition. In addition, every student was expected to participate in classwork. Students were sent to the board to work problems in mathematics. Each child remained at the board until the assigned problem was solved. No flinching was allowed. Students were required to read aloud often, and some group reading in concert occurred. There were no worksheets, but exercises were assigned in the textbook. Straight rows of desks kept them focused on the discipline of education. Interruptions during class time were minimal. Lillie Jones recalled that there simply was not much traffic in the hallways (interview).

Public speaking was also emphasized for Rosenwald students. Edith Darity, a health caregiver in Transylvania County and an active member of the Transylvania Citizens Improvement Organization, described Robert Duncan's emphasis on memorizing and reciting poetry. Each year, she said, one or two poems, such as Edgar Allan Poe's "The Raven" or William Ernest Henley's "Invictus," would be presented to the class to be memorized for performances on other occasions. Darity can recite much of that poetry today (interview, February 23, 2000).

Lillie Madison Jones, who graduated from Rosenwald in 1957, claimed,

Pictured here are Rosenwald faculty members from left to right: Robert L. Duncan, Gertie M. Hemphill, Ethel K. Mills, Synetha G. Benjamin, and William McLaughlin. (Courtesy Bernetha Owens.)

"We did a lot of speaking. There was some anxiety, but speaking was a natural part of who we were. We spoke a lot" (interview). Alice Glaze Robinson, the successful operator of a daycare facility in Yanceyville, North Carolina, believes that she would have grown into a withdrawn and shy adult were it not for the Rosenwald experience. The emphasis on oral presentations helped her overcome her natural tendency to refrain from public speaking. Today expressing her ideas in public gatherings is a normal part of life (interview, February 24, 2000).

Music was another aspect of education emphasized throughout the history of the Brevard Rosenwald School. Members of the Rosenwald community voiced enthusiasm as they recalled musical programs. According to both Selena Robinson and Nathaniel Hall, students sang patriotic and religious songs a capella during their Rosenwald days in the 1920s and 1930s. Eventually the school purchased a piano and an organ, but in the classrooms, music education focused on vocal performance (Robinson, interview, July 16, 1999).

Hall and Dorothy Pierce Hill recalled that often teachers made up songs for the students, sometimes to reinforce learning and often simply for fun (interviews, February 13 and 14, 2000). LaMuriel Andrews spoke animatedly of participating in spring productions that involved the entire school, under the direction of Julia Smith, who arranged for students to perform for a public audience (interview, February 10, 2000).

One song that was sung often, especially whenever the community gathered at the school, was the Negro national anthem: "Lift Every Voice and Sing." Michael Owens said there was music every day (interview).

Hall and Selena Robinson shared the following lyrics from the class song for the 1933 graduates: "We will climb tho' the rocks be rugged / Every step leads us to our goal / Always our hearts beat with gladness / For the help, dear teachers, from you / Sometimes the days seem weary / The night seems dark and dreary / But whatever success we shall obtain / Rosenwald, dear, we owe it to you" (interview, February 14, 2000).

Seasonal plays and operettas were annual events. Every student was involved, and the community turned out en masse to support the production. Those selected for speaking roles felt greatly honored, even if their part consisted of a single line.

Alice Glaze Robinson remembers the sense of accomplishment she derived from saying, "There she goes ... around the corner." She received no bouquets for her one-line performance, but she did get hugs and plenty of praise (interview, February 24, 2000). In the early days of the Rosenwald School, students presented plays to the community at Thanksgiving and at Christmas. On one occasion, Selena Robinson was asked to play the part of a boy in a Christmas program and to help with a special version of "Jingle Bells." The teacher, who invited the entire cast to her home for rehearsals, coached her individually until she learned her part. "She wanted to be sure we learned everything right," Robinson said (interview, February 14, 2000).

Annie Marie Hutchison Hailey, a Rosenwald graduate who returned to teach at the school, explained that the school's productions were selected "to include bunches of children in one extravaganza" (interview, August 21, 2002). Hailey described one character, a little boy named Forgot, who grew and grew until he could not go to bed. According to Hailey, the operetta productions stimulated the imagination.

According to Mills and Frederick Gordon, the halls of Rosenwald came alive with the sound of music after James R. Baten arrived in 1960. Mills described the sounds of the Baten Glee Club as "glorious." According to Pastor Gordon, the entire community felt the impact of Baten's teaching. What began as a choral group in his classroom grew into a school choir of about 75 voices. "I was using music as part of my classroom program, but other teachers wanted their students to have a chance to participate so I was soon

The James R. Baten Glee Club was a source of community pride. First row, left to right: Bruce Young, Keith Norman, Boyce Baker, Greg Robinson, Rosie Hemphill, Bruce Sanders, Althea Mills, and Tommy Smith. Second row, left to right: Clark Wynn, Linda Betsill, Margarete Camp, Alfreida Gordon, Michael Jackson, Ella Whitmire, Margaret Harris, Drucilla Kelly, and Gregory Moore. Third row, left to right: Kay Erwin, Regina Camp, Kay Davenport, Cecilia Whiteside, Thomas Benjamin, Ollie Robinson, Jerry Avery, Charles Hunt, and Judy Mucklerene. Fourth row, left to right: Virginia Norman, Benny Jackson, Carl Mooney, Linda Gash, Dottie Hill, James Johnstone, Tommy Kilgore, Vincent Gordon, and Helen Camp. (Courtesy Mavis Smith.)

teaching music to the entire school," Baten said (interview, October 21, 1999). The group, which traveled occasionally, performed at Hendersonville's Ninth Avenue School on the same program with the high school choral group. Instruction in ethnic, ballroom, and square dancing delighted the students. "I believe that if anyone can speak he can sing.... I felt those students should be able to do more than the hucklebuck," said Baten, a popular member of the Rosenwald staff. According to Baten, who retired after a career in education in Peekskill, New York, his group's concert at the Brevard Junior High School in the 1960s marked the first performance of blacks in that educational facility (interview, October 21, 1999). News of Baten's death, on December 21, 2002, saddened the Rosenwald community.

Rosenwald training, which emphasized the expectation that everyone would help peers, extended from the classroom to the playground. In her primary classes, Mills found that her students learned more when she made them "little teachers" to assist those having difficulty. By explaining concepts to peers, students enlarged their own insight. She also created a town in the first grade room with aisles for streets and desks for buildings. Each child's desk was assigned a street number to correspond to the building it represented. Students were required to spell the numbers. It was Mills' method of reinforcing lessons with numbers and directions (interview, July 9, 1999).

Jones believes there were students at Rosenwald who were learning disabled, but she said that no one targeted that educational handicap. Everyone simply helped each student (interview, November 26, 1999). Baten recalled that the faculty required everyone to learn. "There was no special education," he said. "All students were there to learn." Teachers were stern, and the message was "You will get it before you leave this classroom" (interview, October 21, 1999).

Play was supervised, and everyone had the opportunity to play. Teachers insisted on fairness (Alice Glaze Robinson, interview, February 24, 2000). "The children were never unsupervised," Paul Hunter said. "At recess we had to play out there with the kids. Played softball mostly. We classroom teachers had to do it all ourselves. I taught PE, and we had a little competition between the classes. There were no sports. We just had recess, but all teachers were physical education teachers" (interview). Spontaneous competition also occurred. Julia Smith recalled little girls jumping rope while boys were shooting marbles during recess in the 1940s and 1950s (interview, March 24, 2000).

Traditions went beyond actions to attitudes. Morals and manners had status at Rosenwald. Students were taught to say please and thank you. Devotional periods opened each day, and students memorized Scripture. A strong religious emphasis permeated the Rosenwald experience. In her later role as Guilford County Public Schools Superintendent, Lillie Jones reinforced the value of the Rosenwald practice. Explaining that she has always maintained calm, Jones attributes her tranquility amid turmoil to devotional training at church, at home, and at school. Pondering the Proverbs, for example, has provided Jones with ammunition for dealing with conflict (interview). Both staff and students remember the prayer-meditation emphasis at the beginning of the Rosenwald day with satisfaction.

Discipline frames any effective school setting, and it is often associated with the style of the principal. James Outlaw recalled that Principal Sartor used a board with holes in it, to which LaMuriel Andrews responded, "Man, that tore you up. He didn't spare the rod — but we got spankings, and today we are good" (interview). The Reverend Frederick L. Gordon, whose father drove the school bus for Glade Creek students after consolidation, recalled getting his hand smacked. He said, "I got my hand smacked many times over that water fountain next to the playground. I had the habit of letting the water run quite a while before I drank. Mrs. Mills didn't like to waste water. She would say, 'You don't know how to drink water? If you drink, drink' and she would smack my hand" (interview, February 10, 2000).

Agnes Wilson received a D in a health class because she was practicing poor health habits. During midmorning she repeatedly distributed candy to her friends, which was not a healthy practice. Having admonished her student on a number of occasions, Synetha Benjamin, as a last resort, lowered Wilson's grade in health. According to Wilson, the teacher's grading policy was an effective technique. She did not risk getting another D (interview, February 10, 2000). Another student recalled being paddled only once, but her parents knew what happened by the time she had arrived at home so she was punished again. Paul Hunter was often responsible for administering corporal punishment. One student on the receiving end of a Hunter paddling was Marshall Erwin, current pastor of Bethel Baptist Church. Robbie Gardin remembered being punished twice. "I got whipped twice, for eating before lunch and for getting out of line. I got spanked on the hand" (interview, August 25, 2002). Others affirmed that at the close of the school day, students ran ahead to announce the mischief or successes of the day to the community folk, who were working outside or relaxing on their porches. News traveled fast from the school to the neighborhood.

"We knew the rules. They were not written and posted, but they were imprinted in our minds and in our hearts," said Alice Glaze Robinson (interview, February 24, 2000). Former students frequently called Wilkie Johnstone a strict teacher with high standards. Johnstone was a "legend," according to Lillie Jones, though she never had Johnstone as a teacher. Her standards for each student were high, and there were no excuses for failing to learn. Rumors about her having a daughter who was a professor at a northern university encouraged students to believe in the possibility of elevating their status in life. Lillie Jones knew that Wilkie Johnstone's daughter was a doctor teaching in some university, and that knowledge inspired Jones to earn her doctorate (interview). Other former students frequently referred to Johnstone's teaching them the Bible and having them memorize verses of Scripture. A favorite was II Timothy 2:15: "Study to show thyself approved unto God, a workman that needeth not to be ashamed, rightly dividing the word of truth."

4. Pedagogical Traditions

The name Ethel Mills was spoken with respect, affection, and reverence. The dedicated educator, who passed the century mark in 2001, invested her life in the Rosenwald School community. On the walls and shelves in her living room are numerous plaques and citations documenting years of service to advance African American education in Transylvania County, where she served as teacher and administrator for 45 years. Her total years of service to the state numbered 51. Rosenwald graduate Alice Robinson, director of an innovative day care center in Yanceyville, North Carolina, recalled Mills' strategy for halting students who were rushing through the school halls. She would clap her hands loudly three times, point her finger, and say, "Now, stop, just stop." The technique not only kept boys and girls from rushing madly to recess but also caused students listening from their classrooms to sit rigidly at attention, because Mills had spoken. She respected the children, and they, in turn, respected her (interview, February 24, 2000). "I knew I would miss those children when I retired," Mills admitted (interview, June 9, 1999).

For what infractions were children punished at Rosenwald? Individuals admitted they were punished for talking, for chewing gum, for getting out of line, and for running in the hall. A teacher would ask running students, "Don't you realize you are inside?" (Alice Glaze Robinson, interview, February 24, 2000). Selena Robinson explained that students who fought were whipped (interview, March 23, 2000). According to Michael Owens, "You got a whipping if you didn't do your work, homework or in class. I was lucky. I got only two or three during the whole eight years." He also asserted that no students played any pranks on the teachers because "they just knew better." However, a little mischief occasionally occurred around the water fountain on the playground. By placing fingers strategically on the water jet, the spray went quite a distance (interview).

Over the decades punishments seemed fairly standard at the Rosenwald School. Students were required to write sentences on the chalkboard. At other times, they were traditionally banished to the hall or to the cloakroom if they misbehaved. Alice Glaze Robinson recalled having her ear tugged by Smith (interview, February 24, 2000). Some hands were smacked, some switches were used, occasionally a strap — and there are still reports of Sartor's board with holes in it. Nathaniel Hall said women were inclined to use a switch, but men often used a strap (interview, February 14, 2000). A tradition of discipline helped maintain the standard of acceptable behavior at Rosenwald.

Memories color classroom experiences, but facts document financial limitations, which were a less glorious part of tradition at the Brevard Rosenwald School. As in modern schools, teachers could perform only so many miracles when they worked without the required financial support. Equipment and textbooks require money. The public and the administrators, from state to county, preferred to sidestep this reality. The lack of money limited classroom opportunities and affected students' lives in ways that are impossible to measure accurately.

Financial problems within the education system were a major concern of Du Bois. In his 1938 address to Fisk University graduates, the scholar lamented the lack of mastery of the basic skills of reading, writing, and ciphering. He blamed the shortcomings on a shortage of skilled teachers, a school term of limited duration, and physical environments ill equipped as educational work sites. In Du Bois' delineation of targeted problem areas in the Negro elementary school, he refers to "quarters ill-suited physically and morally to the work in hand ... agility in avoiding race problems ... to see how large a statistical showing can be made without expenditure of funds, thought, or effort...." He urged his audience to labor for modern schoolrooms for elementary students.

The Rosenwald community described a healthy physical and moral environment at the Brevard School, but former students, teachers, and parents also identified problem areas. In the three phases of the school's history, resources and finances were definitely limited, but the people associated with the Rosenwald School were remarkable in their ability to create a vibrant learning environment with high expectations for the learner.

As was true of most rural Appalachian schools, in the early part of the century physical structures housing African American educational institutions in Brevard were often makeshift. Sometimes an abandoned cabin or a church building was used (Hall, 1984). The structure that became the Brevard Rosenwald School was built to function as a three-room school before Ethel Kennedy joined the staff in 1923. She described the building as being "shaped like an airplane" and painted "all white, trimmed in green." She also elaborated on the role of Julius Rosenwald in constructing elementary schools for Negro children in rural communities, including Brevard (interview, June 9, 1999).

North Carolina Rosenwald administrator W.F. Credle's report for the period from July 1, 1921, until July 1, 1922, delineates specifications for the school site in Transylvania County. The site, according to the report, was to contain at least two acres of well-drained property located, if possible, on a public highway. A garden spot with suitable soil and a source of pure water was required. Two sanitary toilets were also specified (Box 8, Rosenwald Fund, N.C. State Archives).

Hall and Selena Robinson recalled that there were five or six rooms by 1933 and that in an earlier time there had been two outhouses, one for boys and one for girls. Sometime in the late 1920s or early 1930s all-weather toilets were built at the front part of the school. The building was substantial, but there was little heat. Warmth was provided by coal-burning heaters, one in each room. Teachers were responsible for firing the primitive furnaces (Hall, interview, July 16, 1999). During school years students collected brush to use as kindling. One boy was allowed to arrive early to start the fire. The assignment was a responsibility of trust, for he needed to arrive in time to warm the building before the others came (Dorothy Pierce Hill, interview, February 17, 2000). James Outlaw recalled assisting Randall Gash with stoking the furnace in the new building. Because local government traditionally provided only a minimal staff, everyone had to help keep the school clean (LaMuriel Andrews, interview, February 10, 2000).

Mills praised the students for being willing to keep the building in good condition. She attributed that attitude to their training at home. She recalled one instance when a student marked on the walls of the new Rosenwald school building.

> Having a new building brought a different interest in going to school ... like going to college. Superintendent Jones thought it [the new building] would be looking old before we'd been there a month.... It's true one girl marked up the walls in the hall with a pencil. The children told me who. I said, "It has to come down," and she cleaned the walls with wet paper towels. That child cried. It was better than a spanking, and it scared the others [interview, July 9, 1999].

In the original building, accordion doors separated the rooms and were pushed back to create an auditorium for special occasions, including public meetings (Hall and Robinson, interview, July 16, 1999). Basketball games were also played inside after partitions were pushed back (Reesie Madison, interview, February 22, 2000). At the back was a small enclosed area for a home economics room. The enclosure corresponded to state school historian Thomas Hanchett's description of industrial rooms in Rosenwald schools (1988). The girls were taught to darn socks, but there were no sewing machines (Dorothy Pierce Hill, interview, February 17, 2000). Winona Whiteside remembered being taught home economics by a Mrs. Murray. "There was a little room where she taught us how to cook and make soup" (interview, March 11, 2000).

Whiteside also recalled that foreign language was required.

> J.M. Harris was the principal, and we had to take a foreign language so I took Latin. Howard Foster almost flunked me ... I never did like Latin. He passed me on condition. I had had diphtheria when I was at Everett School. Nine children had it, but I was the only black. The others died. Mr. Foster had no sympathy for some [interview, March 9, 2000].

On Whiteside's report card, a handwritten note confirms that she was conditionally allowed credit for Latin. Unless she exhibited the ability to do Latin exercises, she would lose the credit. However, the next year she again took Latin and earned higher marks.

Another result of traditional financial limitations was that the school did not have regulation playing fields. Some land was cleared, but the terrain around the school was rough so the play area was limited. At times students played at Brevard High School and also at the Brevard Institute, now Brevard College (Nathaniel Hall and Selena Robinson, interviews, July 16, 1999, and February 14, 2000).

Alumni also talked about playing in the "jungle," an area near the school with trees and marked by the presence of Indian mounds and a cemetery. It was, according to Edith Darity, a "wonderful" place to play (interview). Robbie Outlaw Gardin laughed as she talked about building a playhouse in the woods (interview, August 21, 2002). Dorothy Pierce Hill, remembering the time when there were no swings, explained that she and her classmates played in the woods around the mounds and the graves in the spring. Hill described gathering plants, which the children called "sweet bubbies," and heart-shaped leaves that their teacher, Mrs. Hargreaves, used to make crafts. "I always remember Mrs. Hargreaves, from Saluda. I went there to visit her one time" (Hill, interview, February 17, 2000).

Eventually the school added playground equipment. There were heavy steel swings, a seesaw, and a sliding board. The playing field itself was red dirt so it was easy for clothing to get soiled (Darity, interview).

Financial restrictions also nurtured ingenuity. Fred Mills, husband of teacher and principal Ethel Mills, constructed a stone water fountain at the old school. She said a spring was located nearby and that water was also kept in a bucket inside the building. Students brought their own cups to dip the drinking water, but later the town of Brevard granted a permit for the construction of the fountain, which made drinking more sanitary and provided a pleasant gathering place (interview, March 9, 2000). During Michael Owens' tenure at the new school, the old fountain remained at the edge of the playground. There were fountains inside the newly constructed stone building, but older alumni were pleased that the Fred Mills fountain remained on the grounds because it reminded them of the old school, which had been reduced to ashes. Alumni were dismayed when it was later dismantled.

To supply books and equipment for the school, the county's superintendent of public instruction provided the Rosenwald staff with order forms and a catalogue. Each instructor prepared an individual order, and the principal compiled a school list. When the order arrived, materials were distributed to the teachers, but often, if an item was needed, "you made it or you got someone to" (Ethel Mills, interview, July 9, 1999).

Frequently teachers used their own money to supplement funds provided by the county. They purchased books from the dime stores on Brevard's Main and Broad streets. "We needed something besides the text." Mills explained. "There wasn't enough that kids liked to read about in our library." She and the faculty searched for books with high interest levels for elementary school-age children. Later the superintendent purchased sets of supplementary books at a discount. Mills also recalled the time when students paid a rental fee for texts, probably in the 1940s. (According to the Erwin 1944–1946 report, rental books were established in 1935 [p. 77].)

Mills believes Rosenwald students were handicapped by the lack of reading materials in the their homes. She also explained that the advent of the radio changed everything, and she lamented vehemently that television became the community's babysitter. "Once an insurance man came to the house. He wanted to know if everybody in the community was rich. I told him, 'No, why?' And he pointed to all the antennas on the tops of houses. Television was a cheap babysitter" (interview, June 9, 1999).

Alumni resented that they had to use texts that had been discarded by white students. James Outlaw called them "hand-me-down" books with worn pages (interview, February 10, 2000). A former student remembers that some texts were new, but that most were used. "When I opened my book at the beginning of each year, I would see names of all these students that I didn't know," Lillie Jones recalled (interview). Hall satisfied his curiosity that black students used the same text as the whites by comparing notes with his Caucasian friend Charlie Duckworth. He remembers some new texts, but he knows that most of the time books were rejects from white schools.

The Reverend Frederick L. Gordon also took offense at being provided with used texts (interview, February 9, 2000). Agnes Wilson never doubted the quality of her education, but she wondered if the white students had better books. Her school textbooks were well worn and dog-eared, even soiled (interview, February 8, 2000). Nathaniel Hall's family purchased books in local stores for school use in the 1920s, and the books were passed on to other family members as needed (interview, February 14, 2000).

Used desks were also the norm. However, Mills reported that on one occasion the school board provided new desks for the black school: "A popular white woman said there was no reason for giving those niggers new desks ... they were too good for the likes of them. She said to just give them the old seats that had been stored, but the board didn't listen and we got new desks" (interview, March 28, 2000). "In high school at Ninth Avenue, our football equipment was handed down from Hendersonville High School. It was well used," F. Douglas Cantey said (interview). The lack of new equipment underscored the attitude that African American students in Brevard were undeserving.

Alumna Dorothy Pierce Hill, whose student days date to the 1920s and 1930s, said that books were limited. A New Orleans woman, whom Hill remembers only as Mrs. Rundell, employed her mother during summer visits to Brevard from Louisiana. She sometimes treated young Dorothy Pierce to a book purchased in Asheville. Rundell also sent two boxes of books from Louisiana each year with instructions to return them COD. "Two boxes every year. They (the Rundells) were French" (interview, February 17, 2000). Apparently the woman from New Orleans recognized Dorothy Pierce's intelligence and used her personal resources to encourage the child to read and to study.

Playing at the new Rosenwald School was fun, but one area caused fear: the high wall at the end of the building had a dangerous drop. Edith Darity was frightened when playing near that space as a child (interview, February 23, 2000). Hill also recounted the event that led her and others to request that a fence be placed at the south end of the new Rosenwald School.

> My son and Gayle Mackey were on the school grounds. Gayle's bicycle rolled off the wall. "He's dead! He's dead!" my son screamed. Well, he wasn't, but he got hurt and he knocked out some teeth. We asked the School Board for a fence, but they refused. Later when it got to be what we call the Pentagon (Central Offices for Transylvania County's Public Schools), they put in a jailhouse fence [interview, February 15, 2000].

To supplement the paltry county budgets for equipment and supplies, the Parent Teacher Association sponsored fundraisers. In the early days, parents sold box suppers (Selena Robinson, interview, July 16, 1999). Students saved Blue Horse notebook paper coupons and Popsicle wrappers, which were redeemed for premiums such as balls or classroom games. When the prizes arrived, excited children claimed their awards (Betty Hunt High, interview). Julia Smith recalled that games for indoor play, such as Bingo and musical chairs, were vital during times of rain and snow (interview, March 25, 2000).

The Rosenwald staff built a petty cash fund by selling ice cream and school supplies from the office each day after lunch (Marva Lytle, interview, February 10, 2000). The staff was alert for opportunities to supplement the school's resources—a tradition that continues in many schools, whether in rural, urban or suburban communities.

Nothing ever came to the black school on a silver platter, but the school board made provisions as funds became available (Mills, interview, December 7, 1999). The new building, which cost $61,000, was a stone structure with six classrooms, a library, a cafeteria, and an office (Hall, 1984). According to James Baten, "It was a good building made of rock, but as a facility for lending itself to an educational design ... it was adequate, but it needed a lot. There were the usual drawbacks of a small school such as Rosenwald School — a small faculty — no music, art, or PE. There was a need to broaden and expand the curriculum."

Baten taught sixth grade, but he also taught all-school programs in music, dance, and Spanish. "The state recommended Spanish, and I was the low man on the totem pole ... you will teach Spanish, so I said, 'Sure, I can teach Spanish'" (interview, October 21, 1999).

Mills explained that in the new building, which opened in 1948, the structure that was to serve as a stage had not been "dressed." Splinters abounded because a workman was deliberately careless. According to her, he thought black children should not be pampered. He made hurtful comments such as

> "they won't notice a little roughness ... let them use cobs. They don't need paper." Of course, what he said was told to me, and he was just acting out of ignorance. Another white man, a Mr. Whitmire, made it all right and even built good strong bookcases for each ... classroom. They (the state) were charging a flat rental fee, and he made a separate bookcase for the rental books [interview, December 7, 1999].

Despite limited resources, students managed to compete in sports — all part of a tradition of overcoming obstacles. Principals Mack Dawkins and Javan L. Jones were among those who encouraged students to play football and basketball.

Nathaniel Hall relived experiences of traveling to other communities to play ball. Once the team and its coach traveled through the night to get to a game with Henderson Institute. Players arrived there at 5 A.M. The team slept for a while. Then when it was "good daylight," the game was played, ending with a final score of 37–0, much to the chagrin of the Brevard team. Hall also remembered journeying to Anderson, South Carolina for another game. While traveling through the Rosman community in Transylvania County, the team lay down in the bed of the truck to avoid being seen, a safety precaution designed to avoid any racial incident. He also vividly recalled a favorite white referee named Walt Clayton. Referee Clayton was especially liked because players believed his calls were fair (interview, February 14, 2000).

There were basketball games for the girls as well as for the young boys. Reesie Norman Madison's team played only within the county. She recalled that playing was fun even though there were no uniforms for the girls (interview). Darity regrets that no gymnasium was available for sports-minded black students (interview). Sisters Eversta Smith and Wilkie Robinson relished their basketball games. Sports enriched the school experience of everyone, players and non-players alike.

To develop a fund to purchase a basketball in the late 1920s or early 1930s, Wilkie Johnstone sponsored a chewing gum sale, which was unusual because the school had a rule against chewing gum. Johnstone encouraged students to sell gum in the community, rather than at the school. Young Dorothy Pierce was excited about the unexpected opportunity to become an entrepreneur. Her father, however, did not share her excitement. He told his daughter their family would make a donation for the purchase and required that she return the gum. Dorothy Pierce Hill reported that the campaign to purchase a basketball was successful (interview, February 17, 2000).

Though financial limitations were annoying realities, the barriers to a high school education were more than the Rosenwald community could overcome on its own. The lack of a high school at the Rosenwald site was a major deprivation. To solve the problem, the county provided money to purchase a bus and to pay a driver, who could legally be a teenager, for the 21-mile trek to the all-black Ninth Avenue School in Hendersonville.

"Parents worried about young drivers taking their kids over that dangerous road," James Gardin said (interview, May 30, 1999). "In the winter you'd freeze to death, and that bus was always late," Sherman Crite, Jr. declared. "The bus was not in the best shape. George Owens would pick me up close to the grocery store. Also, he went as close as he could to pick up students at their houses. He made stops at Glade Creek" (interview, November 12, 2002). Audrey Hutchison reported that the bus to Hendersonville picked up a group of students at J.F.W. "Jip" Mills' store at 7:30 A.M. In those days, the road between Brevard and Hendersonville was a treacherous route around winding mountain stretches.

Inadequate finances also curtailed the potential of the library. With the opening of the new Rosenwald School, library space was available, but Wilson reported that neither a formal library nor a librarian was provided. She recalled, however, that students received copies of *Scholastic Magazine* and *My Weekly Reader* (interview, February 8, 2000). By the 1950s and 1960s, improvements had been made. A limited number of library books were available. "It was a nice library for that time," Darity said. "We couldn't go to the public library, but we had books" (interview). After the construction of the Mary C. Jenkins Community Center, which also housed a small library, students had another source for finding books they could check out. The books were used, but their availability was a boost, a luxury to those who enjoyed reading.

Traditionally, people in the school family were the most valuable Rosenwald resource. Early in the century a group of parents purchased land and donated it to the county for use as school property. Wilkie Johnstone, aided in part by Emily Pruden, opened up her home to educate young children and later provided property for the school. The PTA raised money for such projects as cafeteria equipment, stage curtains, and a piano (Mills and Hill, interviews June 19, 1999 and February 17, 2000). Parents willingly sacrificed to improve the school.

Despite the traditional financial shortfall, doors opened occasionally to unique opportunities. A group of Rosenwald students, accompanied by James R. Baten, attended the North Carolina Advancement School in Winston-Salem during the spring semester of 1965. It was an experimental school designed for eighth grade boys who needed special attention, according to Baten. To take advantage of the opportunity, the boys had to have a teacher live on campus with them. The Transylvania County Board of Education paid for substitute Agnes Wilson to assume James Baten's responsibilities so he could chaperone the boys from Rosenwald for the entire semester (interview, March 8, 2000). The classes held in another city were an opportunity for educational enrichment.

Audrey Hutchison noted that students were happy despite conditions at the Brevard Rosenwald School:

> As I remember the days of my attending Rosenwald School, I think of how we played without playground equipment during recess. We didn't go on field trips or visit the public library. We didn't have free or reduced lunches. If we lived close, we went home to eat. Considering all the things we didn't have while attending Rosenwald, I remember all the things we had, and we were happy still [interview, February 10, 2000].

Poverty imposed its limitations on the building and on the school's resources, but an undeterred faculty struggled to unleash the potential of the mind. Records clearly document how the odds were stacked against them through annual financial shortfalls.

A copy of J.P. Sartor's Annual Elementary School Report for 1948-1949, located in Special Collections of the Department of Public Instruction at the North Carolina State Archives, details the resources of the Brevard Rosenwald School at the conclusion of its first year of operation. The report, which covers September 1, 1948, through June 1, 1949, mentions the following facts: There were six full-time teachers, one male and five females. All six faculty members were paid from state funds. Three held primary certificates; one, a grammar grade certificate; and one, a blanket certificate. The principal served as a full-time teacher with four hours of supervisory duties per week. The school had an active PTA. In grades 1–8, the largest class had 34 students; the smallest, 28. The 162 students enrolled averaged a daily membership rate of 91.62 percent and an attendance rate of 55.5 percent. Five students were retained, and 149 were promoted. The figures indicate that eight students had either transferred or dropped out. Other sources mention that polio and influenza fears resulted in absenteeism.

The curriculum consisted of reading, writing, health, language, arithmetic, physical education, music, spelling, social studies, art, and science. Organized activities for the students included basketball, baseball, and public programs. Report cards were distributed every six weeks.

The library contained only 175 books of the expected 500 volumes. There was no atlas or globe and only one set of encyclopedias in the library. There were, however, 28 United States history maps and 10 others. There was a 16mm motion picture projector, but there were no lantern slide projectors, filmstrip projectors, screens, radios, or films. Within the classrooms were crayons, chairs, construction paper, modeling clay, two dozen scissors, and primary pencils, but they lacked paste, staff lines, pitch pipe, paints, brushes, tag board, two dozen rulers, and a full-length mirror.

According to the Sartor report, there were five classrooms, a principal's office, a library room, a health room, four drinking fountains in working order, six lavatories with soap and towels, and two classrooms with lavatories and a fountain. There was neither an auditorium nor a gymnasium. The size of the grounds was one acre, which Sartor rated as inadequate, in poor condition, not beautified, without equipment for the playground or for indoor play.

In the list of improvements for that year, Sartor cited the following: 38 maps, 4 *Encyclopedia Britannica*, 12 *Compton's Pictured Encyclopedias*, supervised lunch, and a piano. Sartor also mentioned that the entire professional staff had attended seven meetings to improve their knowledge of nutrition. Staff assignments were also included. Mills taught first grade; G. Hemphill, Grades 2 and 3; J.J. Smith, Grades 3 and 4; S.G. Benjamin, Grades 5 and 6; and Mrs. J.H. Johnstone, Grades 7 and 8. Superintendent J.B. Jones approved the report.

In the same Special Collections archival file, a report by Principal Annie May Patton of the Pisgah Forest Elementary School provides comparable information for one of Rosenwald School's neighbors. The all-white school had 325 students with nine classrooms and nine teachers. The principal taught two-thirds of the day and supervised one-third. The school had 4-H Clubs and Scouts. There was a "retarded section" of Grade 2, which may suggest remedial work or special education. The principal held an A certificate, as did all of the staff. The average daily attendance was 92 percent.

In the library there were 1,346 books plus magazines. There were also 60 dictionaries and 23 sets of supplementary books. In the list of materials to be used in the classroom only one possible entry of more than 15 was marked no, and that indicated a lack of rhythm band instruments. There was an abundance of maps and globes. The school was located on seven acres in good condition with both playground and indoor play equipment. The school had lunchroom equipment, an electric record player, a projector carrier, blackout shades in four classrooms, and 10 full-length mirrors. Eight of the professional staff had attended four meetings of a workshop in nutrition.

Although its enrollment was twice as large as that of the Rosenwald school, by comparison, the Pisgah Forest School's resources were abundant. The facts speak loudly and eloquently: separate facilities were definitely not equal — a tradition all too familiar to those on short end of the statistics.

Du Bois' lamentation of the lack of adequate resources and finances is supported by Transylvania County statistics. Although all rural mountain schools endured hardships, those serving black students received far less public support than those serving white students. The history of the Brevard Rosenwald School documents community efforts to develop ways of reducing the impact of public indifference and to compensate for widespread inequities.

Parental fund-raising efforts were part of a tradition of community support. Community support and involvement was essential in providing improved educational opportunities for children. Despite the long hours of hard labor and the chains of poverty, parents unearthed ways to provide support. They kept digging for projects to turn concern into cash. Weary from full-time jobs, with little free time or energy to spare, Rosenwald parents still managed to put forth the effort to improve their children's educational opportunities.

W.E.B. Du Bois called for improving the elementary school for black children by placing the school "under the control of those whose children are educated there." School committees composed of prominent black men from the community served as the "board of education" in school matters for Transylvania County's Rosenwald School (Nathaniel Hall and Selena Robinson, interview, July 16, 1999). During the three eras of the Brevard Rosenwald School, parents involved themselves in school life. They provided moral support for teaching, for learning, and for managing classroom behavior. Also, parents organized activities to raise money for resources for the school in addition to attending school events. Their enthusiasm and support was ever-present.

Rural schools have traditionally been the center of community life. Today, according to the Appalachia Educational Laboratory winter newsletter, *The Link*, "meaningful community engagement sets in motion a chain of events that transforms the culture of the school and, often, the community that the school serves" (http://www.ael.org/link/v18n4/index.htm). During the 1950s and 1960s, segregationists exploited this by arguing that school consolidation resulting in integration would be detrimental to the communities involved, possibly destroying them. Now, however, the thinking has changed. According to Wisconsin educators of the Rural School and Community Trust Policy Program, rural educators today are encouraged to view the community not as a culture to affect but as a resource to build bridges for the curriculum (Newsletter, November, 1999, http://www.colostate.edu/orgs/NREA).

The Rosenwald community used the schoolhouse as the hub linking school to community and as a gathering place for voicing community concerns as well as a retreat for entertainment. Both Hall (interview, February 14, 2000) and Hill (interview, February 17, 2000) cited the use of the first Rosenwald school building as a center for events, such as silent movies, magic shows, and variety shows. Hill said,

> We had a magician named Mr. Armstrong—from Spartanburg. We had movies, couldn't go to the Clemson (a Brevard theater constructed in 1929 and open to whites only at that time). Mr. Will Gordon of Marion, North Carolina, brought movies about every month for a while.... We had minstrel shows ... local men performed those. Those silent movies were mostly about cowboys. I remember when Mr. Armstrong cut Bubba Harris in two, and once Bubba got in the trunk, and Mr. Armstrong closed it tight, and then he said, "Bring me that ball," and Bubba walked out from another room. It was wonderful [interview, February 17, 2000].

Hall, who also remembers good times when the community enjoyed silent films and magic shows, recalled programs featuring members of the community, such as barbershop quartets (interview, February 14, 2000). Later, in the 1940s, members of the Negro community were allowed to view movies at the Clemson Theater. The balcony was reserved for black customers.

Through the years the Rosenwald community assembled to celebrate the talents and the accomplishments of their children. Students acted out stories and plays for audiences in the evenings. Parents made costumes and came to watch the play. Jones (interview) and Darity (interview) relived spring performances of simple school plays. Later, concerts and operettas became frequent events. "Our costumes were made of crepe paper—they were the most wonderful thing," Jones said (interview). LaMuriel Brooks Andrews spoke with wonder about performing in an aqua evening dress made of crepe paper. "It was really beautiful," she recalled (interview).

Agnes Wilson said celebratory events spotlighted holidays. She remembered Halloween as a time that was always cold with the ground frozen.

> When it got cold, it stayed cold. Outside trick or treating would be chilly, but the PTA sponsored a school carnival—may have been a fundraiser, I don't recall—we bobbed for apples, had costume parades and contests. Pumpkin seeds were in a jar, and we guessed how many.... Baked goods were for sale, and good hot dogs, lots of fruit ... and decorations such as corn shocks and Indian corn were everywhere [interview, February 8, 2000].

Annie Marie Hailey described a Sadie Hawkins dress-up day that she associated with Halloween. Sometimes teachers joined their students in wearing costumes on that occasion. "Mrs. Benjamin would always dress up. She wore frumpy rags and tatters and had a corncob pipe. We'd congregate in one place and have a little parade. There'd be a prize for the one dressed the funniest" (interview, August 21, 2002).

Another annual event drawing the community into the school was graduation. In the Audrey Hutchison collection of Rosenwald memorabilia is a program used at the 1933 graduation. It cites the time of the annual commencement of Rosenwald High School as May 3, 1933, at 8 P.M. in Brevard, North Carolina. The program, which reflected the ceremonial tradition, included the following parts:

1. Procession
2. Negro national anthem
3. Invocation
4. Salutatorian .... Odell Ballard
5. Class Poem .... Pauline Anderson
6. Valedictorian .... Cornelius Hunt
7. America A World Power .... Winnie Belle Jones
8. Class Will .... Melissia Kilgore
9. Class Prophecy.......................... Gracie Bailey
10. Quartet.................... Rosenwald High School Boys
11. Address to Graduates .... Dr. H.M. Moore
12. Awarding Diplomas .... Principal C.E. Burney
13. Awarding Certificates
14. Awarding Prizes
15. Class Song
16. Remarks .... School Committee
17. Doxology
18. Benediction

ANNUAL SERMON TO THE GRADUATING CLASS
Sunday, April 30, 1933, 3 P.M.
Subject: "THE RECIPE OF LIFE"
Principal C.E. Burney

Audrey Hutchison explained that April 30, 1933, a Sunday, was the date on the outside of the program but May 3, 1933, a Wednesday, was the date printed on the inside. The baccalaureate service was held on Sunday at 3 P.M., and the commencement was held on Wednesday at 8 P.M. (interview, March 8, 2000). Class colors were pink and white. The program also lists 18 graduates with one name inked in. Selena Robinson and Nathaniel Hall graduated that year, but Nathaniel's name was omitted from the list because of disciplinary action (interview, February 14, 2000). The motto is listed as: "*Tout vient a qui sait attendre,"* which Hall translated as "All things come to him who waits." The motto, according to Hall, was a favorite of Professor Javan L. Jones, who later married Winnie Belle, a member of the 1933 class. They relocated to Philadelphia (Hill, interview, February 17, 2000). Other commencement programs are extant, but the 1933 example is a representative sample. It is noteworthy because it shows that the school committee encouraged secondary level classes at the Brevard Rosenwald School. However, Hill pointed out that all students listed on the program were not graduating tenth graders. Some were in lower grades (interview, February 17, 2000).

A year earlier an unusual tragedy marred the traditional ceremony. Winona Smith Whiteside remembered with sadness the death of Maude Killian who was to have graduated in April of 1932. "She was a great big, husky girl. She ran up the hill where Rosenwald was…. When she got to the porch, she fell dead. They said she had a heart attack" (interview, March 9, 2000).

Another high school graduation vivid to alumna Reesie Madison occurred in 1941, soon after fire destroyed the wooden building on March 12. The community assembled in the Bethel "A" Church to give students a successful sendoff (interview, February 22, 2000).

At a typical Rosenwald elementary school graduation, according to Agnes Wilson, everyone sang "Lift Every Voice and Sing," the Negro national anthem used as a standard ritual at formal events. Students wore white dresses and dark suits with carnation bouquets or boutonnières made of colored tissue paper. Programs included prayer and Scripture reading as well as poetry and individual recitations. The valedictorian and the salutatorian delivered carefully rehearsed speeches, much to the approval of the audience. Then the principal conferred "passing" on the joyful class. Sometimes a classroom teacher or the president of the PTA added comments. "The community was very much involved…. Each child belonged to everybody" (interview, February 8, 2000).

Annie Marie Hailey emphasized that graduations were exciting events. There were speeches and awards for high achievement, for good citizenship, and for perfect attendance. "When our names were called, we would strut across that stage and get that rolled up piece of paper. Why, no one ever wanted to miss a day…. Mrs. J.S. Silversteen awarded a citizenship prize. I got one" (interview, August 21, 2002).

Audrey Hutchison, a 1954 graduate, explained that a stage was built to be used for community programs. She recalled that the lunchroom was often used for meetings and that, in the new building, graduation was held in the lunchroom on the last day of school (interview, February 10, 2000).

Michael Owens, an employee at Brevard College and at Pisgah Forest Elementary School, graduated in the 1950s. Reflecting on the traditions of his graduation experience, he described details that were still memorable almost

4. Pedagogical Traditions

Rosenwald graduations were traditional events. This graduating class of the 1950s includes: Front row, left to right: Nancy Owens, Lillian Hemphill, Patricia Hunt, Doris Gardin, Sandra Benjamin, Rosetta Norman, Ella Bernice Smith, Edna Mae Glaze, Gracie Aiken, Lillie Madison, Barbara Baker, Rita Robinson, JoAnne Camp. Back row, left to right: Mr. Robert Duncan, Johnny Mack Whitmire, Frank Earl Penson, Lewis Whiteside, Grady Elliott, Jr., Robert Kilgore, Floyd Benjamin, Robert Camp, Robert Duncan, Jr., Henry Hutchison, Raymond Walker, Robert Hill, Richard Hutchison, Henry Johnson, Jr., Steve Davenport, Nelson Glaze. (Courtesy Bernetha Owens.)

50 years later. "We had blue caps and gowns. We marched downstairs and walked across the stage. We got a diploma.... I don't remember a speaker. There had to be one, probably a preacher. I was so glad and so happy.... There was a good turnout. The whole community came" (interview).

Owens believes that, with perhaps two exceptions, the 15–18 members of his class continued with their high school education.

Pastor Frederick L. Gordon, whose parents attended Rosenwald and served the school in their adult lives, also reminisced about his graduation. The 1961 valedictorian's commencement took place at the church he pastors today. He recalled practicing the march, girls in white dresses and boys in black suits and ties. Marching to "Pomp and Circumstance," the class filed into the center section of the sanctuary. There were speeches, and someone read a poem. Afterward his mother, father, and uncle hosted a party in the family's back yard for the entire class. Happiness prevailed, as was the tradition (interview, February 9, 2000).

Music specialist James Baten described the Rosenwald community as "an extended family kind of situation, with an exceptionally strong PTA" (interview, October 21, 1999). He recalled with appreciation their willingness to make 65 to 70 choir robes for the children to wear as well as the same number of ties. "It was my first teaching job and a beautiful experience." Paul Hunter, also in his first job as a teacher, said, "I got involved with the community" (interview).

In an event that gave the Brevard Rosenwald School state prominence, North Carolina PTA delegates gathered there. According to Audrey Hutchison, the organization was named the National Congress of Colored Parents and Teachers. Reesie Madison, a 1941 Rosenwald graduate, served as a member of the PTA while her five children attended school during the 1950s and 1960s. The community, according to Madison, sent representatives to the state PTA convention. After the conference, they reported decisions and suggestions to the local PTA.

A Rosenwald tradition encouraged parents and students to claim ownership of the school and of the grounds. After going home following dismissal at the end of the school day, students and other family members often returned to the school grounds to play games and to chat around the rock fountain at the edge of the playground.

Of the fountain, Wilson said, "The water fountain from the old school was a pretty heirloom landmark. We would walk there in the afternoon and during time off in the summers. Back then families didn't have two cars. We would drink water, talk, and then walk some more" (interview, February 8, 2000). Hall described the fountain as a stone structure with six water jets (interview, February 14, 2000).

Fred Mills, the husband of Ethel Mills and a talented rock mason, built the fountain, quite an accomplishment for a man with only one arm. Mills was handicapped as the result of an accident at the Transylvania Tanning Company. (Ethel Mills, interview, June 9, 1999). The fountain was a social gathering spot for members of the black community. Its presence on the school grounds enriched their sense of belonging and of ownership when other meeting places were designated as off-limits to African Americans.

Michael Owens and others confirmed that students "always returned to the playground after school." Recalling details of the old Rosenwald school building, Owens described underpinning supports resembling tree trunks that remained a landmark for a number of years following the 1941 fire. He also remembered community sports being special events. "We played on the school grounds plus one empty lot ... played baseball and football mostly."

During his childhood, the boys living near the Rosenwald School formed a team known as Goose Hollow, though Owens is not sure why they used that name. The Goose Hollow players competed with boys from the other side of the railroad tracks at the edge of Brevard, whose team was known simply as "The Corner." Owens explained that those players were from the other corner. "We played just about every evening," (interview, February 29, 2000). Other alumni also referred to after-hours use of the school grounds as a meeting place to talk and to enjoy one another's company.

Teachers were an integral part of the community, and their presence resulted in the extension of school traditions beyond the schoolgrounds. Faculty lived among the families of their students. Principals Mack Dawkins and John Sartor boarded at the family home of Dorothy Pierce Hill. Principal C.E. Burney boarded at Susie Sharp's house (Hill, interview, February 17, 2000). Paul Hunter, then a young bachelor with a lively sense of humor, lived at the boyhood home of Daniel and Michael Owens, which was provided by their mother, Bernetha Owens, near Main Street (Daniel Owens, interview, February 29, 2000). "Once I decided to move out and try it on my own, but I soon returned to Miss Bernetha's," Hunter said (interview, July 1, 2000).

Alice Glaze Robinson remembered that her Rosenwald teachers made her feel special — all but one, "who made me feel I was nothing"— faculty members were accessible and supportive members of the community (interview, February 24, 2000).

Mills, Robinson's principal, maintained contact with her former pupil during her college days. Decades later, Mills continues to stay in touch with Robinson, who resides in Yanceyville, North Carolina. During Robinson's Rosenwald School days, Mills occasionally asked her to retrieve a sweater or an umbrella from her home. As a youngster, Robinson felt a strong sense of trust because she had been selected for such errands. "After I went away to Livingstone, Mrs. Mills made sure I had clothes or whatever I needed" (interview, February 25, 2000). The bonding illustrates that teachers offered extra support for needy students.

Former students Lois Elliott Wynn and Ida Hemphill Ellens confirmed that the Rosenwald faculty routinely befriended students. "Mrs. Mills was my neighbor. She was strict. If she said she'd do something, she'd do it. I was a stubborn child. Sometimes she kept me up there for after-school detention, and then she walked me home. She kept me till I got my act together. I value her for that because it broke a bad habit. Once you left that school, you could go out and conquer anything" (Wynn, interview, March 24, 2002).

Wynn and Ellens both remembered times when Mills provided money to help students. When Ellens was only nine years old, her mother, age 42, died of heart dropsy nine months after giving birth to Ida's sister. "Daddy

Members of the Rosenwald Safety Patrol monitored activities on the school grounds. Pictured are first row, left to right: Richard Smith, Robert L. Young, Morris Young, Paul Hemphill, Steve Benjamin, Jerry Gash, and Buddy Sanders. Second row, left to right: Haywood Moore, Vincent Lynch, Charlie Wynn, Bernard Bailey, and Raymond Howell. Third row, left to right: Thomas Benjamin, Thomas Conley, and Bill Hunt. (Courtesy Mavis Smith.)

didn't dress me like the other girls at school, and my hair wasn't fixed. My daddy did the best he could, but he didn't know how to take care of girls so Mrs. Mills would have my hair fixed every two weeks. Ora Moore fixed it in her house across the street from the school, and Mrs. Mills paid for it" (interview, June 19, 2002).

According to Ellens, it would have been impossible for her to complete the eighth grade and to go on to Ninth Avenue School without Mills' encouragement. "I had to help out at home by cooking and taking care of my sister. My mother taught me to make biscuits while she was sick in bed. After she died, I helped my daddy look out for the family. We didn't always have food to eat" (interview, June 19, 2002). Motivated by Mills' interest, Ellens graduated from high school and took additional college training.

Mills admitted that at times she had to lie to save a child's pride. She wanted each pupil to have a good lunch. If a child did not have the money, Mills would invent a mysterious sponsor who had donated money to use as needed, or she would hire a student to run errands to earn lunch money. At times she had to be quite inventive. "There was one boy who would take nothing. I selected him to be our record boy. He carried messages in exchange for his lunch. His mother had a very poor salary, and he had a dose of pride. The children would have called him a beggar if they had known. Sometimes I had to dig up something to keep their pride" (interview, June 17, 2002).

Other teachers also provided personal help. Ellens described Gertie Hemphill as a kind, compassionate lady, who treated every child as her biological offspring. Ellens also remembered teachers Mary Kilgore and Margaret Avery as exceptional women. "Mrs. Avery remembered me carrying my little sister Nellie around on my hip. She said she felt sorry for me" (interview, June 19, 2002). Ellens' father succeeded in keeping his family together, and his efforts earned him the respect of his children's teachers.

Being invited to visit a teacher's home was an honor. Wilkie Johnstone entertained Alice Glaze Robinson and other classmates in her living room. According to Robinson, to be invited into "the teacher's house" was not taken lightly. During the same decade, music teacher Julia Smith provided housing for Robert Kilgore while he attended high school in Wilmington, N.C.

The community had a vested interest in education. Students were encouraged to take advantage of opportunities at school. Agnes Wilson's father received only a fourth-grade education, but, said Wilson, "he would have slaughtered us" if we had taken school lightly (interview, February 8, 2000). Lillie Jones also expressed appreciation that her father, who had been able to reach "second or third grade," always encouraged his children "to learn, learn, learn." His encouragement paid off: each of his six children earned a college degree, and five have advanced degrees (interview).

As early as the 1920s and 1930s, Rosenwald School parents encouraged their children to improve their minds. Selena Robinson and Nathaniel Hall recalled with fondness their father's simple rewards for doing well at school. The parent stressed the importance of reading, and Hall recalled thanking him for the pennies that were his reward for spelling and reading well (interview, July 16, 1999). Robinson praised her father's willingness to do whatever job came his way to provide for his family and to encourage achievement in school. "If Daddy got a job digging a ditch, he was happy. That meant a week's work, and that was important. Today a machine could dig a ditch in a few hours" (conversation, December 7, 2002).

Conscientious parents supported the school and worked hard to guarantee that children realized the importance of education. "To my father, education was a way out," said Betty Hunt High as she interpreted her parent's view of learning. She knew education would enable her to escape poverty and inequality (interview).

Traditions emerged and became firmly established in the more than seven decades of segregated Negro education in Transylvania County. At the Brevard Rosenwald School, those traditions included classroom procedures, playground activities, evening events, and family involvement. Rosenwald alumni often echoed one another as they related memories of school days marked by limited resources but highly supportive teachers and parents.

In his memoir *A Servant's Journey* (1998), Thomas Kilgore, Jr., states:

> The Rosenwald School for black children in Brevard was inferior in building and supplies to the white elementary and high schools, but teachers like Mrs. J.H. Johnstone, who taught four generations of Brevard

children, her daughter Coragreene Johnstone, who taught me in the ninth grade, and Professor J.L. Jones, who was principal during my eighth and ninth grades, were teachers who had proper credentials and were charged with a deep desire to motivate us to learn, regardless of the handicaps of segregation [p. 12].

One Rosenwald tradition was a morning ritual to mark the day's beginning. Procedure varied with the times, but moral emphasis was typical. Honoring religion and patriotism was another tradition. Betty Hunt High remembers that morning prayers and Bible verses were a part of each school day. As the day began, children sang, "Good morning to you / all in our places / with bright sunshiny faces." Upon leaving for the day, they sang, "Day is done / Time to say goodbye / Until another day / As home we trod / Tripping on our way / We will look before we cross the street / As home we run with skipping feet." It was customary to greet one another and to say goodbye in this manner (interview).

Pastor Frederick L. Gordon described a morning ritual composed of a song, a prayer, the pledge, and another song. Each day began with a devotional period (interview, February 9, 2000). Public schools, both white and black, often used religious instruction to teach character. In small, western North Carolina communities, most families shared the same religion, so there was little or no objection to Christian activities in public schools.

During the mornings in the new Rosenwald building, roll call occurred promptly at 8:30 A.M. Then teachers collected money for lunch and milk. Teachers asked who would be eating in the cafeteria, who brought lunch, and who would be purchasing milk that day. After the information-gathering process, each class had devotions and recited the Lord's Prayer. Following the religious rites, students stood to recite the Pledge of Allegiance and to sing a patriotic song, such as "America the Beautiful" or the national anthem. Sometimes classes recited a motto and sang another song, religious or patriotic. Some days pupils sang the school song, and almost always they repeated Bible verses. Edith Darity remembered taking joy in that routine before "digging into the books" (interview).

At Rosenwald there was "tip toe" recess and "big" recess. At 10 A.M. students had a "tip toe" time to take care of necessary matters quickly and quietly. Any student who socialized was admonished to use the time wisely. After lunch came "big" recess (Wilson and Robinson, interviews, February 8 and 24, 2000). Baten, who served on the staff during Rosenwald's final five years, recalled that the three male faculty members—he, Paul Hunter and Robert Duncan—took the boys to the far playground for a ball game. The men played with the boys, and afterwards all returned to class. "When we went out for recess, we would come up with different activities—nothing formal.... Played it by ear ... very congenial atmosphere" (interview, October 21, 1999).

The Rosenwald faculty fostered a competitive atmosphere. Thomas Kilgore, Jr., recalled vying to outdo classmates Homer Kemp, Cyrus Mooney, and Kemp Smith for the highest grades. Kilgore enjoyed the sweet victory that came to him and Homer Kemp at the end of the 1927-1928 school year when they were proclaimed winners (Kilgore, 1998). On Friday afternoons following "big" recess, a spelling bee, or at times a mathematics bee, took place in individual classrooms. During spelling bees, an important part of school routine, students lined up around the room and spelled until they made a mistake. The last student standing was the week's champion.

The spelling competition was an event of staggering importance to the students, especially in the first Rosenwald building. Dorothy Pierce Hill remembers that other children pinched her, stepped on her toes, tapped her on the head, and hoped that she would develop a headache and have to go home on spelling bee days, because they wanted to outdo her (Hill, interview, February 17, 2000). Nathaniel Hall and his sister, Selena Robinson, remembered the excitement of Friday spelling bees, a team event for their classes, and the sibling rivalry associated with that event. "Spelling bees were terrific. If both of us were on the same team, we always won. If we were on opposite teams, one of us had to out-spell the other. As brother and sister, we'd go at it neck and neck. We were supposed to put it up in the brain to stay" (Nathaniel Hall, interview, February 14, 2000).

Spelling, writing, and penmanship were valued at home and at school. Students wished to write cursively as well as Principal Mills did. Ironically, writing was difficult for Mills when she was a young child. To practice penmanship, Mills wrote on everything, even walls. Finally, she succeeded, becoming the model of cursive writing for teachers, principals, and students.

Lois Elliott Wynn said the Rosenwald faculty emphasized reading, science, and mathematics, but learning to write cursively was more vivid in her memories. For writing practice, employing the Palmer Method, students used special lined paper. Capital letters required special strokes. To master the curves and loops of letters required much practice. Wynn also recalled memorizing and reciting poetry. In science class, peanut and cotton plants dangled from the ceiling, and a sweet potato sent out green vines, showing students how plants grow. Students also studied weather and the changing seasons. One assignment in North Carolina history required that Wynn learn all 100 of the state's counties in alphabetical order and to fill them in on a blank map. She learned her counties in groups of five (interview, March 24, 2002). Though there was a lot of rote memory, students were encouraged to master the material. "They told us there are no dumb children here. If you want to learn, you can learn. And we did" (Ellens, interview, June 18, 2002).

May Day celebrations were also festive occasions. Early that morning or the night before, a parent or a teacher strung colored streamers from the top of the flagpole. Pastor Gordon wondered aloud, "How did they get the ribbons there? I never knew, but we had a time." Holding a streamer in one hand, children danced around the Maypole. They weaved in and out, braiding the streamers. Then children danced in the opposite direction and stopped when the unbraiding was complete (interview, February 9, 2000).

Two alumni recalled the event in this fashion: "I loved the May Day, dancing around the pole. It was a big activity at the school" (Lillie Jones, interview). "When Mr. Baten put on a May Day Program, we wrapped the pole. Then we would do the samba and different dances from different countries" (Marva Lytle, interview).

Neva Whiteside Martin said she could never forget the merriment of annual May Day activities. "One year my sister Cecilia was Queen. She wore a crown" (interview, October 31, 2002). The May Day celebration also included other kinds of "field" activities. "Sack races, eggs in spoons, three-legged races, relays. There was a little track meet. It was great fun," Pastor Gordon recollected (interview, February 9, 2000). It was an opportunity for the children and their teachers to enjoy a festive celebration in the fresh air of spring.

Internalizing the gestures and the stories of faculty members became another tradition. Alice Glaze Robinson still uses Principal Mills' raised finger gesture as an unconscious way of announcing to her staff and children that something serious is under discussion (interview, February 24, 2000). Agnes Wilson, when talking to parents or to her own grandchildren, finds herself using illustrations she learned from Gertie Hemphill. Wilson shared one of Hemphill's stories that she frequently used to emphasize that a parent's love will blind him or her to the child's shortcomings:

> Johnny had grown up and gone into the military. The General was in town, and the Army was giving a full-dress parade — and Johnny's mom had gone to see that parade. The soldiers marched by, looking so smart in their uniforms, going Left, Right, Left, Right in perfect step. Then there came one young man who was going Right, Left, Right, Left. "Looky! Looky! Looky! Everyone else is wrong except my Johnny." Johnny, who had never been right, was perfect in his mother's eyes [Agnes Wilson, interview, February 8, 2000].

Mills, who passed the 100 mark in 2001, is apt to quote one of Hemphill's wise sayings. Mills repeated one of Hemphill's proverbs: "Where there's a will, there's a way so if you don't see a way, take that will and make a way" (interview, March 1, 2001).

Prizes and awards were another traditional practice. Two awards that alumni remember were those for perfect attendance and for good citizenship. Reesie Madison proudly recalled earning a perfect attendance certificate (interview, February 22, 2000). Keith Howell and Samuel Howell, Jr. were also proud of their record of perfect attendance. The accomplishment was especially remarkable because no classes were cancelled because of snow that year. Robbie Outlaw Gardin laughingly reminisced about a day when the snow was knee deep, and she and Ed Sharp were the only students who reached the school. (interview, August 21, 2002). Mills explained that on another occasion the Gash boys braved the elements with their feet and shoes wrapped in tow sacks. Alumni remembered walking through the snow up a steep hill to attend school, sliding down the hill occasionally, and finding opportunities to play in the snow.

Character was also emphasized and honored at the school. Citizenship received annual recognition by the Daughters of the American Revolution, who gave a Good Citizenship award. Mrs. J.S. Silversteen made presentations at awards ceremonies. Annie Marie Hailey recalled being honored with a Citizenship Award.

Repetitive patterns reflected ideology associated with the school as well as with Rosenwald traditions. The school as an entity was comparable to a village. At times alumni called the school a "safe haven," a "security blanket," or "our comfort zone"—terms that implied an image that extended beyond the tradition of financial restrictions. Others talked about the Brevard Rosenwald School as an extension of the home. Several used the word family to identify the close relationship of the children with their teachers, with their principal, and with the community. Either directly or indirectly, the vernacular terms referenced the school as the community's gathering place. The metaphors suggest the staff's success in creating security for each child. A strong atmosphere of safety pervaded the Rosenwald School.

Elementary schools are remarkable in their extraordinary power to impact the lives of children. That power was demonstrated each day and each decade at the Brevard Rosenwald School. The shadow of security was so dynamic that it prevailed despite neglect by the Transylvania County educational system. The strong shadow empowered faculty and parents to forge an alliance that safely led to upgrades brought about by integration. Figurative language suggesting security conveyed a tradition of a healthy learning environment — an abstract embrace that prodded students to achieve.

Chapter 5

Achievement of Integration

WHILE ROSENWALD THE PHILANTHROPIST brought about educational change for African Americans in Brevard, a 1954 court decision meant major change in Transylvania County school practices. No longer was change taking place simply on the western edge of Brevard. A national decision rewrote the regulations and overturned the repressive atmosphere. However, even that change did not happen instantly, as is evident in the events of the 1950s and the 1960s.

The 1953 and 1954 decisions in the case of *Linda Brown v. the Board of Education of Topeka, Kansas* reversed the *Plessy v. Ferguson* decision of 1896. In Linda Brown's state, separate facilities were quite similar. The National Association for the Advancement of Colored People was interested in whether the Supreme Court would find separate, but essentially equal, facilities a violation of civil rights. In the initial arguments, the Court was so divided that further arguments were presented the following year. In the interim, Earl Warren was appointed as Chief Justice.

Convinced that the moral issues far exceeded those of constitutional interpretations, Warren used strong leadership and logical arguments to win a unanimous decision in overturning *Plessy v. Ferguson*. He claimed that "in the field of education the doctrine of separate but equal has no place. Separate is inherently unequal." In reference to black children, separation "generates a feeling of inferiority as to their status in the community" and "may affect their hearts and minds in a way unlikely ever to be undone" (Emmerich, 1998, p. 5).

The Supreme Court decision that segregation in public schools was unconstitutional had a revolutionary impact on education in North Carolina. Reactions ranged from tacit acceptance to delaying tactics to massive resistance. In his Biennial Report, 1952–1954, North Carolina Superintendent Charles F. Carroll suggested:

> Any abrupt jolt to the customary pattern of thought and behavior of a large number of people, regardless of how noble the interest that propels, can produce grave repercussions; change, that is to endure, is born of consent on the part of a firm majority of the people who are to live with it ... the most notable observation is that no responsible North Carolinian has proposed the abolition of public education ... our basic prayer is that each of us will resolve anew that we shall preserve our cherished system of free public education in North Carolina [H.V. Brown, 1964, p. 141].

A second decision, *Brown II*, was required to provide for a speedy end to segregated schools. Resistance was common. Some schools closed. Private schools sprang up hastily. In Norfolk, Virginia, and elsewhere, courts were used to establish integrated schools (Bly, *Journal of Negro Education*, Spring 1998). African Americans became bolder and more aggressive in pursuing their rights. Four black students bravely sat at a lunch counter in Greensboro, North Carolina, on February 1, 1960, and were refused service, but the quartet remained seated until the store closed (Franklin and Moss, 1994). Such "sit-in" demonstrations spread rapidly. Both white and black youth participated in the movement as a peaceful protest. "They sat in white libraries, waded at white beaches, and slept in the lobbies of white hotels. Many were arrested for trespassing, disorderly conduct, and disobeying police officers" (Franklin and Moss, 1994, pp. 495–496).

Gradually they won and others, encouraged by their victories, pursued their own equality. Motions were filed on behalf of minor children in Transylvania County in the United States District Court in 1962 to maintain their eligibility to attend integrated public schools in their county. Consequently, in 1966, the Brevard Rosenwald School was closed, and its students began attending formerly all-white schools in Transylvania County.

The forward step was immense considering the bleak and difficult conditions for black education, as evident in a report dated September 25, 1948, the same year the new Rosenwald building opened. North Carolina Superintendent of Public Instruction Clyde A. Erwin provided Senator John C. Stennis with an outline of problems existing in the education of Negroes in North Carolina. He identified major differences between the quality of white and black education. School buildings, school equipment, and school transportation were unequal. Many white rural schools had been consolidated, but most of the rural schools for black students had not been. An urgent need existed to provide high schools for black communities. Because of the lack of opportunities to attend secondary school, vocational education remained out of reach for most black students. Negro colleges needed additional support, and graduate programs needed to be developed and/or expanded. In some North Carolina communities, local supplements were provided for white teachers but denied to black teachers. Erwin's main point was that there was no equality of educational opportunities for Negro children in North Carolina. The facts were clear, but the neglect continued.

Fourteen years later, in December 1962, the State Department of Public Instruction in Raleigh, issued a comprehensive report prepared by G.H. Ferguson, who had served at the Director of the Division of Negro Education. In *Some Facts about the Education of Negroes in North Carolina: 1921–1960*, Ferguson begins with an analysis of the philosophy of Governor Charles Brantley Aycock, who served from 1901 to 1905. Ferguson highlights events in the history of the state's education of Negroes through 1960. Aycock responded to public criticism of his plan for public school improvement by saying, "We are too poor not to educate our children" (Ferguson, 1962).

During the same time frame, North Carolina Superintendent of Public Instruction E.C. Brooks claimed that North Carolina did not believe in public education. His proof: only 30 districts in the state had been willing to levy a local tax in support of schools.

Ferguson includes this statistical summary:

> The average salary paid to county superintendents annually was less than one dollar a day; to public school teachers, $92.20 for the term.... Practically no interest was manifested in the buildings or equipment of schoolhouses. The children of more than 950 public school districts were ... without schoolhouses while those in 1,132 districts sat on rough pine boards in log houses chinked with clay.... Schools were kept open only 73 days in the year, and less than one-third of the children of school age attended them [Ferguson, p. 1, 1962].

Aycock believed in the right of each child to procure an education. He spoke indignantly about one town that provided taxes for school and, after living with that decision for a short time, voted the tax down. The town celebrated the vote with bonfires and a brass band. Aycock also criticized the willingness for much of the public to provide for the education of white children while exhibiting unwillingness to provide for the education of Negroes. He stated, "These people appear to have been willing to deny education to white children in order that they might keep the Negro in ignorance. Thus, to complicate a situation already sufficiently difficult, the race issue injected its poison into the very vitals of the problem" (Ferguson, 1962, p. 2).

Governor Aycock affirmed "the right of every child born on earth to have the opportunity to burgeon out all that is within him." Aycock's philosophy was reflected in that of C.C. Spaulding, the president of a Negro insurance company, who often advised young Negroes to "apply yourself in your educational endeavor that you will command respect rather than demand respect" (Ferguson, 1962). The philosophy was also echoed in the aspirations of Brevard parents who urged their children to seek an education regardless of the cost.

In 1913, at the request of Superintendent J.Y. Joyner, funds were provided through the General Education Board of New York to support two agents for rural schools. N.C. Newbold was hired to work with the schools for Negro children, and L.C. Brogden, for white children. Subsequently, in 1921, a Division for Negro Education was established within the State Department of Public Instruction. Newbold served as the director with a staff of eight to provide supervision, teacher training, and building construction. The initial problems confronting this division included such facts as poor enrollment of school-age children, slack attendance, tremendous overcrowding during a few months of the school term, rare supervision of instruction, wide range of age groups in many first grades (5 years to 15 years), only seven accredited high schools, few training opportunities for teachers, a frequent high absentee rate for teachers who also served as ministers, and deplorable conditions of buildings and furnishings in rural areas. More truth than fiction existed in the frequently quoted adage that in their school buildings, students had ample opportunities to "study animal life through the cracks in the floor, plant life through openings in the walls, and astronomy through the holes in the roofs" (Ferguson, 1962). Such alarming conditions make it easy to understand why parents valued the Brevard Rosenwald School, limited as it was, especially during the early years, and willingly sacrificed to guarantee its success.

However, Ferguson documents many improvements that occurred under the supervision of the Division of Negro Education. Programs were developed to enhance both teacher preparation and instructional improvement. The change led to an increased number of accredited high schools. One program that proved instrumental in assisting the faculty of the Brevard Rosenwald School was the provision of six-week summer schools located at colleges and at other venues, such as the Hill Street School in Asheville. Instructional levels included high school as well as collegiate subjects. For a period of 15 years, more than 75 percent of instructors attended summer school. More than one third of the Negro teachers from 1924 to 1936 participated in college extension classes.

Another development that impacted the Brevard school community was the interest promoted in providing or improving school buildings. State educational administrators W.F. Credle and G.E. Davis were instrumental in arousing interest in providing better school facilities throughout North Carolina. From 1930 to 1940, the focus was on improved organization and instruction in the elementary schools. From 1940 to 1950, emphasis was on school accreditation and on assisting Negro students and pursuing graduate studies. From 1950 to 1960, bond issues resulted in widespread expansion of school facilities at all levels. In 1939, a fund was established to assist Negroes attending graduate school in other states. A program leading to a doctor of philosophy degree was established at North Carolina College. In 1957, teacher-training programs received impetus from the creation of the Scholarship Loan Fund for Prospective Teachers. However, in 1960, the Division of Instructional Services of the State Department of Public Instruction absorbed the Division of Negro Education as part of an effort to achieve organizational integration.

The history of Negro education before, during, and after the Civil War demonstrates the conflicting conscience of southerners, who felt their slaves should be educated while fearing the empowerment that could result from advanced learning. Industrial education was designed to have a subjugating influence on Negroes, as it forced them to quell any ambitions for advancement.

Philanthropic support, as evident in Brevard, had an elevating impact on the Negro's level of self-worth, but the increasing awareness of inequities in education led to warfare for equality.

It was these historical patterns that African Americans in Brevard and Transylvania County had to overcome. And to defeat the degradation they had witnessed, they needed a building to help them fulfill a dream. That is why the Rosenwald plan appealed to the 1920s leaders. Rather than simply recognizing problems and shortcomings, the possibility of a school building signaled hope: a brighter future for the black children of Transylvania County. Three or four decades later parents were still dreaming of a brighter future when new options became apparent in the 1950s and 1960s.

The 1896 *Plessy v. Ferguson* court decision enhanced the circumstances that led to the establishment and the building of Rosenwald School. It took another court decision, *Linda Brown v. the Board of Education of Topeka, Kansas*, 1954, to close the doors of Brevard Rosenwald School. But this time it was a decision that opened other doors and allowed faculty, parents, and students to step through that door so that they could continue their educational journeys in learning environments newly opened to them. It meant Rosenwald students could join hands with others to pursue learning and to influence the larger community via their special contributions in an integrated public school. It also meant that they could help shape the fame of Brevard High School for the first time as high school students in Transylvania County. To later generations segregation may seem like distant history, but the doors did not open completely until 1966, even though the Supreme Court announced the Brown decision in 1954.

Throughout the South segregated schools for blacks and whites were a long-standing regional tradition. In *The Asheville Citizen* issue on September 1, 1954, a brief article described a small Negro girl requesting to be registered at the Oliver Cromwell Elementary School in Maryland. She was accepted. It was the first time in the history of education that a Baltimore school had both white and black students attending the same school. The path to integration took longer in the schools of Transylvania County, but court decisions paved the way for the establishment of what would become a new tradition: integrated schools with an extended Rosenwald family.

After the *Brown I* and *Brown II* Supreme Court decisions in 1953 and in 1954, the Brevard black population became increasingly involved in fighting for equal educational opportunities for its children. The new Brevard Rosenwald School had been occupied for approximately five years when the first of these two landmark decisions was announced. An analysis of the historical concerns about obstacles that black students experienced in obtaining a high school education shows a sustained pattern of concern about integration and equal opportunity.

Prior to the devastating fire of 1941, Transylvania County's black parents and school leaders tried to provide a high school education within the county for their children. Thomas Kilgore, Jr., said that in 1928 public education ended for him and for all the Rosenwald students at the close of the ninth grade because no standard high school for black students existed in Brevard (Kilgore, 1998). According to Selena Robinson and Nathaniel Hall, at the close of the ninth or tenth grade and, in a few instances, the eleventh grade, a graduation was held that marked the termination of public schooling for the Rosenwald students.

Winona Whiteside retained report cards and other memorabilia from her childhood and youth, valuing the achievement they represented. After completing tenth grade, she was promoted to the eleventh grade, but in those times, students routinely went elsewhere to attend high school. Often girls enrolled at the private, church-supported Allen School in Asheville. Lillie Jones said that attending school in Asheville seemed like being a world away from her home in Brevard, which she visited only on holidays (interview).

After the construction of the Ninth Avenue School in Henderson County, the local board of education made arrangements to transport students there after the eighth grade. In the April 16, 1953, edition of *The Transylvania Times*, Ralph Fisher, the representative to the state legislature in Raleigh, proposed introduction of legislation to establish a high school addition at the Rosenwald site. His efforts were not successful.

Parents of students traveling to the all-black high school in the adjoining county grew increasingly discontent with that provision, especially after the construction of the new Brevard High School. Black citizens rejected the board of education's old excuse that buildings were too small to accommodate black and white students. Sufficient space did exist. According to Agnes Wilson, parents and interested community members formed the Transylvania Citizens Improvement Organization (TCIO) and researched the possibilities for gaining access to equal educational opportunities within the county (interview, February 8, 2000). The TCIO, which continues to function in the twenty-first century, marked its fortieth anniversary with special celebrations on July 1 and 2, 2000.

Infuriated by persistent rejection, African Americans sought legal representation. Nine years after the *Brown I* Supreme Court Decision, Brevard parents filed a civil action suit on August 17, 1962, in U.S. District Court, Western District of North Carolina on behalf of a number of Rosenwald children, including: Georgia Anna Conley; Robert Conley, Jr.; Lenord Ossie Bailey; Cail Elliott; Keith Elliott; James Edward Gardin, Jr.; Frederick L. Gordon; Samuel Howell; Robert L. Hutchison; Edith Roberta Hutchison; Reper Wynn; Gary Madison; Richard A. Robinson; Robert G. Smith III; Neva Whiteside; Steve Wynn; Lewis Howell; Charles Hardin; Willie Howell; Joan Mills; Mamie Etta Robinson; Olivia Whiteside; Tommy Ferguson; Dwight Gash; Herman Howell; Helen Jean Hutchison; Betty Jean Norman; Craig Wilkes; Lindsey Wynn; Harold Chatman; Alvis Louise Robinson; Maggie Jane Smith; Steve Willis Wynn; Norman N. Griffin, Jr.; Judy Shea Robinson; Clara Elizabeth Smith and Kenneth Wilkes.

The parents petitioned the court for action against Superintendent C.W. Bradburn and the members of the Transylvania County Board of Education — E.B. Matheson, Eugene M. Morris, Tom Ramsey, and Harry Morgan. They requested, on behalf of their children, that the public schools of Transylvania County be reorganized on a non–racially segregated basis in response to the Supreme Court's decisions, "without recourse to segregation or discrimination on the basis of race or color" (attached to Board of Education minutes).

The suit also documents the black students' dilemma — they were forced to leave the county to attend high school even though a high school existed within the county. After July 19, 1962, gradual integration was allowed at the secondary school level. Before that time no black student was permitted to attend public schools in Transylvania County above the elementary school level. The segregated Rosenwald School existed to educate students in the lower grades, one through eight.

The case was decided in favor of the petitioners in 1963. Selena Robinson, who has received widespread recognition for her role in fighting for school integration, recalled approaching the board of education on three separate occasions to request that black students be allowed to attend Brevard High School. She said the board agreed to talk to concerned parents only in small groups and that the board's initial argument against integration was the lack of space at Brevard High School.

That reason was acceptable to the TCIO until the new building was constructed. At that time the committee discovered that there was unused space in the Brevard High School building. The school board agreed to take one or two students in a token gesture of gradual integration, and a few African American students began to attend Brevard High School. However, others continued the 42-mile round trip to Ninth Avenue School in Hendersonville.

Feeling their rights were being violated, TCIO members retained the services of Reuben Dailey, an attorney from Asheville who agreed to meet his clients in Brevard and to represent them in a possible court action. Samuel Raper, who pastored the Bethel "A" Baptist Church but resided in Shelby, monitored the situation to ensure that all proper procedures were followed. Because of fear of losing their jobs, some citizens opted out of the court battle, but 40 remained.

Samuel Raper, almost 90, related the long and slow court battle while seated at his kitchen table. "We stayed in court for almost four years," Raper said. "During that time five got on the stand, like Johnsie Lee Mills. She was outspoken and clear.(Others do not recall Mrs. Mills being called to testify.) I remember Selena Robinson told Judge Warlick, 'I have 14 children,' and the judge said, 'How many?' And Selena told him that all her children were in school and that they left before daylight and that they came back after dark—and that when they were playing football, somebody had to go get them after practice" (interview, October 24, 2002).

Robinson told the judge of the burdens the black community had to bear because their children were forced to attend school in another county. "If there was a game we had to be there to drive the children back home late at night. And if my child got sick, they just had to stay there all day because we couldn't go over to Hendersonville and pick them up," Robinson said (interview, July 16, 1999).

Robinson recalls Samuel Raper, Vinie Gordon, Cornelius Hunt, then employed at Ecusta, and herself taking the stand in court.

> When they called me to the stand, I was so scared. I didn't know what would happen. He asked me to state the names and ages of my children, which I did, and then he said, "You have a nice school." And then the judge said no more busing to Henderson County. We were all so happy. Ralph Ramsey was their attorney. He said, "But we were going to let them go one at a time" [interview, July 16, 1999].

The Reverend Raper said when he heard Judge Warlick declare, "I've heard enough. Transylvania County must integrate its schools, but not now" that he turned as white as the judge. Laughingly, the gentleman explained that he expected another long delay and was relieved to learn that the schools must be integrated in the fall of 1963. He hastened to add that the TCIO got lots of help from white people, about fifteen, and three men in particular. Raper was unable to remember all their names, but he mentioned Fannye Harris, Alcovia McCall, and their husbands.

> We didn't march. We just prayed. White folks prayed with us. We were too small to march. We were in court for four years, and I had to work hard to keep our folks together. It taxed their patience, and when I heard the judge say, "We're going to integrate that school, but not now," I got a sinking feeling. He looked at me and said, "School is about out. We can't do it now, but go home, old man, and we'll integrate in the fall." I wasn't old then, but I guess I looked old, I was so scared [telephone interview, September 29, 2002].

Civil Rights champion Samuel Raper lives in Shelby, North Carolina. (Photograph by Betty Jamerson Reed.)

The Asheville Times reported, on March 11, 1963, that in the United States District Court, Judge Wilson Warlick handed down the decision that Transylvania County junior and senior high schools should be totally desegregated for the 1963-1964 school year. He directed attorney Reuben Dailey to prepare the order for his signature and indicated he would sign it. Judge Warlick stipulated that any students wishing to continue attending school in Hendersonville would be free to do so.

According to Samuel Raper, Transylvania County became the state's first public school system to integrate totally. "It may have been the first in the South to achieve total integration," he said (interview, July 7, 2000). On the front page of the March

14, 1963, edition of *The Transylvania Times*, the headline stated, "Judge So Orders: Brevard Junior, Senior High Schools Completely Integrated." The story noted that Judge Warlick made no ruling on the elementary schools in Brevard which, according to the reporter, "are expected to remain segregated."

The reporter added, "Negro students in grades first through the eighth will continue to go to the Rosenwald school here as in the past. Last year Reuben J. Bailey, Asheville attorney, petitioned the courts to admit all 40 Negro junior and senior high school students to the Brevard schools. The courts ruled that eight be permitted to attend during the 1962-63 term." Integration of the elementary schools did not occur until Transylvania County was forced to comply with the Civil Rights Act of 1964.

Students struggled with their own pressures during these critical years. Edith Hutchison Darity described her inner turmoil during her eighth-grade year as she thought about making the transition from Rosenwald to Ninth Avenue School, a school that each of her seven brothers and sisters had attended.

While she was preoccupied with the school transfer as a 13-year-old, Darity recalled that the TCIO and Pastor Samuel A. Raper led the black community into court for the right to attend high school in Transylvania County. She recalled transferring from Ninth Avenue to Brevard High School for her senior year, 1964. There had been partial integration in 1962, and the court decision of 1963 paved the way for full integration of the high school. Consequently, after her junior year at the all-black high school in Henderson County, Edith Darity completed her high school education in Transylvania County. "It was my first and my last year at Brevard High School," she said. "I remember being very concerned about having enough units to graduate" (interview).

Betty Hunt High, a resident of Zebulon, North Carolina, said that the entire process required for bringing about integration seemed insignificant to her at the time. She remembered that her father, Cornelius Hunt, was active in the battle to gain equal access to educational facilities within the county for black students. She recalled that he spent a lot of time talking to prominent people and helping organize a strategy for winning the fight (interview).

Reesie Madison, a parent of one of the black students first selected to attend Brevard High School, remembers that the experience was not pleasant.

> They said they [the board of education] would start with seven kids.... One of my sons ... in the twelfth grade was picked to go to Brevard High School. It was hard, very hard, but with the help of the Lord, we

Cornelius Hunt, the first African American to be elected to the Brevard City Council, poses with his sons and daughters. Left to right: Charles, Margaret, Cornelius Hunt, Betty Jean, Cornelius, Jr., and William. (Courtesy Brenda Hunt.)

made it through in spite of obstacles.... I would get calls every morning at 8:15. Nobody answered. It (the telephone line) was silent ... went on for quite a while ... finally stopped. My son James stuck it out. Eloise, my daughter, was at Rosenwald when full integration came. She went to Brevard Junior High [interview].

The silent threats may have influenced Madison in her decision not to participate when the TCIO suit was tried in court. "I didn't go back when they went to court," she said (interview).

In a speech at Brevard College, alumnus Keith Elliott described his experience as a part of the 1962 token integration: "I felt like I had the weight of the world on my shoulders" (January 20, 2003).

From his office at the *Florida Sun Review* in the Orlando area, James Madison described his experience with the token integration at Brevard High School. He recalled that there were some "incidents," but all the black students were placed in classes designated as average. The standards in such classes did not provide a great deal of challenge. "My being able to excel surprised them, but our classes were more advanced even in a black school" (interview, November 14, 2002). An honor student, Madison had not found great challenge at the Ninth Avenue School, but he discovered even less in the average classes at Brevard High School. Also, Madison was disappointed that he had not been allowed to try out for the football team. In Hendersonville, he had been a starter, but there was fear that a black student would have difficulty dealing with the academic rigors of an all-white school, and that, if such were the case, a movement against integration might develop.

Leaders at the Brevard High School realized that James Madison should have been placed in an honors class, but it was too late. When they learned of his disappointment at not being permitted to play football, he was offered a chance to go out for baseball, but Madison, who graduated in the spring of 1963, declined.

> Some of them seemed to realize they had made a mistake so they asked for my reaction. I told them that the only thing was that I really wanted to play football. I grew up playing football. I missed being a starter, but they didn't think I could be a student and an athlete both. There was no opportunity so they apologized and tried to make it up to me. I could have played baseball, but I didn't want to. I couldn't stand baseball, too slow. I did quite well. I guess they finally realized "they can walk and chew at the same time." My younger brother Gary played. He was a standout player [interview].

Pastor Frederick L. Gordon, whose father was one of the petitioners in the civil action, first went to Brevard High School in the fall of 1962 and graduated from that institution in 1965. Speaking about the policy of gradual integration, he said that when his brother graduated in 1967, total integration existed in Transylvania County (interview, February 9, 2000).

The faculty was also affected by the integration. While African American students were finally permitted to enroll at Brevard High School, African American teachers felt the continuing effects of discrimination. Teacher James R. Baten was offered what he regarded as a token position when full integration led to the closing of the Brevard Rosenwald School.

> I had a master's degree when Rosenwald students were integrated, but Superintendent Bradburn didn't think I was qualified to be a regular teacher. Others weren't offered a position. I could be a counselor. That meant I would be hired to keep those black boys in line. All the Rosenwald teachers at that time were college graduates, grade A certified teachers... [interview, October 21, 1999].

Baten also reminisced about the attitude toward talented black football players at Brevard High. Baten recalled that after integration occurred black players helped the team compete for the state championship, a game which he attended (interview, October 21, 1999).

The Reverend Raper also remembered that the Brevard High School football record for the next two years was amazing after black players joined the Brevard Blue Devil team. "After integration, they had a really great football team," Raper said (interview, September 29, 2002).

In addition, Baten evaluated the policy of gradual integration, which would result in all students who completed the Rosenwald School program being eligible to attend Brevard High School within four years. The plan resulted in two highly competent teachers, Robert T. Duncan and Mary Bolden, losing their positions. Dr. Lillie Jones cited the former as being her most memorable teacher, the person who despite Jones' poverty, encouraged her to pursue her dreams. She remembers his words this way: "'Lillie, you have a lot of potential. Don't let anyone say there's something you can't do'" (interview).

Integrated classrooms eventually extended down to the sixth grade, a change that also marked the end of Paul E. Hunter's tenure at Rosenwald. "I wonder sometimes if integration really bettered the quality of education for children. At Rosenwald they knew they had friends, instructors willing to give anything. For a teacher, it was a mortal sin not to give all," Baten reflected (interview, October 21, 1999). Students heartily endorsed the conviction that the teachers at Rosenwald were united in their desire for students to learn.

James Gardin and Samuel Howell recall that there were some problems following integration on the school bus and in the cafeteria. Resentment surfaced—apparently as a result of feelings that often emerge when someone different has moved to new turf. Pastor Samuel Raper, the Brevard High School principal, and a Bethel "A" church deacon were able to work out the problems (interview, July 15, 1999).

Dee Brittain, a white teacher active at the time of total integration, recounted the principal's dilemma as to how to handle a problem of racial hostility on the school bus. He found the solution, she said, when a Negro mother offered to ride the bus to keep order. An unidentified outside group persuaded a female student from South Carolina to enroll at Brevard High School, but the matter was addressed and the girl withdrew (interview, July 15, 1999).

As plans were under way for the 1966 closure of the Brevard Rosenwald School, Superintendent Bradburn offered Principal Ethel K. Mills a position at Brevard Elementary School. She declined because she had only one year remaining until retirement. She described her experience with integration in this way:

> Like anything else, there was little say so ... it was occurring all over. High school had always been a problem. We just never had enough students to justify having one at Rosenwald. Integration ... I think we went

at it in too big a hurry. Needed to start slow. Both sides needed adjustment. Doing it all at once made a lot of difference. I don't like a sudden dose of anything [interview, July 9, 1999].

Integration brought the demise of the Brevard Rosenwald School, but recollections keep it alive in the hearts and minds of its alumni, former faculty, and community members. A Rosenwald Homecoming was held in the summer of 2000.

Integration did not create paradise. For some, the Supreme Court decision simply led to more heartache and financial discrimination. The ideal was hopeful, but it took decades to achieve positive results for both adults and children. And for sure, the painful memories of discrimination continued. In fact, they still continue, according to former teachers, parents, and students.

Du Bois' 1938 address, though challenging and provocative, rings with resentment that educational institutions provided for black children were inferior in staffing, in resources, in length of term, in academic standards, and in lack of community involvement. The same resentment resounds among the voices of former students and staff of the Brevard Rosenwald School. Decades later, they still speak of the bitterness they harbored because the Transylvania County Board of Education exhibited little interest in equality and in equity of educational opportunities for its black community.

Former teacher James R. Baten, who lived in Asheville till he died in 2002, recalled, "Perhaps the superintendent may have attended one Christmas concert" (interview, October 21, 1999). Other people recall no interaction with the Board of Education. In the 1990s, Selena Robinson spoke to the Rotary Club. She reflected on the absence of a picture of the Rosenwald School in the display of photographs of old schools of Transylvania County at the Eugene M. Morris Education Center. Rotarian Mickey Church, then the superintendent of public schools, borrowed a picture of her alma mater, had it copied and framed, and then added it to the display — and it remains there today (Selena Robinson, interview, March 23, 2000).

Rosenwald personnel, from students to leaders, also believed that the indifference of the board sanctioned white people in Brevard to mistreat blacks in similar ways. Ethel Mills recounted an instance when she entered Patterson's, a local retail store. "I was interested in a handbag. Two young employees looked at one another and grinned so I knew to be prepared for war." The clerks offered her other bags, but apparently the one that attracted Mrs. Mills was not one they were willing to sell. "They suggested another handbag, but I said, 'No, thank you' and left. As I was walking away, one said, 'That's one nigger that knew what she wanted.' They didn't want me to have it."

Mills also recalled planning to purchase a skirt in the same store. "The owner's wife said, 'Wait until I come back. I promised my friend I would have lunch with her, but I'll take care of you when I get back,'" Mills said. "I just laughed. What kind of idiot was I? But her sons were always nice to me. They said thank you, and they smiled. When folks mistreat you, you can be sure somebody led them wrong" (interview, October 1, 1999).

The *Sylvan News* and other county newspapers announced frequent teacher meetings in the county. Mills, when asked whether she and her staff attended the county faculty meetings, said, "It depended ... very seldom. Some would, and some wouldn't. You see, we were used to it ... not being expected. Several times I reported to the school board. They just wanted to see what I could talk about." Concerning the lack of references to the Rosenwald school in newspapers, Mills simply commented, "We were not often recognized" (interview, October 1, 1999).

Other African Americans who lived in Transylvania County tell similar stories. One example of second-class treatment regarded as acceptable centered upon two local movie theaters, the Clemson and the Co-ed. The Co-ed remained open to white customers only, but sometime after World War II, black customers were admitted by a side door to view movies from the balcony area of the Clemson. Fred and Ethel Mills were employed for a time to take up tickets at the balcony entrance "I would work at school during the day, and then I would work at the theater during the evening," Mrs. Mills said (interview, March 15, 2000).

Although the general attitude of the white community was one of superiority to blacks, it was not shared by everyone. Stories endure about white people who respected and cared for their black neighbors. A white woman, Fannye Harris, frequently supplemented college student Lillie Jones' monthly gift of $3 from her parents by sending her $30. Later, when Jones offered to repay Miss Harris, she was told to help out another needy person when she had the opportunity to do so. "Just do a favor for someone else in need." Both Fannye Harris and Alcovia McCall, two white educators who were missionary-spirited individuals, extended friendship and religious instruction to young ladies. They arranged for young Lillie Madison, Alice Glaze, Agnes Lynch, and Betty Jean Hunt to spend their summers traveling to Baptist mission stations in other cities in the South, an experience that broadened their horizons.

Former Rosenwald students describe used desks and ragged texts that were no longer good enough for the white kids but more than good enough for black students. Seeing names of children unknown to them in their new texts strengthened the Rosenwald students' belief that the white community and its governing bodies viewed them as inferior and perhaps less than human. James Outlaw vehemently affirmed this:

5. Achievement of Integration

Both Brevard's theaters were segregated until the mid–1940s when the Clemson began to accommodate African Americans in its balcony. (Courtesy Transylvania County Archives.)

I remember when we went to school in church basements and annexes. We wanted a school, but the Board of Education "down-trodded" us. They said, "You don't need a school." I remember they decided to build a school and had to remove two houses to build ... laying concrete, steel, rock. I remember they told us school would be late ... no furniture ... no left over books from the white school. I remember ... having nothing to work with ... always had to wait for hand-me-downs from the whites.... There are still members of local government that don't want this story told [interview, February 10, 2000].

No high school education was provided in the county by the board of education. J.H. Michael of Buncombe County had sought construction of area high schools for Negro students, but the scattered population made the attempt extremely difficult. According to Dorothy Pierce Hill, the secondary education offered at Rosenwald during her last year there in the 1930s was a sham. She felt that the high school students had not done any secondary level work and that they were simply putting in time that was essentially wasted.

Fannye Harris befriended many African Americans. (Courtesy Roberta H. Ashley.)

In her opinion, strife developed because the students did not have adequate supervision by Principal Nathaniel Sessoms.

Hill shared an unpleasant experience that happened at the old Rosenwald building. The group in the "big room," the classroom for the upper grades, decided to put on a play. Because only one copy was available, it was passed from student to student. When Hill asked for the book to copy her part, another student refused to give it to her and called her a name. Hill picked a pan of hot water off the heater and hurled it across the room at her antagonist. It missed its target, but Principal Sessoms grabbed her and was going to paddle her when Charles Erwin grabbed him. According to Hill, Erwin said, "If you hit her, you will be dead tonight. Her father will kill you." Dorothy Pierce Hill cried all day, and her father arrived home just in time to hear her story when the principal came to the house, only to be ordered away by the angry parent. On another occasion, Sessoms did not give Hill a report card when they were distributed to the other students. Her father found the principal in front of Mills' house, a short distance from the school. The principal responded to Mr. Pierce's query about the missing report card by taking it out of his inside coat pocket, and saying, "Here, I was bringing it to her." In reply, her father said, "I'll let you slide, but you have missed death by inches" (interview, March 14, 2000). Hill believes that education at Rosenwald was not properly monitored by the powers responsible for the school.

The long trek to Henderson County to attend Ninth Avenue High School was damaging to Rosenwald students, but in the new building each student who successfully completed eighth grade was assigned to Ninth Avenue. Students felt they were sacrificing part of their identity by traveling to another county to attend high school, but being assigned to the public schools of Hendersonville City Schools was a routine matter.

In an envelope postmarked July 12, 1957, at 5 P.M., addressed to "Parents of Robert Emory Hill," a message on a narrow strip of paper states: "The following named student Robert Emory Hill is assigned for the 1957-58 school term to Ninth Avenue High School in Hendersonville, North Carolina." It was signed by S.E. Varner, Jr., Chairman, Board of Education. Dorothy Pierce Hill still has the notice in the papers she collected pertaining to her children. In succinct fashion, each rising freshman became the responsibility of the board of education in another community. In Transylvania County, their educational rights had been terminated.

Agnes Wilson, who as an adult was employed by the Transylvania County Board of Education for many years, said, "Even as a child, it galled me to think of having to ride a bus to a different county. High school students had been cheated. Our parents were taxpayers in Transylvania County. We felt like quitting rather than getting on that bus, but we didn't" (interview, February 8, 2000). Such emotions found a justifiable outlet in the battle to win the right to attend the all-white Brevard High School.

Alice Glaze Robinson, a Rosenwald student who later served as a teacher at the school, evaluated being sent away to high school in this manner:

> It was an injustice for me to go to Hendersonville. I didn't like riding the bus ... walking to the store. The bus was cold, and it was a long way. At Ninth Avenue, the closeness was not found that we had at Rosenwald ... but there we found some teachers who accepted us. Others didn't. I still had the team from Rosenwald. I get unpleasant flashbacks at times, but I blot them out [interview, February 24, 2000].

At the time of integration, the attitude of whites irritated the blacks. Audrey Hutchison heard a white citizen remark in reference to the area around the Rosenwald School: "It's too dangerous for white children to come through that neighborhood" (interview, February 10, 2000). Dorothy Pierce Hill heard a board of education member being quoted on radio station WPNF. She remembered his comments in this way: "We will have to do something about that building within three months. You know it is in a bad neighborhood." She reflected, "That man is still living. Our school was the best kept one in the county" (interview, February 17, 2000). Both staff and students confirmed that the Rosenwald building was well maintained.

Another point of contention is the current use and name of the Brevard Rosenwald School building. Black citizens resent the fact that the building ceased to exist as a school. It became the site of the administrative offices for the Transylvania County Board of Education. To be used for that purpose, the building required extensive remodeling. "I was in there today," said Michael Owens. "It just doesn't seem like I was ever a student there.... Now, I wish they would keep it Rosenwald. That's what it was originally.... I enjoyed it. I liked it a lot" (interview, February 29, 2000).

Other sources echoed the wish that the building had been retained as a school, that white students could have attended Rosenwald. Audrey Hutchison believed that the school board felt that it would have been too dangerous for white children to travel to the Rosenwald School (interview, February 10, 2000). Recalling the pleasant community in which she grew up, LaMuriel Andrews was shocked that anyone would call her former neighborhood unsafe (interview, February 10, 2000). Baten interpreted the closing of Rosenwald this way: "The black school simply closed down. It was not good enough to bring white students there" (interview, October 21, 1999).

The building no longer retains the name Rosenwald, a strong point of grievance. It is called the Eugene M. Morris Education Center, in honor of a former board of education member who lost his life during a robbery at the Asheville drugstore where he was filling in for another pharmacist. The April 21, 1981, school board minutes reveal the intent to name a school facility in honor of Morris. According to the December 1, 1981, minutes, the dedication program for the Eugene Morris Education Center was held at Brevard High School. "Folks resented that the school was shut down and the name not retained," Pastor Frederick L. Gordon said.

To the black community, the only name worthy of replacing that of Julius Rosenwald would have been Ethel K. Mills. They contend that a plaque honoring her tenure from 1923 to 1966 should be placed on the building. They also resent the poor upkeep of the grounds. "Mable Armstrong died still upset at all the weeds ... the honeysuckle ... growing on that property. And the people drive out of there like maniacs at times ... and they're not kids" (Dorothy Pierce Hill, interview, March 14, 2000).

Ethel Mills sees no wrong in using the building for administrative offices, but she does wish it could have been used for the children (interview, March 14, 2000). She remembers the closing of the school:

> While the knob was still warm, teachers came from all over the county to take what they could use. The superintendent had us sort supplies, rulers, scissors, and even the damaged ones were taken. That surprised me. Of course, all that the PTA purchased was public property the minute they gave it to the school. It tickled me at how excited the high school was to get our kitchen equipment [interview, March 28, 2000].

Although Edith Darity believed the Brevard Rosenwald School should have remained open, she would like to see the building become a historical site, perhaps a cultural arts center for Transylvania County, to chronicle the history of the Negroes of the county. Said Darity: "That building is just bubbling with history" (interview).

In March 2000, the Brevard City Council designated the former Rosenwald school as a local historic landmark. In a letter dated August 21, 2001, Transylvania County School Superintendent, Terry K. Holliday, wrote in support of the Community Development Block Grant for the Rosenwald

Community: "The Board of Education has an interest in giving the building [Eugene M. Morris Education Center] back to the community to be used as a community resource center," Holliday said. "We have been working for over a year to have the Rosenwald School designated as a national historic landmark. The building and land have been valued at more than $350,000. With renovation, the facility could meet all of the community needs listed in the grant application." Holliday indicated that the school system would be willing to provide parenting education, mentoring and tutoring services, and programs addressed to meet the needs of disadvantaged youth.

Integration requires a greater sensitivity to the needs of all students and parents. In Transylvania County, the mix of students brought together by integration now contains not just blacks and whites, but Asians, Latinos and others.

Chapter 6

Adjustment to Integration

THE HISTORY OF THE EDUCATIONAL experience for Rosenwald students was reflected throughout the nation in the inequities of the black educational experience. The Brevard community did not place as much value on opportunities for black students as it did on opportunities for white students. The practice inadvertently dishonored the humanity of the black community, but probably was not done out of a sense of hostility, hatred, or cruelty. Black education was traditionally neglected, and the white community was blind to the damage of discrimination. The small size of the black student population made it difficult to target pupil needs in a separate school. In addition, dual institutions created unnecessary financial demands. Had racial prejudice been less prevalent, economic wisdom would have dictated merging the schools.

In the minds of segregation proponents, however, viewing blacks as inferior lent legitimacy to separate schools. There is historical evidence that the white community had been well-indoctrinated with the philosophy of white supremacy, such as that encountered by Ethel Mills when she went shopping, or by Edith Hutchison Darity, who was restricted from using the public library. By 1966, students intent on integrating the white high school did not require the escort of armed guards, such as those used in Little Rock, Arkansas, when Patricia Pattillo Beals and her companions sought entrance to a segregated school. Integration in Transylvania County did not provoke the violent response and threats that it did in other parts of the South.

During the battle for integration, support for the movement existed in the white community, but even before that time, African Americans were befriended by whites. Of course, Julius Rosenwald dealt generously with a people whom he had never met. State administrator N.C. Newbold built his career on efforts to improve educational opportunities for black children in rural communities, but during an early visit to Brevard, he conducted workshops for white, not black, teachers. Locally, two women sought occasions to build relationships with members of the black community.

Fannye Biddy Harris, a white woman, became a member of Bethel "A" Baptist Church and assisted Samuel Raper in his campaign to bring about school integration. She worked with the young girls in the church. According to Harris's daughter, Roberta Ashley, her mother became interested in the local black community after completing a UNC-Chapel Hill course dealing with the problems of blacks. After finishing the course based on the text *An American Dilemma*, written by the Swedish social scientist Gunnar Myrdal, Harris, who taught in the public schools for 32 years, became a familiar face in the black community.

A survivor of cancer, Harris kept on giving of herself until her death. Roberta Ashley, her daughter, said,

> Mother was always doing work in her community. She attended services in black churches. She attended Bethel "A." When she died, she had been working and attending at Glade Creek. She taught for 32 years in the public schools, but she had so much energy that when she was 70, she started volunteering at Schenck Job Corps, and she volunteered four days a week for 12 years ... that woman had more get up and go than I will ever have.... She said, "I'll go down, but I'll get up" [interview, October 17, 2002].

Harris, whom Selena Robinson viewed as a woman of great courage, still elicits respect and affection in the Rosenwald community. Harris encouraged young black women to improve their lives by pursuing a college education. Harris' life was difficult, but she rose above her circumstances and helped support dozens of young black people with money and with encouragement.

Alcovia Orr McCall was another white woman who worked in the Rosenwald community. Not only did she attend services at the Bethel "A" Church, she also encouraged the educational growth of young girls by providing opportunities for them to travel and to teach in Vacation Bible Schools. Following her retirement as a teacher and principal in the public schools, McCall served in numerous ministries. After her death on April 30, 1995, the North Carolina Baptist Foundation honored the educator by establishing the Alcovia Orr McCall Endowment. Funds from the endowment are designated for interracial projects (Transylvania Heritage, 1995).

Members of the Rosenwald community serve as advocates and friends. When Mary Cowal moved to Brevard in the 1980s, she worked at Transylvania Community Hospital. There she became acquainted with ministers serving the African American community, such as the Reverend David Suber. Their interest in her patients impressed her. Gradually Cowal became familiar with the story of the segregated hospital and the efforts of the Transylvania Citizens Improvement Organization [TCIO] to gain equal access for medical treatment in that facility. Cowal was moved by accounts of hardships involving social and economic deprivation.

Cowal viewed diversity as an indisputable avenue of enrichment. Upon learning that the Ku Klux Klan was planning a public march in Brevard, she and others decided to create a counter-diversion. During the KKK parade a small group of women, black and white, met at St. Philip's Episcopal Church to talk. They decided that the interaction was so enjoyable that they would continue to meet. Calling themselves simply "Friends," the women met in one another's homes. As they socialized around their dinner tables, the women formed lasting friendships despite racial differences.

On such occasions, Cowal learned from her black friends—Maggie Scruggs, Wilkie Robinson, Ruth Johnstone, Indiana Conley, Cornelia Howell, and Reesie Madison—about the harsh treatment they had endured. Cowal learned that white students on a passing school bus had yelled verbal insults, had hurled objects at her friends, and had spit on them when they were young girls walking on the sidewalk. Their helplessness to resist such assaults disturbed Cowal.

Cowal became a member of the TCIO. Recently, the organization has focused on providing scholarships for African American youths. The goal required fundraising: "That's how I learned to fry chicken. We'd meet at the Mary C. Jenkins Community Center and fry chicken to sell as a lunchtime snack. We'd raise a few thousand dollars." Cowal, the recipient of the Girl Scout's Mable Armstrong Award, also led a troop that met in the basement of the Sharing House (interview, November 21, 2002).

Personal good will does not underwrite changes in education. Despite the lack of official support, black leaders encouraged improvement of schooling for Negro students throughout the twentieth century by initiating and sustaining efforts to educate their youth. Anderson (1988) concluded that the desire of African Americans for an education indicated great faith in the good that would come from knowledge. Black students confronted overwhelming odds as they persisted in their efforts to acquire knowledge.

Although generally at odds about the best kind of education for Negroes, W.E.B. Du Bois and Booker T. Washington held similar attitudes about the importance of elementary schools. Washington suggested that Rosenwald use his funds not to construct other Tuskegees, but to accommodate the urgent need for elementary school buildings. Du Bois, himself a recipient of a Rosenwald grant, was convinced that the plight of the Negroes as a people would be greatly improved if Negroes were well educated at the elementary school level. In Transylvania County, the Negro community struggled to secure a quality education for their children at that level, the only level available to them before the 1960s.

During the 1960s and the following decades, the Brevard schools were enriched by the inclusion of black students. When they crossed the color line to participate fully as equals with white Transylvania students, they finally benefited from the full force of integration. Today, the black students still recall the trauma and the adjustment.

The "Friends" first met as a counter diversion to a Ku Klux Klan parade. Pictured from left to right are Indiana Conley, Mary Cowal, and Cornelia Howell. (Courtesy Mary Cowal.)

Teachers also had to make the adjustment to integration. Joyce Owens, a white teacher, recalls her feelings as she faced her first integrated class. "We were scared of each other. The only black people I had known were gardeners, yardmen, and maids at my mother's home in Tifton, Georgia," she said. Owens explained that Principal Joe McGuire mandated that every class at Brevard Junior High School should have an alphabetical order of seating. "Poor eyesight, poor hearing, nothing was to be considered except alphabetical order. I had some really 'stand-out' black students—well-behaved and smart—who did their homework and minded their manners. They were exceptional" (interview, July 8, 2002).

Outstanding students who were in her first integrated class included Dottie Hill, Linda Gash, Charles Hunt, and Carl Mooney, Jr. A few years later, in a reversal of roles, Linda Gash, an African American teacher, taught Owens' daughters, Cathy and Carol.

Owens said that the black students had been advised to take general math, but she felt that a number would have excelled in algebra. She is convinced that they were misguided to ensure success. When Owens was assigned hall duty, she enforced the rule that mandated no lingering in the hallway by saying, "Boys, go to your class." One of the black students astutely asked why she never ordered the girls to go to class.

Owens recalled one attempt at typical middle school mischief. A small black boy asserted that he would have his large black friend beat up any white classmate who refused to sharpen his pencil. On another occasion, Owens' touching a student on the elbow to guide him back to class brought a threat: "Don't touch me. The last person who did that got it!" (interview, September 26, 2002). She realized that tensions existed beneath the surface of seemingly smooth integration efforts.

Students, both white and black, taunted members of the other race. Eric Crite, a black student, recalled being threatened by two white males. "They just always wanted to fight me. I kept to myself. I wasn't ... outgoing. I remember their names to this day.... Things got heated. We did fight.... And later, not on the school grounds, there was another fight. It was nothing racial, just stupid" (interview, November 8, 2002).

After integration took place, Ethel K. Mills worked for a time in the integrated Head Start program. She was pleased that black and white children could be friends at school. "I remember two little children who loved to talk to each other. She hadn't discovered that he was black" (interview, March 1, 2001). On one occasion, a small child wanted to know if Mills were white. "Can't you look at me and see. Look at my hands and my hair. She claimed she didn't know, and I didn't say. I wanted her to decide. Small ones generally accept you as a person."

However, on another occasion, Mills was injured. "We had a rule not to spank. Something hard and sharp hit me on the back of my hand. It drew blood. I asked, 'Who threw that?' Everyone sat up straight, but one little head went down. 'You were the one who shot me, weren't you?' He was terribly embarrassed. I felt sorry for him, but I hit him across the hand" (interview, March 1, 2001). Integration in Transylvania County was a peaceful transition, but adjustments had to be made.

There was little fanfare when the Brevard Senior High School integrated in 1963. A few black students had been enrolled for the 1962-1963 school year. A lot of credit for the successful integration goes to N.A. Miller, principal at the high school. He realized problems could develop with little warning so he approached the school board to explain that in his judgment it would be foolish for seven people to expect a call to provide input into the right course of action. "We were the first school in the western part of the state to integrate. I told them (the board of education) I needed to make decisions as needed. Back me or I'm out of here" (interview, November 20, 2002).

The local police and the sheriff's department offered to be on hand, and eight state troopers told Miller they would be stationed near the school. "I chose to have them stay away, but I told them I would call if necessary." Miller also spent hours talking to the officials at WLOS-TV in Asheville, and they consented to stay away from Brevard during the opening day of school.

"Open TV causes problems. We talked a good two hours or more, and they agreed there would be no TV crew the first day," he said. "I really didn't know what to expect. Every night I was getting phone calls from the KKK in Pickens, South Carolina. 'We'll blow you up.' That went on for a long time" (interview, November 20, 2002). Miller credits the community, the students, and the staff for the successful school integration. He cited the contribution made by Bob Armstrong, Randal Lyday, and Cliff Brookshire. "I had three good men, and I had enough sense to stay out of the way."

Miller said he and those three arrived at the school every morning at 6:30 and went to different areas of the school to build a presence. Miller also held a Monday meeting with all the black students in the auditorium. "They could talk about anything. I listened, and I learned. We worked at it. It was my school with my kids. There would be no dual standard. Not while I was there" (interview).

Miller insisted on equal punishments for blacks and whites. Early in September a fight broke out between two students, a white and a black. It was the first fight, and the policy was equal punishment for both offenders. The rule was suspension for ten days. After the suspension ended, parents were required to accompany the offenders back to school for a conference with the principal. Students received a zero on all work missed and were required to make up the time one hour a day after school.

There was an option. Miller allowed students to choose between the suspension and the school punishment, and he told them they had two minutes to decide. Each chose the school punishment. Bob Armstrong, the assistant principal, took them to the gym and had them do 50 sit-ups, 50 push-ups, and wind sprints. One got sick. "I don't remember if the white or the black got sick first, but the other one said, 'His kind can't take this.' Armstrong kept it up until both got sick." Miller emphasized that identical punishment was administered to both students. That, he feels, explained why another fight between a white and a black did not occur until two days before school closed after Brevard High School's first year as a fully integrated institution.

Another potentially disruptive experience occurred prior to a school dance. Before Miller related the experience, he cautioned, "This was in the '60s." Miller still remembers what he told the black students during a Monday meeting: "Now, I can't tell you not to date a white girl, but, I'm telling you, some guy will come out of the mountains with a gun and try to kill you. I'm your principal, and I'll try to stop him, but I'm not ready to go just yet."

Later, his secretary told him, "Reggie Lynch needs to talk to you." A handsome young man, Reggie explained that he had thought long and hard about Miller's comments and had decided he was not ready to die either. Miller pressed him for information. It seemed a white classmate had been aggressively pursuing him. She persisted in efforts to persuade Reggie to escort her to the prom.

Enlisting the assistance of teachers, Miller gathered information about the pursuit. "The teachers saw Reggie trying to stay away from her, but she wouldn't leave him alone. She kept right after him so I took care of it." Miller received no cooperation from the teenage girl. She was adamant about forcing her attention on her black classmate, in spite of the fact that he wanted nothing to do with her. When all else failed, Miller suspended her, but her father fought the action. The irate parent began making threats by telephone, but Miller explained that warnings had been given well in advance. "Her father was at school by 6:30 the next morning after I suspended her. He insisted she couldn't be suspended, but I had already suspended her. All the paper work was done."

It was one of the few times Miller lost his patience. It was his custom to keep a softball bat in the wastepaper basket next to his desk. That morning the irate parent, using very strong language, made personal threats. Miller stood up, taking the bat in his hands as he did so. He said, "Now, I'll let you have the first blow, but it better be a good one or you'll be carried out of this office. So take your lick now, or sit down. Thank heavens, the man decided to sit." The man's daughter served her suspension, and her father accompanied her upon her return to school. The young black student never knew how much effort it took to protect him from the 1960s taboo of interracial dating.

It was also necessary to suspend some black students. "I suspended two girls for 'riot talk.' And there was another instance. Fred Mills—we played together when we were children—was my choice for bus driver, but he worked shifts at Ecusta. Art Loeb, the plant's vice president, agreed to shift his schedule. I told Fred just to give me the names if there were any problems. Quite a while went by, but then Fred gave me five names of students who had used profanity on the bus. I sent for Lindsey Warren. As he entered the office, Warren immediately asked, 'What'd I do? What'd I do?' When I told him what he was reported as having said on the school bus, he said, 'That's not true. I said that before I got on the bus.'" Miller's investigation revealed that the profanity was stimulated by misbehavior the night before, but he punished all five students for using foul language on the school bus.

During the first year of integration, there was a gun incident. Miller had been away, "probably on Southern Association business." After Miller's return, the chief of police called to report that a black student was threatening the principal's life. The word on the street was that the boy was taking a gun to school. "The chief offered to take a warrant and handle the situation, but I told him, 'No, we'll handle it, but you be two minutes away.' Can you imagine being that foolish? I asked Bob Armstrong, the assistant principal, to be listening at the door. I met the student as he got off his bus and invited him to the office. He sat across from my desk. I said, 'Do you have a gun?'

He said, 'Yes.' I said, 'I need it,' He reached in his pocket, took out the gun, and handed it to me. I stood up and told him he was expelled and that he had one minute to leave. He had the gall to ask, 'Why?'"

Later that day Miller discovered that his family thought he was still in danger. In fact, his sons were sure they knew more than their dad knew. "The funny thing is when I got home, my wife said you better talk to the boys. Well, they had heard that a high school boy was taking a gun to school. When my wife and I asked why we weren't told, they said, 'Dad said never to say anything about what we heard about school.'" Miller's conviction was that the principal should handle any problem that occurred at school. "It was my school, my kids, my problems."

The gun incident was a bad experience, but Miller protected the school from bad publicity. Ironically, the same "gun-toting" student had a second opportunity to express his resentment. He was randomly selected to be interviewed by a visiting Southern Association team. "'You know how the Southern Association works," Miller said. "They take every fifth kid, and the one black they got was this guy. They asked, 'How do you like this school?' He answered, 'I don't give a damn about this school.' 'Why?' 'Because the principal is always trying to run me off.'" Decades later, Miller still concludes, "Well, you can't win them all." Conflict is a normal part of school life, but this near-crisis exceeded reasonable expectations, especially for the era.

For most African American families, though, integration resulted in greater opportunities for their students. Grady Elliott, a black parent whose son began the integrated experiment in 1962, visited Miller prior to the opening of school. He was happy that his children no longer had to travel outside the county to attend high school. Elliott wanted Principal Miller to know that he would support the school and that his children would be expected to respect the faculty and to value the opportunities offered at Brevard Senior High School.

"Keith Elliott's daddy came before school started. He didn't want his boy to get into any trouble. I remember he said, 'Young'uns are like chickens. If you don't know where they are, they won't do you any good.'" Miller explained that chickens used to be allowed to roam at will, to run free and that their nests had to be searched out in order to gather the eggs. If the nest could not be located, the eggs would spoil. Grady Elliott wanted to know immediately if any problems arose so he would be able to help his son. Elliott shared with Miller that he and his wife hoped to provide a college education for each of their children. "He worked at Ecusta, and he and his boys had a garbage service. He said, 'I am trying to send all of mine to college'" (interview). Miller respected and admired Grady Elliott and his family.

Brevard High School continues to have increased athletic strength, and talented African Americans have frequently set the pace for success. After

Brevard High School's football team first integrated in 1963. First row, left to right: Coach Jim Johnson, Don Peevy, Danny Shook, Brock Kitchen, Ollie Johnson, Ray Siniard, John Garren, James "Tank" Whitmire, Don Metcalf, Ricky Trent, Paul Scruggs, Robbie Sales, Manager Roger Metcalf. Second row, left to right: Manager Rodney Franks, Dickie Roberts, Mike Metcalf, George Leopard, Tommy Ferguson, Dickie Edwards, Rad Bramlett, Rickey Skerett, Keith Elliott, David Cantrell, Jim Buchanan, Spencer MacFie, Coach Cliff Brookshire. Third row, left to right: Coach Bob Armstrong, Manager Mike Driscoll, Tommy Burell, Reginald Lynch, Wayne Hunter, Larry Hamilton, Ronnie Brown, Robert Conley, Lloyd Fisher, L.H. Hughey, Larry Reece, Buddy Huff, Kenneth Parker, Charles Saleeby, Johnny Peterson. (Courtesy Cliff Brookshire.)

integration, the Rosenwald community stepped into the white domain. Athletes were eager to take advantage of more rigorous training and higher levels of competition. Sports opportunities had existed for interested youths at the Ninth Avenue School in Hendersonville, in part due to the dedication of Principal John Marable, but at Brevard Senior High School, Rosenwald youth faced possible discrimination in the sports arena.

The first integrated football team in North Carolina, and maybe even in the South, was formed at Brevard High School in 1963. Cliff Brookshire, who was inducted into the North Carolina High School Athletic Association's Hall of Fame on April 26, 2003, coached football that fall.

Brookshire explained that seven young blacks tried out for the football team. "A lot of folks thought there would be trouble," he said. "Some policemen showed up, but the principal asked them to leave. And he was right. We didn't need 'em. The white kids, and they deserve a lot of credit, accepted the black athletes.... I told them they were welcome to be a part of the team as long as they were there for the benefit of the school or themselves, and not for some outside organization. One of them did quit — I can't remember his name — but the others stuck it out. We had an excellent principal. N.A. Miller knew how to run a school, and Bob Armstrong was an excellent disciplinarian" (interview, September 23, 2002).

Obviously the staff had no experience coaching integrated teams and did not know what to expect. In the minds of coaches and players, football was the top priority. But there were concerns about how the youths would react to one another. "You know I was sitting there with Coach Armstrong, and I just happened to think those white boys have never been in the showers with colored boys," Brookshire said. "How are they going to react? Well, we decided to wait and see. There were a dozen showerheads. At first they kind of hesitated, but then they started taking showers, and that was it. No problems." Racial slurs were anticipated, but among the boys on the squad those remarks simply did not occur.

The easygoing manner of the black students helped defuse any potential insult. "Tank Whitmire was sittin' there, and Keith Elliot. I was sittin' between 'em. Tank only weighed about 135, and he had small legs. Keith was 185, one of the finest kids you'll ever meet ... an excellent football player. I had 'em leave their shoes outside so they wouldn't track mud into the field house," Brookshire said. "They were putting 'em on or taking 'em off. Something was said about Tank's legs lookin' like matchsticks, and he said, 'Yeah, burnt matchsticks.' Had a sense of humor. Little Tank is dead now. Keith made All-American at Western Carolina University. Robert was a tall, lanky fellow. I had a lot of fun with him" (interview).

N.A. Miller remembered Robert Conley's kickoff talent. "He would kick from the end zone, and boom, it was gone." Brookshire described Conley's first play: "The other team was about to score on us, and Wayne Hunter, the co-captain and a good lineman, got hurt. He was okay, but the official sent him out for one play. I looked up to pick someone to replace Wayne, and I called to Conley to fill in. I said, 'Come here, Conley. I want you to get in the gap on the left side ... and then shoot through the gap and tackle the first person, whether he's got the ball or not. Just shoot through and hit somebody.' Well, he hit the ball carrier. It was amazing! Later, after the game he acted out the play. It was a lot of fun." Brookshire said Conley developed a ritual of exaggerating the events of that one play to entertain his friends.

Brookshire and his helpers warned the African American players to be prepared for hostility at their games. Integration was new to the region, and it did not occur voluntarily. "I remember telling Paul Scruggs that he could expect physical and verbal abuse from our opposition. 'And when it comes, what are you going to do?' Well, he said, 'I'll grin and take it. Then I'll hit 'em harder on the next play, and then I'll help 'em up'" (Brookshire, interview).

All of them — Paul Scruggs, James "Tank" Whitmire, Keith Elliott, Tommy Ferguson, Reginald Lynch, and Robert Conley — were pioneers in integrated high school athletics. That role required both courage and common sense.

Coach Brookshire shared his memories of several key games that demonstrated the fearlessness and the courtesy of the six young blacks on Brevard's first integrated team. "We had newspaper men showing up at our opening game against T.C. Roberson ... from Greensboro and Charlotte. There was lots of shoutin' in the stands. First, Paul scored a 30- to 40-yard touchdown. Next Keith blocked a punt, scooped it up, and scored. We had 39 points that night. Those colored boys scored four of our touchdowns. It set the tone for the whole season."

Kays Gary of the *Charlotte Observer* wrote about the season opener between Brevard and T.C. Roberson. His article was reprinted in *The National Observer*. Wayne Hunter and Lloyd Fisher, an all-state candidate, were co-captains, and Danny Shook was quarterback. Gary focused on Paul Scruggs while crediting the other members of the team for their achievements. Scruggs did not start, but Coach Brookshire put him into the game with the score tied 6–6. According to Gary's article, a hush fell over the crowd, and there was a "scattering of hoots" to which Scruggs did not respond. Scruggs took a pitch from quarterback Danny Shook and "scooted" through a hole created by tackle Wayne Hunter, running 50 yards for the tie-breaking touchdown.

> ... When it ended with Brevard ahead, 39–13, the T.C. Roberson High players ... shook hands ... especially the hands of Paul Scruggs and guard Keith Elliot.

"We'll play against you any time and anywhere.... You are real gentlemen."

And Keith and Paul shyly smiled their thanks.

It had been perhaps the biggest night in their lives.

It was the first time they had ever played against white boys.

But more important, it was the first time they had ever played on the same team with white boys.

And now Brevard figures it won more than a ball game Saturday night [September 1963].

Two races were represented on the football squad, but bonding made them a team. The hurdles were difficult to overcome, but by the end of the season the championship game was a celebration of unity.

Coach Brookshire expressed admiration and gratitude for the support given him by Cornelius Hunt, a member of the black community. "He was a lot of help to me. He introduced me to the parents down there. He was a super guy, a fine gentleman."

Brookshire had a tradition of attending church with his football squad at churches in the community. After the team became integrated, he and the principal decided that it would be wise to attend only churches to which they were invited — in writing — and there were few invitations. Principal N.A. Miller sent out letters to 22 churches to explain that the football team would attend worship services only if invited by letter. Brookshire recalled receiving only three invitations in the fall of 1963 (interview).

"The only church where a group got up and walked out was mine," Coach Brookshire remembers, laughing. He recalled that being invited to Bethel "A" Baptist Church by the Reverend Samuel Raper was a special experience. Pastor Raper told a story and took up a collection. Later the team was invited to the Mary C. Jenkins Community Center for pregame refreshments. "I never saw so much food. It was a feast, more than enough for three or four football teams. It was wonderful."

Traveling to away games that necessitated staying overnight brought a different set of difficulties. In one community in the Leaksville, North Carolina area, the black team members had to be housed in private homes because no motels or hotels were open to blacks. Some restaurants welcomed the white players but warned the coaches that blacks would not be served. Brookshire recalled his white team members, on the return home from Leaksville, insisting on "to go" service so they could eat aboard the bus with their black teammates. "All of 'em brought their food out and ate on the bus with the black kids."

Another game pitted the newly integrated Brevard Blue Devils against East Forsyth in Winston-Salem. King Cotton was the only public hotel facility that would accommodate black members of the team. "Dr. Miller said,

'I don't care what it costs. Take the team there.'" There was a pregame meal, and Congressman Charles Taylor, then a young law student at Wake Forest University, asked if he could come by and meet the team. Taylor, a Brevard resident and a Blue Devil fan, spoke to the players. "He gave 'em a pep talk." The Brevard Blue Devils won the game. Brookshire remembers that *Sports Illustrated* had enough interest to send a reporter to cover the game.

Once Brookshire and his team returned to the lobby of King Cotton, they were amazed at the number of people who had congregated there. "I wondered what in the world was going on," Brookshire said. "Some black guy took Keith by his arm and was leading him out of the room. 'What are you doing with my player?' I asked. He said, 'I just want to talk to him.' 'Well, you come on up to'—I gave him the room number—'and you can talk to the whole squad....' He asked, 'Are you afraid of what he might say?' Well, I figured I'd be proud of whatever Keith had to say, but I didn't want someone pulling one of my players off by himself. Later someone told me the black man was from the NAACP. Some of those other folks I had to ignore" (interview).

The week prior to the assassination of President John F. Kennedy, the Brevard team made the playoffs. The next week the big match was to take place in Buncombe County, but the game had to be postponed until the next day, a Saturday afternoon, because of the assassination on Friday. According to Coach Brookshire, the atmosphere was like a wake. Everyone was silent. The game ended in a 0–0 tie. At that time there was no sudden death tiebreaker so Reidsville and Brevard were declared co-champions.

There was an incident at the championship game that seemed to typify the hostility and pressure the team had felt all year. Someone in the stands threw black ink or paint on the Brevard team as the players were coming out of the dressing room. Despite numerous scrubbings, Brookshire never succeeded in removing the stain from the uniforms (interview). This permanent stain on the Brevard uniform seemed symbolic of much of America's hostile reaction to integration.

The success of former Rosenwald students in sports helped bring together the white and black communities, but there was still much prejudice to be overcome before an integrated team was fully accepted. During the 1963 fall season, the Brevard Blue Devils traveled to Greeneville, Tennessee. Coach Brookshire can never forget the events of that night, because his football team was treated brutally. He recalled penalties that defied explanation but forced defeat on his team. "But my players just kept right on playing—and playing hard." During the game the visitors' dressing room was flooded, and their clothing was scattered. When the team manager requested dry towels, he was told that none were available.

Boarding the bus was also memorable because an angry mob was blocking the way. After the players were on board, the hostile crowd beat on the bus with stones. The crowd also broke windows. Tennessee state highway patrolmen disbursed the crowd. "I remember cars with North Carolina tags were damaged that night," Brookshire said. "My sister and mother drove over for the game. Their paint was scratched up, probably with keys, but definitely with some kind of metal.... It was a bad scene, but the next year, the Greeneville team came to Brevard, and we had our revenge."

The coach added, "The Greeneville team — we called them the 'Jolly Green Giants'— outmanned us in every position. They looked like a college team. 'Little Tank' just weighed 135. We had stacks of clean dry towels in their dressing room and dozens of drinks in a tub of ice" (interview). Brookshire was determined to teach his players how to properly react to hostility.

Principal Miller also has vivid recollections of the Greeneville, Tennessee, game. He explained that Coach Brookshire had rules. One rule pertained to dress. Going to away games meant that team members wore suits and ties. "There are not likely to be fights when you're in your Sunday best," Miller said. "Another rule penalized anyone involved in unsportsmanlike conduct on the court by being taken out of the game and doing laps. At the Greeneville game, the team captain begged to be taken out. He said, 'Take me out, or I'll kill them, for they're trying to kill Keith Elliott.'"

Miller identified the Greeneville game as the only one lost that fall. He also confirmed the damage to cars with North Carolina plates. He thinks the cars were damaged when Tennessee fans dragged nails along doors and fenders. Miller also remembers that when the Greeneville team came to Brevard, the Brevard staff met them at the gate and extended them every courtesy. And the Brevard Blue Devils won.

Miller explained that a number of schools refused to play Brevard's team because of its black players. At least two schools offered to pay for a chance to play an integrated team. The Brevard team was invited to Bennett High School at Kingsport. The Tennessee school offered to pay $6,000. "I said 'no' because I felt they only wanted publicity. It was more than we would make in three games, but no. I didn't think it was right," Miller said. Teams in South Carolina also invited the Brevard football team to play them.

When the integrated Brevard team traveled, many restaurants refused to serve the black players, instead offering hateful racial epithets. Miller had had a similar experience in the early 1950s when he and his friends, on the way from Connecticut to Washington, D.C., were told their African American companion was not welcome in a Maryland restaurant. "We all got up and left," Miller said.

The principal and the coaching staff always provided a pregame meal. With an integrated team, they had to find a way to feed the team while avoiding a rejection by local restaurants. Sometimes the meal was served in Bre-

Keith Elliott emphasizes his point to team members Rad Bramlett and Buddy Huff. In the background from left to right are Mike Metcalf, Ollie Johnson, (obscured), John Garren, Dickie Roberts, Don Metcalf, Johnny Peterson, (obscured), Charles Saleeby, Reggie Lynch, (obscured). (Courtesy Cliff Brookshire.)

vard High's gym to enable the team to eat together. A key to the success of the integration process may lie in the fact that the Brevard High staff made a concerted effort to avoid publicity about the negative treatment they were receiving. Both black and white leaders worked diligently to sidestep unnecessary problems.

Success in football brought blacks and whites to the same stadium to root for the same team. Early pictures of the crowds at those games show African Americans standing in front of the bleachers while white fans filled the stands. Total integration occurred incrementally over time. A seat in the classroom was a right, but a seat at the football stadium had to be earned. Similarly, for students there were still color barriers for organizations that reflected popularity, as opposed to athletic skill.

Integration of the cheerleading squad and the homecoming court took more time. The 1970 *Brevardier*, the high school yearbook, pictures African Americans Andrea Mackey and Carl Mooney, her escort, in the homecoming court. Millicent Norman, another African American student, is featured as a

6. Adjustment to Integration

member of the cheerleading squad in the 1974 *Brevardier*. Although African Americans were not entirely welcomed into the Brevard High School community immediately after integration occurred in 1963, four decades later the races study and socialize with minimal awareness of past differences. Newspaper stories now give equal attention to African American students who earn distinction. In 2002, Cortney Corley reigned as homecoming queen. In athletics, Wendell Moss and Pierre Deshauteurs won numerous honors. Their accomplishments would not have been possible only a few decades earlier.

Former Rosenwald students earned respect, but the white community, after integration, failed to honor the history of their elementary school in simple ways, such as the inclusion of a picture of the Brevard Rosenwald School in the gallery of early schools on display at the education center. To have the building renamed for a white man who opposed desegregation may also be interpreted as insensitive, and that decision occurred 15 years after school integration became a court-forced reality.

Somehow, despite insults and financial shortcomings, a distinctive sense of community developed. The Brevard Rosenwald School was a community unto itself, and school spirit emanated from its site into every home in the black neighborhood. The school was the gathering place for all black citizens. In the era of the original Brevard Rosenwald School, Negro citizens gathered in its rooms for an evening of entertainment or played croquet with family and friends on the school grounds. The school's spirit accompanied the African American students when they were finally allowed to enter the integrated Brevard High School.

Chapter 7

Patterns of Success

As FORMER STAFF AND STUDENTS recounted their memories of Rosenwald days, school pride was reflected in numerous references to community members who had made remarkable progress in their professions. Measuring such achievements is one approach to measuring institutional success. A school's effectiveness is measured by its ability to unleash the talents of its students and to inspire them to strive for greater heights. The caring, nurturing environment of the Rosenwald School in Transylvania County was extraordinary. Within its halls children mattered most. When Robert, Walter, and Sandra Hill painted nursery rhyme illustrations on a bed sheet, it was placed on display on the walls of Rosenwald so that the total school community could see and appreciate their efforts (Dorothy Pierce Hill, interview, March 14, 2000).

Within the community what counted most were the children. When a group of Rosenwald teenagers formed a band — the Tams — and received invitations to perform from Washington, D.C., to Mississippi, their parents contracted Rockefeller Kilgore to travel with them. They encouraged the young musicians to develop their skills and to take advantage of exciting opportunities, but a respected adult had to accompany them.

All the performers were in their teens. Charles Whitmire was the vocalist; Charles W. Hemphill, the guitarist; William English, the drummer; and George Bishop, Jr., a young man from Asheville, the organist. Other members were Eddie Moss, Jr., Johnny L. Roseman, William "Po Bill" Mills, Dennis Robinson and Everett Lee Adams. The group was popular in the South (William Wynn, interview).

Describing an evening performance at the Brevard Country Club, Dennis Robinson said, "It snowed while we were playing for a group from Brevard

High School, and you should have seen those white kids helping us pack our instruments and trudging with us black kids in that snow to get back home. We played at fraternity parties. I don't know how some of those guys ever graduated with all the drinking they did. We played at Royal Pines and at El Tango in Lake Lure. It was a great experience" (interview, December 27, 2002). The community always spotlighted music.

Throughout the history of the Rosenwald School, black youths had to overcome seemingly insurmountable obstacles that blocked every avenue to success. Economic and social barriers confronted them, but African Americans succeeded despite the barrage of discrimination. Motivated by parents, ministers, and teachers who claimed that there was no horizon too distant to be attained, young people moved forward to realize their hopes and dreams. At home and in school, academic prowess was valued, perhaps demanded. Character was modeled by faculty, by parents, and by church and community leaders. Integrity and compassion were part of daily conduct. When confronted by inadequate facilities and resources, Rosenwald teachers willed their students to learn in order to build a brighter future for themselves and for members of their race.

"I remember how those teachers walked down the halls, like they were somebody," Alice Glaze Robinson recalled. "They walked with authority, all of them. I remember those shoes with block heels, all laced up" (interview, February 24, 2000). The phrase "like they were somebody" is reflected in an experience shared by the Reverend Thomas Kilgore, Jr., in *A Servant's Journey* (1998). Working as a butler, waiter, and chauffeur in the Dickerson Boarding House to build a nest egg for his college fund, Kilgore was shocked when he overheard his employer's response to a guest's compliment about his competence and good manners. Mrs. Dickerson replied, "Yes, and he is so different from the former butler, who often tried to engage guests in conversation, as if he was somebody" (p. 17).

Kilgore felt challenged to show that he was indeed somebody. For the youth, that meant being assertive when demanding duties conflicted with his ability to perform each in a manner pleasing to his boss, Mrs. Dickerson. In later years he was named one of the most influential black leaders of the twentieth century and won as many, if not more, honors than any other resident of Brevard, North Carolina. Perhaps he was inspired by Professor Javan L. Jones, Wilkie Johnstone, and Coragreene Johnstone — individuals who projected the ambiance of being "somebody."

However, in the 1930s, Thomas Kilgore, Jr., at age 15, became the victim of accusations that he was guilty of criminal conduct. Sheriff Tom Woods charged him with making lewd and insulting remarks to a white woman. The young Kilgore, on an afternoon break from his job at the Wallace boarding house and unaware of any problem, was socializing with Herschell Thomas and two girls a few miles out of Brevard when the sheriff and his deputies suddenly appeared and carried the young people to jail.

All were released except Thomas Kilgore, Jr., who was placed in jail and kept there for three days. He was indicted and brought to trial and found guilty. Kilgore's accuser never appeared, but Sheriff Woods, who, according to Kilgore, was not well thought of in the black community, presented testimony to the magistrate; the young boy was found guilty and sentenced to serve six months on a chain gang. Intervention by his attorney led to Kilgore's sentence being switched from performing hard labor to being banned from Transylvania County for one year. Happily, that led to his attending Stephens Lee High School in Asheville, North Carolina (Kilgore, 1998). Kilgore later became a well-known minister and civil rights activist.

Teachers were important people in the Rosenwald community. To attend church with them, to shop in the same grocery store, to live in the same community suggested that, by rubbing elbows with those professionals, some of their worth marked everyone in the neighborhood. Wilkie Robinson was named for Mrs. Johnstone, a teacher known for classes where becoming bored was simply not permitted. "She told me, 'I gave you my name. Now, don't you be messin' it up.' She wanted me to be a good girl and not get ruined. Oh, she wanted me to be my best...." (interview, August 27, 2002). Mrs. Johnstone inspired young Wilkie, one of the Rosenwald School's basketball players, to set high personal standards of conduct and achievement. Ann Jamerson, a white businesswoman, described Johnstone, who personified excellence, as "a true lady" and as a mother whose daughter was "one of the most beautiful women I have ever seen" (interview, December 13, 2002).

Most of the Rosenwald teachers modeled confidence and success for their students. State requirements demanded that instructors continue studying in formal settings to renew their teaching certificates. Not only did they create learning environments for their pupils, but also they sought learning opportunities for themselves. In addition, the Rosenwald teachers served as positive members of their democratic society, despite their lives being impacted by the negative aspects of segregation.

One example was the faculty's support of soldiers who protected and defended the nation. During the days of World Wars I and II, female teachers knitted socks and sweaters for the men in uniform. To knit seemed a simple way to make a contribution, but to do so required learning a new skill and sacrificing personal time, as Ethel K. Mills explained. "The Red Cross wanted people to knit. One person would learn to knit. Then she taught someone else. It spread like wildfire. It was like catching a disease. During World War I, I couldn't turn those toes on the socks, but when World War II came, I knew how. We would meet and knit socks and sweaters for the soldiers. We needed four needles to do the heels. There were no circular needles.

During World War II, I knitted 18 sweaters for the Red Cross, used four needles to make round collars. I learned it" (interview, March 1, 2001).

Seemingly ordinary people were remarkably accomplished, and the manifold achievements of Rosenwald graduates are a trophy for the men and women who taught at the school. From a community of fewer than 1,000 have come ministers, educators, attorneys, medical professionals, artists, and businessmen and -women. The professional achievements of former Rosenwald students are evident in the following sample of successful individuals:

Educators: Arnella Benjamin, Barbara Garrett, Nathaniel Hall, James Arthur Hefner, Robert Hutchison, Lillie Madison Jones, Gary Madison, Rosetta Madison Henderson, Neva Whiteside Martin, Gwyan Mooney, Alice Glaze Robinson, Lois Elliott Wynn.

University administrators: Archie Erwin, James A. Hefner.

Ministers and religious workers: Justine Conley, Frederick L. Gordon, Cail Elliott, Keith Elliott, Marshall Erwin, Thomas Kilgore, Jr., Morris Young, Sr.

Business leaders: Floyd Benjamin, Sherman Crite, Jr., Vernon Gardin, James Outlaw, Lewis F. Whiteside.

Community leaders:. Mable Armstrong, Edith Darity, Cornelius Hunt, Audrey Hutchison, Ella W. Jones, Thaddeus Kilgore, Marva Lytle, Reesie Madison, Selena Robinson, Winona Whiteside, Charles Whitmire, Agnes Wilson.

Artists: Loretta Aiken (Jackie "Moms" Mabley), Joan Mills Bell, Stephanie Crite, Arthur Lynch, Johnsie Mills, William Mills, Charles Moss, Robert Norman, Rosetta Norman.

Other professions: Olivia Whiteside Boyd, nurse; F. Douglas Cantey, attorney; Althea Gordon, social service worker; Dottie Hill Harris, medical technician; Betty Jean Hunt High, librarian; Beverly Hill, speech therapist; Luretha Knox, nurse; Penny Lytle, probation officer; James Arthur Madison, journalist/businessman; Linda McCants, secretary; Carl Mooney, chemist; Shelia Mooney, counselor; Cliff Outlaw, Peace Corps worker/computer consultant; Edna Sandler, secretary.

Their success illustrates the potential of a school that allows learners to interact equally with devoted teachers, as these students did during their days at the Brevard Rosenwald School. As Agnes Wilson, substitute teacher during the spring semester of 1955, said, "At Rosenwald we tried to ensure that each student knew to be himself" (interview, February 8, 2000). Michael Owens shared a similar conviction, "If it was in you, those teachers brought it out" (interview). Faculty members often succeeded in helping students identify and develop their strengths.

The above list of Rosenwald students who achieved success in professional areas is far from complete. At best, their names constitute a random sample. Of course, all graduates did not achieve success. One former Rosenwald student said, "Some walked the streets. Some turned to alcohol. Some could not face life." Teachers also admit there were some lives that were disappointing, but Rosenwald had its share of success stories.

One man who figures prominently in the early history of the community successfully ran a number of businesses and took an active role in overseeing a school for black children. James P. Aiken was born March 1, 1861, and died August 25, 1909. According to Selena Robinson, Aiken was the son of a slave, Jane Rhodes Aiken, and her white owner. The Aiken family provided financial support for the establishment of his business (interview, October 10, 2002). The Transylvania County archives contain a business card of James Aiken's, and he was a well-respected businessman. He operated several successful businesses on Main Street in downtown Brevard. In *The Transylvania Times*, a feature article, "Transylvania Blacks Were Pioneers," by Ruth Penney (June 12, 1986) cites Aiken as the owner of a barber shop, a café, a bakery, a cider and gingerbread business, and a dray service.

Selena Robinson explained that a dray service was an old-fashioned taxi service. Mr. Aiken's wagons picked up folks at the depot or provided transportation of people and goods to other parts of the county (interview, October 10, 2002).

She also shared a family story of remarkable tolerance concerning this entrepreneur, who was her uncle. James Aiken was born while his mother was enslaved, but he was a free Negro. Jane Aiken had been a slave from the age of nine and had served four masters. The last one brought her to Transylvania County. After she was granted freedom, she married Dennis Cleveland Hall. "Uncle Jim used to come by our house ... and we always wondered about his light skin," Robinson said. "We would ask our grandma. 'How come Uncle Jim is so light and Daddy is so dark?' She said, 'When you get old enough, I'll tell you.' And ... later she sat us down and told us that he was born by her boss and you couldn't do anything about it then. You had to do what the boss said. And she said they let me keep my child and that made me so glad. And they never did beat me. She also said, 'No matter what anybody does to you, don't you ever hate them because hate will destroy you.' And I remember her saying that to this day" (interviews, July 16, 1999 and October 21, 2002).

James Aiken, a school committeeman for the Brevard #2 Colored School, quickly branched off from selling gingerbread and cider into other endeavors. An advertisement that appeared in an early Transylvania County newspaper and was published in *Transylvania Heritage Today* (summer, 1999), affirms his fight to achieve "shoe supremacy ... to secure for my patrons' shoes attractive and good — every pair made to wear" with an invitation to check out his stock at the second door below the post office in Brevard. He also advertised fashions, groceries, notions, tinware, coffins, and toothsome dainties. An astute businessman, he knew how to turn a profit.

City records of disbursements indicate that the town government offices often hired Aiken's dray service. During the Christmas season of 1908, Aiken placed an advertisement in the *Sylvan Valley News*. The ad stated: "Meet me at Jim Aiken's Headquarters for / Santa Clause / During the holidays. Don't fail to see his line of / Candies, Fruits and Toys / Before buying elsewhere / Dry Goods, Notions, Hats and Shoes / Have arrived and the prices can't be beat / In town."

Despite the racial chasm that existed in the mountain town of Brevard in 1909, Aiken's death brought forth from the white community acclaim for the character of their Negro neighbor. Working as a volunteer fireman, he was killed by a horrific explosion that threw him ten or twelve feet, broke his neck, and severely mutilated him. His funeral was conducted in the white First Baptist Church and, as a token of respect for the deceased fireman, all businesses were closed during the services.

Further evidence of the attitude of the white public is found in the August 26, 1909, *Asheville Citizen*. The reporter described Aiken as a "well known colored porter." Actually, in the United States census for 1900, Aiken identified himself as a merchant. In similar language, the writer of an editorial in *The French Broad Hustler,* dated August 27, 1909, referred to Aiken as a man who "knew his place ... one colored man who left the world better than he found it ... one Negro who voted for his friends ... esteemed colored man...."

Following his death, the Aiken family retained ownership of the house they had helped purchase and offered no assistance to his widow and children, which may explain why one child left the community in search of success (Selena Robinson, interview, October 21, 2002). The widow, Mary Aiken, thanked the community for the outpouring of sympathy and requested that they continue their patronage of the store, which she continued to operate. In the April 8, 1910, *Sylvan Valley News*, the editor alludes to "good grub during Court Week served in Mary Aiken's store."

On May 6, 1910, this ad appeared: "I have on hand a full line of / New Goods / SHOES, HATS, NOTIONS, CANDIES, NUTS, FRUITS and GROCERIES / at the J.P. Aiken old stand.... Mrs. Mary Aiken, Proprietor." A later ad recommends her business for hats, shoes, shirts, warm meals, and states that fish and oysters were available each Wednesday and Saturday. Her name appears this time as Mary Aiken Parton, indicating that she had married

George Parton. It is striking that in the early 1900s a black woman was successful in operating a Main Street business (William Wynn, interview).

Two high achievers from the African American community were educated in a school for colored children in Brevard, but the exact school is unknown. Loretta Mary Aiken was born in Brevard on March 19, 1897, and Coragreene Johnstone was born in Knoxville, Tennessee, on September 26, 1908. Aiken became famous as Jackie "Moms" Mabley, performing as a dancer, a singer, an actress, and a comedienne. Billed as "the funniest woman in the world," Moms visited her hometown as often as possible. In the October 22, 1971, edition of *The Asheville Citizen*, Bob Terrell described Moms Mabley as "one of America's finest comediennes."

Encouraged by her great-grandmother, Harriet Smith, a woman of Cherokee descent who lived near the Davidson River, Loretta Aiken decided to find out what kind of world lay beyond her mountains. First, at age 14, she moved to Hill Street in Asheville. Already a mother and pregnant with another, the young woman moved from there to Cleveland to be with her own mother, Mary Parton. Although a victim of rape, after a long struggle she opted not to have an abortion. Terrell (1971) cites her comments: "I was brought up in a very Christian family. I wasn't taught to throw away children, but I was going to. I was going to Detroit to have an abortion and something told me not to.... I got down on my knees.... Suddenly a voice came to me ... 'Go on the stage....'" And that is what she did. Pregnant and with no prior experience, Aiken joined a touring troupe in Chicago and got her start in show business. For a period spanning five decades, Moms Mabley entertained thousands, including prisoners at Sing Sing at Christmastime. Her career included roles as singer, dancer, actress, and comedienne. Annie Marie Hailey described Moms' typical costume as "frumpy clothes, sagging stockings, and beat up shoes. No dentures" (interview, August 21, 2002).

Winona Whiteside praised Moms for her continued interest in the affairs of her friends and relatives in Brevard. "A lot of folks who made it to the big time would have forgotten us, but not Moms," Whiteside said (interview, March 13, 2000). Mabley's death on May 23, 1975, in White Plains, New York, saddened the community.

Her friend, Coragreene Johnstone, made remarkable inroads in academia. An educator, Johnstone earned a B.A. summa cum laude from Talledega College in 1932, an M.A. from the University of Michigan in 1935, and a Ph.D. from Michigan in 1952. After leaving the Brevard Rosenwald School, she taught at six colleges, including Spelman College, 1945–1951 and 1952–1954; Fisk University, 1954–1957; and Cheney State College, 1964 until her retirement in 1975. At Cheney, she was a professor of English and director of the Division of Humanities. Johnstone, who was a member of numerous scholarly societies and was active in St. John's Episcopal Church, studied at the University of London and at Oxford University. The Rosenwald Community reserves a special place of pride for Mabley and Johnstone.

On March 23, 1995, the Rosenwald community lost one of its strongest civic leaders when Mable Kilgore Armstrong died. Mable Armstrong, the wife of Oscar Armstrong, was active in so many projects that she told *Transylvania Times* reporter Pete Shiflet, "I'm like a jumping bean, always jumping from one thing to another" (November 17, 1986). Her parents were John and Elizabeth Garrett Kilgore, and her stepfather was Bill Jackson, who helped to install the first water system in Brevard.

A faithful member of Bethel Baptist Church, Armstrong wrote a cookbook to assist in a fund-raising promotion for the church. She entitled it *The Kitchen Mechanic.* Armstrong was a member of two civic groups: the Jolly Twelve and the Uplift Club. The latter was organized in 1936. Members of both organizations united their efforts to provide services to the community, but the Jolly Twelve was primarily a social club. Armstrong, who served on the boards of the Mary C. Jenkins Community Center and the United Way, was also active in the 4C Program and the Brevard City Beautification Committee. She served as president of the Garden Club and was a Girl Scout leader.

Richard Stricker and his family had a special relationship with Mable Armstrong. Stricker's parents were doctors. Mable went to work for the Stricker family six months before Richard's birth and remained there until her death. Because Richard was chronically ill, his care was turned over to Mable, who treated him like her own child. "Mable was a lovely lady and a real leader," Stricker said. "She was close to all of us, but probably closest to me. She was a wonderful cook. She didn't really work for us. She worked with us. It was a totally 'family affair'" (interview, October 30, 2002).

When speaking of her, Stricker revealed his affection for Mable. He assessed her interests and achievements. Her church, Bethel Baptist, was a special place for her. Married at the age of 13, Mable had a limited education, but in her 60s she earned a high school diploma by correspondence, and she took piano lessons in her 70s. Stricker said she was a highly intelligent person who was knowledgeable about many subjects, especially nature, botany, and biology. Mrs. Armstrong had a high level of culture, perhaps because her husband Oscar worked for wealthy, educated people. According to Stricker, Mable was keen on improving conditions in the world around her. Her foresight in collecting artifacts of the history of the Rosenwald community is praiseworthy. Her collection remains today, carefully guarded by her friends, Audrey Hutchison and Edith Darity, who carry on the Armstrong tradition of preserving the history of the African American community.

Reesie Madison, another community leader, completed her Rosenwald education in 1941. Her six children were raised in Brevard and attended her

alma mater. Madison, a homemaker, devoted herself to community service. She was active in the Parent-Teachers Association and was a Girl Scout leader for 30 years. She participated in the ministries of Bethel "A" Church, such as the Alternative School Program, the Bus Stop Ministry and the Rise and Shine program.

A Sunday school and Vacation Bible School teacher, Madison was active in the Christian Women's Club and in Bible study groups. A member of the Garden Club and the Johnsie Lee Mills Memorial Mass Choir, she supported both Habitat for Humanity and the Sharing House. Madison, who died April 1, 2001, made a major contribution to the TCIO's battle to integrate the schools. Her children are in the process of establishing a scholarship fund in memory of their community-minded parents.

A Rosenwald alumnus who made his home with cousins in Washington, D.C., while attending high school there, Nathaniel Hall graduated from Cardoza Business High School in 1938. He enrolled in Miner Teachers College, also in Washington. During World War II, he served in the United States Army. He was shipped to England in 1943, serving there until 1945 when he was relocated to a base near Munich, Germany.

Following his discharge, he completed requirements for the bachelor of science degree at Miner Teachers College. Later he earned a master of arts degree at the Catholic University of America. He taught social studies and worked in administrative positions in summer school programs until his retirement in the late 1970s. "I taught social studies mostly, history, geography, civics," Hall said. "Little old books were used for state history. There was no real D.C. [District of Columbia] history ... we put together a history of the District of Columbia ... a good book."

Hall also authored three books: *They've Been Neglected Too Long* (1969), *Helping Johnny to Read* (1981), and *The Negroes of Transylvania County*. The latter was published as a major appendage to *Transylvania Beginnings: A History* (1984). Hall viewed his history of the "colored people of Transylvania County" as his most worthwhile accomplishment because it preserved important details about the lives of his people. Hall also takes pride in the accomplishments of his son Winston, who is an educator, and of his late son Bernard, a Catholic priest who died in March 2002 (interview, July 16, 2002).

Hall, skilled in caning chairs and in basket weaving, has also written a

Opposite: Rosenwald teachers Julia Smith, Ethel Mills, and Wilkie Johnstone were members of the Uplift Club, a service organization. First row, left to right: Julia Harris, Belle Benjamin, Julia Smith, Edith Mills, Bernetha Owens, Llellyn Jeter. Second row, left to right: Callie Mills, Lessie B. Riley, Wilkie Johnstone. Third row, left to right: Henrietta Turner, Edna Glaze, Victoria Hutchison, Flora Aiken, Agnes Hunt, Marie Davenport, Ethel Mills, Wilkie Robinson, Catherine Mooney, Mable Armstrong, and Trilby Elliott. (Courtesy Patricia Austin.)

collection of poetry based on personal experiences. Currently he is writing a biography of his sister, Selena Robinson. Hall is also involved in civic and church activities. Since retirement, he has lived in Brevard, where he shares his vast knowledge of local history with the community.

Hall's sister, Selena Hall Robinson, also has practical skills. Mrs. Robinson knows how to make soap, how to quilt, and how to sew. Her latest project is making "Dammit Dolls," a toy used as a stress reliever. Owners relieve tension or frustration by slamming the colorful doll against a wall. Robinson learned much about life from her grandmother, a former slave who "lived with us and lived to be 104 years old." Robinson's grandmother was a midwife who delivered both white and black babies. The mother of 14 children, Mrs. Robinson recalled promising God that she would help someone else when she got her babies out of diapers and weaned from bottles.

Believing that "we should leave this world in better shape than we found it in," Robinson built a career with Western North Carolina's Community Action as an outreach worker who was required to make home visits. She remembers her first visit to a section of Transylvania County notorious for its racial hostility. "I was the first one to be sent and I was scared," Robinson said. "But I said to myself, 'I am going to take God with me.'" She was going to meet a school principal to get information and the addresses of some students. A group of students on the play area taunted her with "Hey, Nigger, Nigger, Nigger," but one boy jerked loose and told her, "Go, say something." Robinson simply asked how to contact the office: "Do you mind showing me the principal's office?" The child was afraid to go, but pointed in the direction. The children ran away. Such incidents strengthened Robinson's resolve to face whatever opposition confronted her with a calm spirit.

Sometimes Robinson was responsible for allotting food stamps to struggling families. If the breadwinner were on strike with no income, he or she would need to sign up with Mrs. Robinson, who was required to confirm the truth of their circumstances. She explained the consequences of filing a false report. "Sometimes they would give me their story and call back later to explain that they had discovered a son had money in the bank and that I should tear up the application," she said.

On one occasion a white client, in need of fuel, was repulsed by the prospect of touching Mrs. Robinson's hands. The woman carefully held her social security card up by its corners to be copied. Later the same person complained that some items were missing from her purse and wanted Mrs. Robinson's searched to retrieve her property. Her purse was searched, as the white woman requested, but no stolen goods were found. Although her duties brought her into frequent fire, Mrs. Robinson never gave up. "That job made a woman out of me" (interview, July 10, 2002). It also helped prepare her to battle for the integration of the public schools and the local hospital.

Robinson was honored by the United States Forest Service's National Volunteer Award for hours donated to the Schenck Job Corps Center, where she served as a volunteer for 31 years. Reported in a *Transylvania Times* article by Jon Hildreth, the presentation was made on April 24, 1997. John Ramsey, U.S. Forest supervisor, called Robinson the "first lady of Schenck Job Corps Center." Schenck Principal L.T. Allen credited Robinson with taking measures to promote good will for the Job Corps within the community. Robinson's vision led her to establish the Corps' Community Relations Council, which provided an important tool for communication between the Center and the community. According to Allen, the council helped ensure the success of the existing Job Corps program, which has an operating budget of more than $4 million.

In his speech praising Robinson, Allen recalled that in 1965 only one in ten Appalachian citizens had completed high school and that Robinson's efforts had aided in developing offerings that included at least one college program for the Job Corps site. Allen expressed appreciation for Robinson's service as advisor, counselor, and teacher to both staff and students. He remarked, "We used to say she had about 250 children" (*Transylvania Times*, April 28, 1997).

In addition, Selena Robinson has contributed to the Land of the Sky Regional Council and Transylvania County's Human Relations Council. She is often asked to speak to groups about her role in the movement to integrate the public schools of Transylvania County and to share her memories and skills about the past. Robinson has demonstrated the craft of soap making for the Transylvania Historical Society activities. Selena Robinson, now a much-admired senior citizen, is something of a local celebrity.

Cornelius Hunt was another esteemed resident of Transylvania County. He was born on November 19, 1919, and died on June 17, 1990. Hunt, who was a student at the Rosenwald School in the 1930s, became an outstanding member of the greater Brevard community. He ensured that African Americans were allowed to vote by taking his concerns to Raleigh. Hunt, according to Mrs. Selena Robinson, was threatened with the prospect of jail when he first attempted to participate in the voting process. Infuriated at the treatment he had received, Hunt visited politicians in the state capital. After that trip Brevard's African Americans were allowed access to the voting booths (Robinson, interview, July 16, 1999). When the Hendersonville School Board expanded its Advisory Board in April 1959, Hunt became a member of the group, which made recommendations directly affecting the education of black children.

In the 1960s, Hunt helped found the Transylvania Citizens Improvement Organization (TCIO), the vehicle for seeking affirmative action for African Americans in Transylvania County. Serving as its first president, Hunt, with

Scouting provided an extension of educational opportunities. Boy Scouts and their leaders pose in front of Bethel "A" Baptist Church. Front row, left to right: Wendell Johnstone, Charles "Eagle" Moss, Keith Howell, David Baker, Terry Crite, and Tyrone Gordon. Back row, left to right: Samuel Raper, Rufus Norman, Eddie Moss, Stevie Norman, Richard Smith, Paul Hemphill, Cornelius Hunt, Sherman Crite, Jr., and Grady Elliott.

the assistance of the Reverend Samuel Raper and others, led the fight to integrate the public schools and to open the local hospital on an equal basis to members of the extended Rosenwald community. Later Hunt worked to integrate the annual Fourth of July celebration for Ecusta workers at Straus Park. In 1974 Hunt and his TCIO supporters won recognition of the needs of the area's African Americans for affordable housing.

Mary Cowal, a Brevard resident who works with Hospice and Home Care in Transylvania County, expressed her admiration for Hunt: "I was privileged to know Cornelius Hunt. He was a deep inspiration to me. He cared about everyone. He drew no lines based on color or economics. As a councilman, he stressed not working for one issue, but for the good of all" (interview). On the other hand, if he were moved to do so, he could organize resistance to the point of stirring up strong opposition. The high school principal described him as a tough man who demonstrated unusual resilience (N.A. Miller, interview).

An employee at the Olin Corporation for more than 31 years, Hunt was a remarkable example of the relentless courage required to fight a system in which white supremacy was the norm. The charismatic Hunt prodded others to upgrade the community by providing equal opportunities. His leadership won him the respect of both white and black citizens. The grandson of slaves, Hunt was elected to the Brevard City Council in 1973. At the time of his death in 1990, he was serving as Mayor Pro Tem of the Council.

Hunt was also involved in Habitat for Humanity, which illustrates that his concern for fair housing exceeded mere lip service. Hunt also provided support to send young people to World Peace Camps. He was director of the United Way in Transylvania County and served locally on the Board of Directors of the American Cancer Society, the American Red Cross, and the Mary C. Jenkins Community Center. A member of the Executive Council of the Land of the Sky Regional Council, he also worked on the Community Relations Council of the Schenck Job Corps Center.

In 1992, Hunt was honored when the Cornelius Hunt Memorial Endowment was created within the Transylvania County Education Foundation. The purpose of the fund is to provide motivational and enrichment opportunities specifically for African American youths in Transylvania County. Community colleague Dorothy Mock worked tirelessly to ensure the endowment's success, orchestrating regular fundraising to honor the memory of Cornelius Hunt. Among the prizes for the 1993 fundraiser was an acrylic painting by Stephanie Crite, an award-winning local artist who briefly attended the reconstructed Rosenwald School.

Hunt was again honored when Mayor John Peterson proclaimed that June 3, 1995, be observed as Cornelius Hunt Day. The event, designed as part of the celebration of the thirty-fifth anniversary of the TCIO, featured the sale of raffle tickets to fund two annual scholarships for high school seniors. Proceeds were placed in the Cornelius Hunt Endowment Fund.

Numerous Rosenwald graduates have pursued careers in teaching and in educational administration. Lillie Madison Jones, the oldest of six children who grew up in Brevard, felt compelled to be a role model for her siblings in the pursuit of education. She succeeded, and her five brothers and sisters also graduated from college and completed advanced study. After finishing the elementary program at the Rosenwald School, Jones completed her high school education at Allen School in Asheville. She earned a bachelor's degree from Bennett College, a master's degree from North Carolina A&T State University, and a doctorate from Virginia Tech. Jones has been recognized for her accomplishments in education.

When Jones was named Highpointer (NC) of the Year, Steve Huffman of the *High Point Enterprise* praised her as an educator who "has displayed concern for the oppressed, spoken out on issues of poverty, participated in

At Alice's Educational Wonderland in Yanceyville, North Carolina, Jahlen and Thomas enjoy a special moment with the beloved Mrs. Alice. (Photograph by Paul Robinson, Jr.)

civic affairs, and promoted community and human improvement." As superintendent of the Guilford County Schools, Jones helped establish three alternative learning centers for the public schools. Now an ordained minister, she serves two congregations in Mooresville, North Carolina.

Alice Glaze Robinson, an outstanding educator and businesswoman, has won accolades statewide for her achievements in early childhood education. During her childhood she shared the home of her grandparents, Quillie and Pinkie Glaze, located near the site of the Rosenwald School. Vividly recalling the poverty of those years, she described walking up the steep hills in the Rosenwald community with the loosened soles of her shoes slapping against the ground. A 1962 graduate of Livingstone College, Robinson is now the owner and director of Alice's Educational Wonderland in Yanceyville, North Carolina. "I give all the credit for that to God. He made it possible," Robinson affirmed (interview, October 25, 2002).

Citing Ethel K. Mills as the definitive influence that led her into teaching, Robinson said, "I had been teaching, but I decided I wouldn't continue. Well, Mrs. Mills said, 'What is this I hear, young lady?... You will teach, and there is a job waiting for you here at Rosenwald'" (interview, October 25, 2002). Alice Glaze accepted that position and taught for one year in Brevard and then accepted an invitation to return to Caswell County. Her former principal had been fielding numerous requests from parents that he persuade her to come back.

There, in 1975, she was honored as Teacher of the Year. Since then, she has journeyed on a mission to convince each child who comes her way that he or she is special. "I had one teacher at Rosenwald who made me feel like nothing ... like nobody, and I will not allow a child in my school to feel that way" (interview, October 25, 2002). The walls at Alice's Educational Wonderland abound with messages relaying the idea that each child is worthy of respect and admiration. Inscribed on the sidewalk is the school's manifesto: "Welcome. Every child is special here."

When the state ordered Robinson to remove a large toy train that was prominent on her playground, she redesigned the area so the children would not lose "their" train. The play area at Alice's Educational Wonderland is the property of the children. From Robinson's perspective, a playground that must be immaculately maintained reflects the priority of outsiders rather than the needs of children.

At Yanceyville's Gunn Memorial Library, Rebecca Dellinger called Robinson "our local angel" and "our community treasure." Dellinger, the Children's Librarian, described Robinson's teaching philosophy this way:

> She is about children respecting children and growing up to respect others. Robinson stresses literacy, and she gets her entire staff involved. Each week she brings the children to the library for story time. If the weather is good, they walk here. And if it snows, she calls and invites us to come to the school for story time. She is something else. She lets us know when we're doing right and when we're not. [interview, October 25, 2002].

People throughout the Yanceyville community entrust her with their children. Robinson does not need to advertise. Her clientele handles that by word of mouth.

Robinson bonds with anyone who shares her view of a child's value, but when anyone steps out of line in her presence, she acts quickly. Robinson contracted with a photographer to visit the school to shoot pictures. The young man traveled from Winston-Salem to Yanceyville, but he was rushing through the shot and not showing the children respect. Robinson sent him packing. "I want my children treated like somebody. He was jerking them around. When he told one, 'You look like a hotdog,' I told him he needed to be some place else and that he should pack his things and leave" (interview, October 25, 2002). Alice Robinson expects others to treat each child as someone of special value, as she does.

In its November 1, 2000, issue, the *Caswell Messenger* summarized

Robinson's experience in education: primary teacher in Caswell County, first grade teacher in Brevard, leader in Early Childhood Learning Institutes at Salem College, study of the Rural Disadvantaged Child at the University of Rhode Island–Kingston, training personnel and directing Vacation Bible Schools for the Southern Baptist Convention in North Carolina and in Louisiana. An active member of her church, Robinson has also participated in Zeta Phi Beta Sorority, NAACP, Eastern Star, Board of Health, Human Relations Council, Caswell County Arts' Council, and the Caswell County Partnership for Children. She serves the community as well as her children.

Attributing her success to God, Robinson, twice a survivor of breast cancer, stated, "God is not a part of my life. He is my life" (interview, October 25, 2002). Like so many of the former Rosenwald students, an unfaltering faith in God and in His ability to control the circumstances of life provides the keystone of Robinson's philosophy.

Another teacher who has been effective in her interaction with young people is Neva Whiteside Martin of Reidsville, North Carolina. Mrs. Martin attended the Brevard Rosenwald School in the 1950s. She enrolled at Ninth Avenue School but transferred to Brevard High School and went on to graduate from Livingstone College with a major in English. The instructor in Rockingham County's Title I Reading Program, she provided intensive reading instruction for disadvantaged students. "I loved teaching those students," Martin said. "It was never really a chore. I loved the kids. They were very special" (interview).

In reviewing her various educational experiences, Martin lauded the preparation she received at Rosenwald as "very good for the elementary level," but she also felt community-sponsored events enriched her education. "I gained a lot from participating in the church choir and also from belonging to the Girl Scouts," she said. "My mother, Evon Whiteside, was our troop leader. We went camping, and Mable Armstrong was involved. We had a lot of fun, and we learned a lot."

Neva Martin retired from teaching after 26 years because of debilitating health problems. She has dialysis treatments each week, but she remains as active as possible. Describing her professionally, Alice Glaze Robinson explained Martin's effectiveness by observing that she found personal fulfillment in working with students who needed a bit of extra help. "Neva is such a compassionate person and tries to fix everyone's problem," Robinson said. "She never says no. She is resourceful. Neither time nor money is a factor when she is helping others. In fact, because of her health problems, we have to tell her no" (interview, November 11, 2002).

Several Rosenwald graduates taught for a time and then went into other areas of service. Two of those were Lewis Whiteside and James Madison. Whiteside taught at Brevard High School and at Brevard Middle School, but he moved on to succeed in a business career in Shelby, North Carolina. James Arthur Madison, Jr., a former teacher, is the editor of the *Florida Sun Review*, a newspaper in the Orlando, Florida area, and also manages investment properties.

Madison, educated at the Brevard Rosenwald School from 1952 to 1959, attended Ninth Avenue School in Hendersonville from 1959 to 1962, when Cedric Jones was serving as the principal. Madison transferred to Brevard High School and graduated in 1963. He earned a bachelor of science degree at North Carolina A&T State University. Madison, active in the college's ROTC program, was commissioned into the United States Air Force and served in the Vietnam War. A recipient of the Bronze Star, with the rank of major, he is a retired member of the Air Force Reserves.

In 1975, Madison's book *Heirs of Truth* was published, and he has completed a work of fiction, *Wheat Fields of Harvest*, which is also to be published. He also created Formulation, a mathematical board game. Madison described his father as a fantastic role model, a man who strongly supported his children and encouraged them to strive to achieve their dreams. Madison explained that his father was a self-taught man with limited formal education, but that he was skilled in finance and was an intelligent individual. "Any other role model was unnecessary. He said what he meant and did what he said ... and he maintained that position throughout his life" (interview).

Madison has discovered the value of variety in his life. "I was in education. It was great. What happens in the classroom is fine, but you can learn a great deal by going out into life and doing things," he said. "For example, I used the GI Bill to take advanced flight training, rather than to go to graduate school. I have enjoyed the freedom to do as much as I can the way I can do it. Education can take a lot of different forms."

In 1991, James Arthur Hefner, a former Rosenwald student, became president of Tennessee State University. There he has established a Chair of Excellence in both the College of Business and in the College of Engineering and Technology, and a Chair of Entrepreneurship in the College of Business. During his tenure, the College of Business was accredited by the American Assembly of Collegiate Schools of Business. In 1993, he succeeded in establishing Phi Kappa Phi, an honor society encompassing all academic disciplines, on campus.

Prior to accepting the presidency at Tennessee State University, Hefner was president of Jackson State University in Mississippi, a professor of economics at Morehouse College in Atlanta, and Provost at Tuskegee Institute. James Haney, in the *Metropolitan Times* of Nashville, Tennessee, shared a story of Hefner's elementary school days: There were few books in his childhood home so his principal, Ethel K. Mills, invited him to stop by her home to read her encyclopedias. "For eight years while I was in elementary school,

I would stop at her house on the way home, and I would read the encyclopedia," said Hefner, who graduated from Ninth Avenue School in Hendersonville as salutatorian. He attended college at North Carolina A&T State University in Greensboro.

After earning a master's degree from Atlanta University, Hefner earned a Ph.D. in economics at the University of Colorado–Boulder in 1971. He has authored more than 50 articles on economic issues and has published two books: *Black Empowerment in Atlanta* and *Public Policy for the Black Community: Strategies and Perspectives.*

Hefner was elected to the Board of Directors of the American Council on Education in March 2000. He was the first professor to hold the endowed Charles E. Merrill Chair at Morehouse College and has been a visiting research associate at Harvard University, at Princeton University, and at the University of Wisconsin–Madison.

Morehouse College established the James A. Hefner Award, which provides scholarships for worthy students. In May 2000, a group of 180 students received more than $205,000. Hefner has received the Ida B. Wells Institute's award for his support of journalism, journalism education, and freedom of speech. Of this honor, Dr. Hefner expressed great pleasure because of its emphasis on freedom of speech and of the press, which he called "cornerstones that ... made our nation great."

Hefner has also been praised for his aggressive leadership in hiring Vivian Fuller, the first African American female to become athletic director at an NCAA Division I School with football (http://www.tnstate.edu/jhaney/hefner.htm and http://www.tnstate.edu/opr/hefner.htm). Hefner was awarded the W.E.B. Du Bois Award by the National Association of Social and Behavioral Scientists at its 1997 national conference in Nashville. Michael R. Williams, outgoing president of the organization, cited Hefner's scholarship and leadership in black studies as the basis for the award.

Hefner attributes his success in part to encouragement from such men as Hugh Gloster, former president of Morehouse University, who recommended that Hefner consider a career in higher education administration, and Tuskegee's Benjamin Payton, who expressed confidence in Hefner's ability to run a university. Today Hefner voices a strong conviction that young black males should be targeted in college recruitment efforts. Hefner advocates the efforts as a good recruitment strategy from a compassionate point of view, and he also believes that providing a young African Americans with a college education boosts the economic output of our total society. By recruiting black males, the college is waging a war against poverty, unemployment and ignorance (http://www.tnstate.edu/jhaney/hefner.htm and http://www.tnstate.edu/opr/hefner.htm).

Former Rosenwald students have also achieved success in the business arena. James Outlaw was educated in the segregated schools of Transylvania County. He attended classes in church basements and in one church annex until the new Rosenwald School opened its doors in 1948. Outlaw still harbors a sense of betrayal that no furniture and no new books were provided for the school when it first opened. Despite the limited resources, Outlaw is convinced that he was well-educated at Rosenwald, which he described as having been "very dear to us black kids" (*The Transylvania Times*, February 19, 1998). During a session of the Transylvania County Human Relations Council on which he serves, Outlaw said, "The happiest day I remember from my childhood was the day we moved into the new Rosenwald School, and I was in fourth grade" (January 7, 2003).

After graduating from the Ninth Avenue School in Hendersonville, Outlaw enlisted in the United States Air Force because he had no money for college. Later he enrolled at North Carolina College in Durham. There he took part in the "sit-in" demonstrations at Woolworth's. After receiving his degree in business administration with a minor in economics in 1960, Outlaw was unable to find a job in the area near his home so he went to New York City.

Building a successful career, Outlaw worked for the Writers Guild of America, Shell Oil Company, Caliex Petroleum Corporation, and the New York Life Insurance Company. New York Life hired James Outlaw, to comply with an affirmative action program. Eventually Outlaw was transferred back to North Carolina, first to Charlotte and then to Brevard, where he managed a branch of New York Life in an office on Main Street.

A community-minded citizen, Outlaw has served on the board of the United Way and on the Human Relations Council. He is a mentor with the M2K Middle School Mentoring Program sponsored by Neighbors in Ministry, Inc. The mentoring project allows Outlaw to develop a friendly relationship with middle-school youth. He has been a volunteer tutor and an active member of Bethel "A" Baptist Church.

Not willing to remain idle since his retirement, Outlaw has worked at Schenck Job Corps and at College Walk, a retirement center. His son, Sidney, served as drum major for the Brevard High School Marching Band and has performed in musical productions at UNC-Greensboro and with the Greensboro Opera Company.

James Outlaw has also been a member of Mountain Lily Lodge #117, which originated as a branch of the Masons (Hall, 1984). Outlaw attributes his personal success to God and to the encouragement of his mother, Bridget Outlaw. "All that I am or will be I owe to God and to my mother. She's 90 years old, and I am now her caregiver" (interview, January 7, 2003).

After attending the Brevard Rosenwald School, Floyd Benjamin earned a bachelor's degree in biology and a master's in microbiology from North Carolina Central University. He served as president and CEO of Pasadena

Research Laboratories in San Clemente, California, before joining Akorn, Inc. of Chicago as its CEO. Benjamin is the only black CEO of a pharmaceutical company in the United States.

Settled comfortably in a chair in his Hillview home, Sherman Crite, Jr. talked about growing up in the Rosenwald community. He and his wife Carolyn purchased the J.F.W. Mills grocery and operated a business there for about ten years. The couple stocked the store with staples and with grocery items as well as with a few radios and television sets. Crite enjoyed running a business that served as a gathering place for members of the community. While buying items on their grocery lists, the customers, mostly black, visited with one another. No one felt rushed to do business and leave. Crite identified extending credit as a problem for small grocery stores. "Sometimes you would be paid, and sometimes you wouldn't. It was always a risk" (interview, November 12, 2002). Eventually the Crites converted the store into apartments and continue to use them as investment property.

Religious leaders are also among the graduates of the Rosenwald Elementary School. National church leader and civil rights activist Thomas Kilgore, Jr. came to Brevard in 1925 when his family moved from Woodruff, South Carolina. One of the 12 children of Thomas and Eugenia Kilgore, he attended Rosenwald and graduated from the all-black Stephens Lee High School in Asheville. In 1935, he graduated from Morehouse College in Atlanta. He was ordained in Brevard by the Reverend A.H. Wilson and served as the assistant pastor at Bethel Baptist Church (Agnes Wilson, interview, October 13, 2002). A public school principal for three years, Kilgore headed the New Bethel Baptist Church in Asheville, North Carolina from 1936 to 1938. He served the Friendship Baptist Church of Winston-Salem and the Rising Star Baptist Church of Walnut Cove, North Carolina from the late 1930s to the mid–1940s. From 1941 to 1944, he was chaplain for Winston-Salem State Teachers College (Kilgore, 1998).

Later he was pastor of the Second Baptist Church in Los Angeles, California, which is the oldest black Baptist church in that city. Kilgore was elected president both of the American Baptist Churches, USA, and of the Progressive National Baptist Convention. From 1947 until 1963, the Reverend Kilgore served in the Friendship Baptist Church in New York, where he helped to raise bail money for the civil rights workers who had been incarcerated in the South. Kilgore helped to organize the 1963 march in Washington, D.C. (http://www.usc.edu/isd/publications/now/stories/66.html). From 1956 to 1988, nine honorary doctorates were conferred on him.

A lifetime member of the NAACP, Kilgore helped register voters and provide union opportunities for tobacco workers in Winston-Salem, North Carolina, in the 1940s. In 1957, he directed the Prayer Pilgrimage for Freedom in Washington, D.C. In April 1968, he organized a memorial service for

National civil rights leader and Rosenwald graduate Thomas Kilgore, Jr., was chaplain at Winston-Salem State Teachers College in the 1940s. Rosenwald teachers attended classes on the campus. (Courtesy Forsyth County Library Photograph Collection.)

Dr. Martin Luther King, Jr., and established Operation Unity as a means of preventing the outbreak of violence. He was the recipient of numerous awards, including the 1986 Distinguished Christian Service Award, the Guardian Angel Award, the Community Achievement Award, and the 1989 Nelson Mandela Humanitarian Award. A $200,000 endowed scholarship has been established in his honor at the University of Southern California, and the Thomas Kilgore Jr. Center has been dedicated at Morehouse College (Kilgore, 1998).

Another outstanding leader in religious service is Frederick L. Gordon, pastor of the Bethel "A" Baptist Church. Gordon's parents were Fred and Vinie Gordon, strong supporters of the Brevard Rosenwald School and two of the petitioners for the integration of local public schools. The oldest of seven children, Gordon majored in psychology at Western Carolina University and graduated from Shaw Divinity School magna cum laude. Since his conversion at age 14, he has been involved in the Christian ministry. At 16, Gordon participated in summer missionary programs sponsored by the Southern Baptist Convention of North Carolina. He spent summers in remote mountain areas where he conducted Vacation Bible Schools for African American children. In November 1970, he became an ordained minister. In 1972, he married Frankie M. Lewis of Waynesboro, Georgia. The couple parented eight children. One was their biological child, and they adopted four children and were foster parents of three others.

From 1965 until 1974, Gordon was Associate Pastor at Bethel "A" Church, and he returned there as pastor in 1992. Achievements in his pastorates include building programs, financial growth, and the development of outreach programs. Currently he could be compared to the CEO of a corporation because at Bethel "A" there are numerous outreach ministries, such as the multifaceted Neighbors in Ministry. The vital work of Neighbors in Ministry provides an intensive after-school program of tutoring and recreation for minority children. It enables children from low-income families to attend a nine-week summer day camp. In addition, the program sponsors forums and provides health screening and health education for the entire community. Programs of evangelism, foreign mission service, women's concerns, and programs for all school-age children exist. Gordon has also pastored churches in Black Mountain, North Carolina, and in Kingsport, Tennessee.

Regarded as an asset to Transylvania County, Gordon has served on more than 20 boards or committees, including the Task Force for Better Schools, SAFE (an organization providing shelter for abused individuals), Transylvania County Citizens Concerned for Children, Western Carolina Community Action, Inc., and the Ethics Committee of the Transylvania Community Hospital. Gordon is also a guest lecturer in Old Testament Studies at Brevard College. His willingness to serve has enriched the lives of many individuals.

From a small population, numerous individuals have achieved diverse levels of success. Mary Alice Wilkes Mooney was the first African American to enroll at Brevard College. Later she was hired at the Olin Corporation and worked there for 29 years before retiring in August 2002. "All of us at Rosenwald were successful in one way or another," she said.

F. Douglas Cantey, Mooney's cousin who served in the U. S. Army, is another Rosenwald alumnus and was the first African American to graduate from Brevard College. After graduating from Ninth Avenue School in 1959, Cantey first worked and saved money for college. He attended North Carolina College (now Central College) in Durham, for two semesters before his money ran out. He went to work again, this time at Brevard College, to save money for his education. Returning to school in Durham, Cantey used up his financial resources after only one semester. He dropped out for an extended period of time.

After serving in the United States Army, he enrolled part-time at Brevard College, planning to earn enough units to transfer as a junior. According to William Wynn, Jr., Cantey worked at DuPont on the second shift and attended classes during the day (interview). In 1973, Cantey graduated from UNC–Chapel Hill and went on to complete his law degree there.

Formerly a public defender, Cantey is senior assistant attorney for Charlotte. His wife, the former Minnie Davenport, also attended the Brevard Rosenwald School, where her mother Marie Davenport supervised food services. The couple has two sons, both college graduates. One is a writer, and the other works for the Federal Bureau of Investigation (interview).

Defining success is a complex chore. Parents, pastors, teachers, and community leaders all left their imprint on the children and youths of the Rosenwald community. Often the influence of individuals continues for generations. The lessons children learn at school and from their community affect not only their interaction with others but also their responses to challenges. Talent and intelligence play an intrinsic role in an individual's struggle to climb the ladder of success, but parental and community support is also a strong motivational force.

Alumni of the Brevard Rosenwald School learned the values of responsible employment, hard work, personal enrichment, and concern for others—values that outweigh other considerations, such as wealth. Rosenwald success stories offer colorful evidence that men and women who have known the cruelties of social and economic deprivation can overcome such circumstances. Their sense of achievement continues to empower them to help others.

Chapter 8

Revitalization of Community

REVITALIZATION HAS BEEN THE BUZZWORD in Brevard's City Council chambers. On December 17, 2001, Governor Michael F. Easley notified the councilmen that Brevard had been awarded a Community Development Block Grant (CDBG), which has a value of $1,750,000 to be allotted over a period of five years. Continued use of the money depends on evidence of improvement in the designated area of Brevard's West End, now commonly referred to as the Rosenwald community.

The city council invested time and energy to develop projects that would allow the citizens of this community to "play in the winner's circle" (*Focus 2020*, 2001). According to City Clerk Glenda Sansosti, the Land of the Sky Regional Council administered the project during its first year.

During the five-year period, according to pamphlets circulated by the city council, leaders will accomplish designated projects: Neighborhood Charette; Sidewalk, Landscaping, and Public Area Improvement; Community Development Corporation; Multi-Purpose Community Center and Park; Community Resource Guide; Health Services and Education Programs; Housing Rehabilitation Program; Condemn and Demolish Dilapidated Houses; Emergency Home Repair Program; Water and Sewer Improvements; Financial and Job Training Assistance; Incentives for Development and New Affordable Housing; Infrastructure Funding for New Affordable Housing; New Home Buyer Program; Home Maintenance Course; MicroEnterprise Program; Job Training Center; and Neighborhood Museum.

Citizens who live in the newly invigorated Rosenwald community have provided input into the plans for revitalization, and community members have been appointed to the Revitalization Advisory Committee. Others provide counsel and expertise as component champions and project coordinators. Each street has volunteer block leaders who keep neighbors informed about the status of the grant and recruit assistance as needed (*Focus 2020*, 2001). The total community has been drawn into revitalization plans.

Numerous organizations and individuals support the revitalization of Brevard's West End, including Blue Ridge Community College; Greg Walker-Wilson, executive director of Mountain MicroEnterprise Fund (which will assist in the establishment of small businesses); and Ben F. Ormand, a retired Presbyterian minister who served on the Board of Directors for the Mary C. Jenkins Community Center for eight years, and who was historically a friend of the African American community until his death in 2003.

Children will benefit from the renewed emphasis on assisting and expanding early education centers. The Hillview Children's Services Center is located on a 34-acre plot of land owned by Western Carolina Community Action, Inc., in the Rosenwald neighborhood. David White, WCCA's executive director, endorses the block grant program as a means to improve the economic situation of needy local families. Greg Young, executive director for the Boys and Girls Club of Transylvania County, points out the great need for additional space to house the program he directs. Currently Young's after-school program meets in the Mary C. Jenkins Community Center with about 25 students in attendance. Summer programs there have an enrollment of approximately 125 students.

The dilemma for the Boys and Girls Club is the shortage of space at the existing community center. The plan is to erect a new community center and to convert the current one into a museum. In addition, the construction of office space for public school administrators at the Transylvania Center of BRCC will permit a usage change of the Eugene Morris Education Center, which originally housed the 1948 Rosenwald school. The historic Rosenwald building will be restored to the Rosenwald community. Plans include the possibility of a community center that would help revitalize the neighborhood. Also, the building may showcase archives of African American life in Transylvania County.

On September 5, 2002, as part of the $1.7 million grant to improve the Rosenwald neighborhood, residents interested in becoming homeowners received information about how to enroll for assistance. The recruitment effort complied with the project's goals for the first year. Allowing interested residents to buy homes is a key component of the revitalization program. To give the neighborhood a facelift, dilapidated houses and businesses will be demolished to promote the construction of new buildings.

Circumstances have improved greatly for African Americans in Brevard and Transylvania County in the twentieth century. They now live in a world of integrated education and expanded opportunities in a rural community. But as African American citizens Rufus Norman and Valeria Gardin stated, much remains to be done. The Transylvania Citizens Improvement Organization (TCIO) continues to be unflinching in its resolve to obtain justice for black citizens. Celebrating its fortieth anniversary, the organization chose as its theme "Rosenwald School Remembered" with an assembly at the Eugene Morris Education Center as a kickoff point on July 1, 2000. Meeting at the site that housed the Brevard Rosenwald School from 1948 to 1966, former students and staff reveled in the day's activities. Marshall Erwin served as Master of Ceremonies as the audience sang "Lift Every Voice and Sing," the Negro national anthem, and the school song, "Oh Rosenwald." Ella Whitmire Jones summarized the history of the school with assistance from Nathaniel Hall.

Pictures of teachers marked the location of their former classrooms in the Morris Education Center. Those in attendance reminisced about their school days. Later, an historical tour stopped at sites of homes, stores, churches, cemeteries and other places that had been a vital part of daily life. Newspaper articles, mementos and pictures transformed the Mary C. Jenkins Community Center into a temporary museum. The experience reminded viewers of the days before civil rights legislation. Dorothy Mock, a white advocate of civil rights for all, described the activities as an effort for the TCIO to "retrace its steps from segregation to integration."

That evening, at Brevard College's Myers Dining Hall, president Judy Griffin led the TCIO in additional celebrations at the 40th Anniversary Awards Banquet. The Reverend Larry Harris of the Open Bible Church of God gave the invocation and the closing prayer. The event featured Larry Fortenberry's speech: "Without Vision, the People Perish." Linda and Rodney Locks and Dorothy Mock presented honorary awards.

The TCIO recognized its founding members, named courageous champions of civil rights. They included James Avery, Grady Elliott, Marie Davenport, Evon Kelley, Jimell Hall, Fannye Harris, Cornelia Howell, Cornelius Hunt, Mary B. Kilgore, Rockefeller Kilgore, Ruth Johnstone, Allie B. Mackey, Reesie Madison, Johnsie Lee Mills, Marjorie Moss, Jacob Norman, Samuel Raper, Selena Robinson, Walter Robinson, Wilkie Robinson, Maggie Scruggs, Evelyn Smith, Josephine Wynn, and Ulysses Wynn.

Seeds of revitalization, planted long before the announcement of the Block Grant in 2001, grew into major accomplishments of the TCIO. The earliest seeds germinated when the TCIO nurtured integration of public schools and equal access to Transylvania Community Hospital and to Ecusta's Camp Straus recreational facilities. In 1974, the organization negotiated the development of public housing for the African American community. In 1983, the group began an annual tradition of honoring the community's senior citizens. In 1988, the TCIO scholarship fund became a reality. In 1992, the group established the Cornelius Hunt Memorial Endowment. Later the

8. Revitalization of Community

A housing development now stands on the site of the original Brevard Rosenwald School. (Photograph by Juanita Spanogle.)

TCIO honored Ulysses Wynn, another former president, by establishing a scholarship bearing his name at Blue Ridge Community College. Strong leadership in the past and in the present has been an asset that continues to make the TCIO a thriving organization.

Almost 100 years later, the powerlessness reflected in Martha M. Slowe's 1909 announcement in *The Sylvan Valley News* would be totally inappropriate in today's newspaper. Slowe, who expressed hope that members of the Colored Domestic Science Club would become better citizens and servants, appealed to willing white friends to visit the class to share words of encouragement with her students. Now, despite the sharply curtailed employment market in Transylvania County, Brevard's African Americans frequently serve as administrative assistants or as executive directors of enterprises. A number who grew up in Brevard pursue professional careers elsewhere. As in all communities, African American individuals work in the service industry, but now they do so alongside Caucasians who are paid at the same rate. Economic progress is another factor that has stimulated the revitalization project.

Currently the African American presence in Brevard is routine. Transylvania County's African Americans serve on juries and participate in political activities. In 2002, Helen Kilgore Rout ran for a seat on the local board of education. Although unsuccessful, she made a respectable showing and has been encouraged to run again to become the first African American to serve on the Transylvania County Board of Education. In the early twentieth century rarely did African Americans find likenesses from their community in print. Today it is common to see photos of African Americans on the social page in the Brevard newspaper. Sports sections of local newspapers feature action shots of talented African American athletes and cheerleaders. During the 2002 homecoming at Brevard High School, a young African American, Cortney Conley, reigned as homecoming queen. Apparently youth now cast their votes without discrimination against a person of color.

Personal kindness has also been a behind-the-scenes part of the revitalization process. Former Brevard resident Mary Witmer Dawson was a white artist who drew Rosenwald School personalities. In the early 1990s, Dawson's niece, Louisa Cartledge, donated one of her aunt's works as a prize for the Fabulous Drawing to help establish the Cornelius Hunt Endowment. The prize was a portrait of Condry Sharp, the African American who owned a Carver Street boarding house and who had previously worked for the Witmer family. The lucky winner presented the portrait to the family of Condry Sharp (Annie Marie Hailey, interview, August 21 and 22, 2002).

As a result of a chance encounter, another of Dawson's charcoal portraits brought fulfillment to a former student of the Rosenwald School. As reported by Mark Todd (May 6, 1993) in *The Transylvania Times,* Cartledge saw Nellie H. Robinson at a Bethel "A" church service and was impressed by her striking resemblance to the woman in one of her aunt's portraits. When Nellie Robinson viewed the portrait, she did not recognize the individual. Later, Robinson showed the picture to her sister, Ida Hemphill Ellens, who recognized the subject immediately. It was a portrait of their mother, Rosie Mae Hemphill. Neighbor Marjorie Moss confirmed the identity. Hemphill had died when she was 47, leaving a nine-month-old baby, and no family photo of the mother existed. Robinson had often longed to know what her mother looked like. When Cartledge presented the portrait to her as a gift, Robinson's desire for a concrete image of her mother was at last fulfilled (Dorothy Mock, interview).

While memories of the past have stimulated revitalization efforts, newcomers have also helped expand the vision. Descendants of Transylvania County's original African American settlers reside in Brevard and Pisgah Forest, but other notable citizens have moved into the area. Two men, Larry Fortenberry and Rodney W. Locks, had an energizing effect on the black population. Although neither is a native of Transylvania County, the new residents focused their talents on supporting the community and worked shoulder to shoulder with "natives." Their attitude inspired the community to set new goals and to meet challenges.

Fortenberry, a quality services specialist for AGFA before he relocated to Raleigh in 2003, was the motivating force behind many TCIO activities. The organization's education committee chair, he delivered the keynote address at TCIO's fortieth anniversary celebration. In addition, Fortenberry chaired the Board of Directors of the Neighbors in Ministry program. Since 1994, that program has expanded from an outreach ministry of Bethel "A"

Baptist Church to an ecumenical program sponsored by the American Association of University Women, Bethel "A" Baptist Church, Bethel Baptist Church, Brevard–Davidson River Presbysterian Church, First United Methodist Church, Lutheran Church of the Good Shepherd, Sacred Heart Catholic Church, and St. Philip's Episcopal Church. Fortenberry led the organization in promoting the Damascus Road Anti-Racism Process, which seeks to combat racism through community education and planning. He frequently conducts workshops to heighten the awareness of community diversity.

Rodney Locks, who moved to Brevard in 1989 to work as senior systems engineer for the nearby Rosman Research Station, managed by the Department of Defense, drafted the proposal for the Revitalization Block Grant. After the Rosman Research Station was closed, Locks and his wife, Rosenwald alumna Linda Gash, moved to the United Kingdom, then returned to Brevard in the late 1990s. Locks was elected to the Brevard City Council and continues to exert his leadership in that position.

In his role as city councilman, Locks orchestrated efforts to secure a Community Development Block Grant to revitalize the predominantly African American neighborhood in Brevard. Now he supervises the Rosenwald project. A tireless civil servant, Councilman Locks has served on the boards of Kids in Camp, the Children's Center, the 4-H Advisory Council, the Shelter Available for Family Emergencies (SAFE), and the Transylvania Dispute Settlement Center, now called the Center for Dialogue. He has volunteered in the Neighbors in Ministry's Rise and Shine Program and in Brevard's public schools. Both he and his wife are active members of the TCIO. Each has served as president of that organization and supports all of its functions.

One of the goals of the revitalization project is a restoration of neighborhood vitality, including institutions that were community favorites. "I miss the neighborhood stores," resident Thomas Gardin said. He described shops where a resident could buy crackers, candy, and a soda while visiting with other customers. "The area needs a new community center that can serve the needs of adults as well as children and young people," said Mary Cowal, a supportive friend of the African American community. With the completion of the Rosenwald Revitalization program, both Gardin's and Cowal's wishes may become a reality. The plan calls for opening new stores and a new community center.

At a special celebration of Black History Month at the Mary C. Jenkins Community Center on February 23, 2003, Rodney Locks presented an update of the project and announced that the next segment of funds had been approved. Locks also contended that racism still exists in Brevard, and creates a situation in which the black community continually struggles to overcome low expectations. Locks pointed out that the city has 911 registered black voters, and encouraged the black community to vote and to concentrate on closing the gap between blacks and whites in education. He urged citizens to continue to pressure the school system to meet the needs of African American students. Outside organizations, like the Boys and Girls Club, supplement the school system by providing after-school programs.

The Brevard City Council offers opportunities for home ownership through the CDBG project as one means of revitalizing the African American community. Locks said that nine individuals have had applications for purchasing homes approved and that 14 have been approved for assistance with home repairs. To train entrepreneurs to establish small businesses, the city council sponsored three classes with 16 students attending. A new eatery, Soul Food Restaurant, has opened its doors near Greasy Corner. The construction of a new playground is another revitalization project. According to Locks, Helen Kilgore Rout has been gathering information to determine what features the community would like in its new play area.

In October 2002 Ethel K. Mills discussed early childhood education with Ida Ellens and Juanita Spanogle. At the age of 102, Mills still believes "that you can't beat the devil out of a child, but ... you can sure beat it into him." (Photograph by Juanita Spanogle.)

A revitalization grant is not a magic wand that one waves over a community, instantly wiping out all scars of the past. Although integration is a fact of life, residential segregation exists. Often African Americans prefer the comfort of the old neighborhood, with its memories and traditions. While African Americans reside throughout Transylvania County, the majority live in the southwest area of Brevard, on the streets that hosted their historical educational centers: the Johnstone School, the Colored Industrial School, Brevard #2 Colored School, and the Brevard Rosenwald School. That section also housed the historical black churches of the area, with the exceptions of the French Broad and the Glade Creek Baptist churches.

The revitalization grant functions within the framework of a strong historical foundation underlying the Rosenwald community. In North Carolina and throughout the South, Rosenwald provided architectural assistance by supplying seed money to encourage school construction and renovation. Rosenwald funds were awarded only to communities willing and able to invest their own money in the project, which showed an awareness of the importance of intellectual achievement to the black population. Like their white counterparts, African Americans viewed education as a panacea for healing the wounds of economic and social deprivation. Willingly, parents sacrificed to provide schools for their offspring. Empowering the weak through expanding educational opportunities was a significant means of building a stronger community.

Decades after the Rosenwald name disappeared from the historical Brevard school, via a decision of white leaders, former students testify to the positive influence of interaction at the Rosenwald School. Instructors were role models, and prodded their students to achieve success. Former pupils regret that they did not realize the true worth of those professionals until many years after they were in their classes. Middle-aged adults and senior citizens praised their former teachers' dedication, intelligence, and character. Stories recounted the kindness of Synetha Benjamin, the humor of Paul Hunter, the encouraging comments of Robert Duncan, the sweet spirit of Mary E. Bolden, the willingness of Gertie Hemphill to allow fun in the midst of learning, and the monetary gifts of Ethel Mills to needy children. When people think of revitalization, they think of contributions from the Rosenwald community that resulted in a life-changing atmosphere, not simply a landscape-dominating structure.

Revitalization means more than a return of the monuments of the past. For residents, it builds on the strength, courage, and compassion of their elementary school teachers. As a symbol of their belief in the leader's ideals, the congregation of Bethel "A" created the Ethel K. Mills Citizenship Award in honor of the former principal/teacher.

Revitalization should also mean more than nostalgia, and should include recognition that not everything was ideal. Racism resulted in unequal treatment that continually hurt the school, and not every member of the faculty excelled professionally. N.A. Miller, who served as Director of Instruction prior to becoming principal at Brevard Senior High School, observed teachers in action at the Rosenwald School. "Some teachers were okay, and some weren't. Attendance was always the big problem, and records weren't always accurate" (interview).

Revitalization should also recognize the abstracts that were important. Instructional quality was essential, but even more important was encouragement, a key component found in the homes and in the churches of the school

community. By uniting efforts, ordinary people exerted an amazing power to transform Brevard, North Carolina into a community of equality — and that spirit of collaboration is an important aspect of the Rosenwald legacy. The current attempts to rejuvenate the community will preserve pride in its history, in its traditions, and in its accomplishments.

In the first half of the twentieth century, the "colored school" also functioned as a community center. For black southerners, it was necessary to recruit or to create their own entertainment, so community programs took place at the segregated school. In Brevard, Mary B. Kilgore's visionary concept led to the creation of the Mary C. Jenkins Community Center as a complementary site to the school's stage area in its cafeteria. With encouragement from white supporters, interested black citizens raised funds, and the Center opened in 1953.

In the April 26, 1966, edition of *The Transylvania Times*, Kilgore presented a progress report detailing activities at the center. Robroy Farquhar, founder of the Flat Rock Playhouse, coached a children's theatrical group. Young people practiced at the center to participate in the Sylvan Valley Festival. Rosenwald students in the group included Carolyn Harris, Edith Hutchison, Ethel Ann Hemphill, Mamie Hall, Clifford Outlaw, Gloria Brooks, Everett Adams, Maxine Robinson, Agnes Lynch, John Rosemond, Harlan Hutchison, Shirley Wilkes, Norma Hunt, Joyce Gash, Maxine Benjamin, Betty Hunt, Laura Smith, and LaMuriel Brooks. The theater project shows that a large number of school children are served by a neighborhood community center, demonstrating the importance of such a facility.

The Allen School Choir and the Stephens Lee Orchestra performed at the center. In addition, the building was a site for young people to square dance and to clog. With a dreamy look in her eyes, Lois Elliott Wynn recalled dancing into the wee hours at the Mary C. Jenkins Community Center to the music of the Tams, a local group composed of Brevard Rosenwald School students who had gained widespread recognition in the 1950s and the 1960s. "Their music was just wonderful! And it only cost 50 cents or a dollar to get in" (Lois Wynn, interview, December 17, 2002). The center also showcased sports events, such as wrestling matches and donkey ball games.

Though the center was independent of the school, it functioned as an

Opposite: Kindergarten classes assembled at the Mary C. Jenkins Community Center. Teachers are (left) Josephine Wynn and (right) Juanita Hutchison. First row, left to right: Brandon Crite, Timmy Madison, Rudy Norman, William Mills, Eric Crite, Richard Kilgore, Brad Wynn, Ronald Norman, James Smith, and John Hemphill. Second row, left to right: Jennifer Sanders, Michelle Hemphill, Rhonda Moore, Nyoka Smith, Karen Blocker, Michelle Norman, Justine Conley, Laura Gardin, Alma Norman, Stephanie Sanders, Francine Mills, LaTonya Moore, Sylvia Smith, and Frenchie Hutchison. (Courtesy Patricia Austin and Eric Crite.)

adjunct that stimulated excitement for the community. The spirit of enthusiasm within the community is something that citizens long to restore, and it is one way they would like the block grant to enrich their lives.

In addition to community experiences, community facilities also disappeared, leaving another hole in the community. For years there was a swimming pool at the center, but Selena Robinson said it had to be closed because of maintenance expenses. State health requirements overburdened the community council for black citizens. Robinson remembered that Cornelius Hunt suggested swimmers use the pool at Franklin Park in the white community. The proposal met with opposition, but the conflict was eventually resolved (interview, December 6, 2002).

Though the swimming pool closed, a neighborhood playground opened with assistance from a white friend, Dorothy Silversteen Bjerg. The Silversteen Memorial Park provided busy parents a nearby spot for their children to play on swings, in sandboxes, and on sliding boards. At that time the playground filled a great need, but the area has deteriorated. With funds from the revitalization project, better playgrounds will be built. In addition, recreation projects and programs will be provided for all ages. Newly paved streets and sidewalks, also paid for by CDBG funds, will make travel safer within the community.

Towering historically above the houses of local blacks, the Brevard Rosenwald School illustrates the power of Julius Rosenwald. It is a power that extends from the erection of a school building to the dynamic of a lifestyle that supports both education and entertainment. It is a power that transforms both the streets and the spirits. And still today, the Rosenwald image causes the black community to long for something more vital than opportunities in an integrated school. It is a power that causes people to discern the relationship of advantages to the attainment of results. It is an enriching power that creates newborn dreams via the Community Development Block Grant.

The Rosenwald Fund casts its shadow on a grant process that revisits the idea of sharing funds. Rosenwald's wealth enabled him to endow aspiring communities with lasting educational resources. His power, though, did not lie in generous donations of money. Wisely, Rosenwald sponsored innovation only in communities willing to collaborate in school construction. His practice challenged the African American population to raise money, to volunteer labor, and to enlist the assistance of the white community. The improved school facility was not a gift. Rather, it was an achievement in which each citizen could take pride.

A tradition of involvement continues to stimulate action in the Brevard community. Town citizens, a combination of black and white leaders, generated a proposal for a block grant. State officials responded positively to the idea of building for the next century by capitalizing on the deeds of the past century. Now leaders work together to achieve the dreams initiated by the block grant. Residents remember the past, but they anticipate the future. They yearn for an ongoing Rosenwald mindset to achieve educational, social, and economic results, and they want the ideas espoused by Julius Rosenwald to continue to shape the profile of the community, one where all can enjoy life equally.

Chapter 9

Contributions to Education

No LONGER DOES A "COLORED TOWN" hide in the western corner of Brevard, now an active town attracting retirees and families who want to raise their children in a secure environment. But the area is still a hub, one that thrives because a school was once the center of life in the neighborhood and because residents both experience participation without limitations and anticipate improvements that will cement the quality of life in their mountain suburb.

Change has permanently transformed the landscape in Brevard. The Rosenwald community extends into the ranks of the white world in the twenty-first century through interracial partnerships and marriages. Work sites are integrated. Restaurants and movie theaters practice open access. Water fountains are unrestricted. The Transylvania County Public Library is a public-access building. No flaming Ku Klux Klan crosses terrorize the community. Advocates of segregation may still dwell in Transylvania County, but their voices have been muted.

Admittedly, there are still moments of discomfort and sneak attacks that threaten the stability brought about by positive changes. There have been complaints of inequitable treatment in recent years, including complaints about the slim ratio of black teachers in the public schools. Twice the Ku Klux Klan has marched publicly on the streets of Brevard. Members of the African American community objected to Marion "Mal" Crite's dismissal from the public school system. White versus black is not a prevalent issue, but racial disagreements do arise.

Although unnoticed by Brevard's famous white squirrels, the permanence of progress now colors the town. The history of the Brevard Rosenwald School and its precursors, educational institutions serving the black children of an Appalachian county in western North Carolina, extends back for more than a century. From well before 1910, the school influenced the present via its influence on former students and staff. Its impact continues even though the school was officially closed in 1966, when Transylvania County complied with the 1964 Civil Rights Act.

That year, 1966, also marked the end of the Pearsall Plan, ratified in 1956, which had empowered local boards of education to control the enrollment and assignment of children in public schools. A delaying tactic, the plan also proposed vouchers to provide private schooling for students who preferred not to attend an integrated school. The Pearsall Plan was ruled unconstitutional as a result of the federal Civil Rights Act of 1964 (http://www.dpi.state.nc.us/State_Board_history/chapter 3.html). In 1965 Brevard teachers were told that, if they were unwilling to teach integrated classes, their resignations would be accepted.

Efforts to educate black children of the region are a part of the Rosenwald heritage. Julius Rosenwald himself is a part of their chronicle. His contributions to building improvement were honored by the school family. On occasion lessons focused on his accomplishments. Philanthropy, civil rights movements, and court decisions influenced the classroom and the community. One vital element in the black child's education was the auxiliary support provided in homes where parents viewed scholastic success as a way to improve the quality of life.

Glaring inequities existed between the educational options for blacks and whites. Racial discrimination was an accepted fact of life throughout most of the twentieth century for the residents of Brevard, North Carolina. Asked if she recalled having felt the pain of segregation, Brenda Elliott responded, "When all you know is one way, it's hard to say I felt the pain. Segregation was what it was. I hardly had any contact with the white populace of Transylvania County or the surrounding counties of western North Carolina" (questionnaire, August 2002). When Dennis Robinson was asked if he had trouble getting a permit to keep his Brevard restaurant open, he responded, "No, the problem was getting the white customers to eat in a black-owned establishment. They simply weren't willing, and that was in the nineties" (interview, December 27, 2002).

Thomas Gardin first experienced an integrated society when he joined the army, which, he explained, had banned segregation as a result of Harry S Truman's 1947 creation of the President's Committee on Civil Rights. The Truman committee's denouncement of racism led to desegregation of the armed forces (http://examiner.net/stories/o30102/new_030102009.shtml).

Historical accounts frequently record neglect and indifference by the white community and document the struggle by black students to secure their rights under the Constitution. Supreme Court decisions of the 1950s and

1960s brought a remarkable period of change and turmoil to the mountain communities of western North Carolina. Negro citizens were no longer content with their status as less than equal, and their ability to create a united front, unflinching in the demand for justice, led to major victories over racial discrimination. White resistance did not include bombings or fires, but scare tactics were used. Pressure kept some sympathetic whites from publicly voicing personal convictions. At times both whites and blacks felt maintaining two separate worlds was better than the agony of building a new one.

Joyce Owens referred to that dilemma as a "fear of changing worlds" (interview, September 26, 2002). A teacher during the early stages of integration, Owens described her experience with segregation as the norm of daily life as she grew up in Tifton, Georgia. She remembered a growing realization that discrimination was wrong. At her orchid warehouse, Owens employed both whites and blacks. "I was feeding the white teenagers who worked for us, but the black men went home for lunch. Well, when I found out that one fellow was going to Pisgah Forest to drop off one worker and then driving to Brevard to eat and then back to Pisgah Forest to pick him up and then here to work, I decided that was ridiculous. If I could feed those white boys, I could fix lunch for those two men — and I did. I set two tables, one outside and one inside. I didn't tell them where to sit, but the black men sat out on the carport. All I had ever known was segregation. You see, I had to change my point of view." Her eyes moistened as she recalled this moment of enlightenment.

Pride in the Brevard Rosenwald School surged to new heights when its existence as an African American school ceased. Pride in the Rosenwald students was bolstered by their courage in confronting the white population of the integrated public schools and by their successes in that foreign arena. Initially there was little social interaction between the two races. It was only natural for students to sit with their friends and to interact with them. But as time passed, that changed. White students came to enjoy the songs performed by black students during breaks in the school day. The whites asked their teacher to allow the singing to take place more often (Joyce Owens, interview, September 26, 2002).

Not only did whites notice the musical talent of their new classmates, but also they quickly became aware of athletic talent. Robbie Gardin recalls that her daughter Ruby played basketball at Brevard High School and that the white players came by the Gardin home to pick up their teammate. "They all loved my daughter," she said (interview, August 21, 2002).

Moving into the white schools did not necessarily improve the quality of learning for African Americans. Although the educational process may be enhanced by a fine structure, a school is not simply a building. The school is a community of teachers and learners, supported by parents. Their relationships create the school and impact the quality of education. If efforts are successful, the joy of learning emanates from interaction within the scholastic community. In their classes at Rosenwald, many students had acquired a strong educational foundation.

The Brevard Rosenwald School extended beyond walls, floors, ceilings, and a roof. The school was greater than the buildings where classes were conducted. It permeated the homes and families of the school's pupils, teachers, and employees. Far greater than the sum of its buildings and books, the school was a pervasive spirit that emanated from the schoolyard to the greater community. Eventually that spirit also became a force of enrichment for the white community.

The history of the educational experience for Rosenwald students was reflected throughout the nation in the inequities of the black educational experience. The Brevard community did not place Negro education on the same level as that for white students. Perhaps the practice was not intended to dishonor the humanity of black neighbors out of a sense of hostility, hatred, or cruelty. Certainly, though, tradition and blindness to the dictates of discrimination played a role. The small size of the black student population magnified the difficulties of dealing with student needs in a separate school system.

Dual systems created unnecessary financial demands, and the budget often sidestepped the needs of black schools. Had racial prejudice been less prevalent, economic wisdom would have dictated merging the schools. However, in the minds of segregation proponents, viewing blacks as inferior lent legitimacy to separate schools. The experiences of black residents indicate that the white community in Brevard had been well indoctrinated with attitudes of white supremacy.

Rosenwald students intent on integrating the white high school did not require the escort of armed guards and no one was forced to hide out in other states to avoid the threat of violence due to integration. No doubt a great deal of hostility existed in Transylvania County in the 1960s, but time has allowed those negative memories to fade.

As indicated by Samuel Raper, there were exceptions to racial prejudice among the white populace in Transylvania County. Nathaniel Hall played with whites, and so did others. Nell Ashworth's son, Donald, loved his African American neighbor, Zeb Hemphill, affectionately calling him "Uncle Remus." N.A. Miller grew up playing with his friend Fred Mills. David Price viewed his black playmates as best friends. However, not one indicated that the relationship continued into adulthood.

An analysis of the school's history raises these questions: What was the Brevard Rosenwald School like? How can it be best described? A description of the physical setting of the school can be derived from deeds and the minutes of the board of education, and, more importantly, from the memories and comments of the staff and alumni. A frame structure was built to supplement space in the home of Wilkie C. Johnstone, who conducted classes to train black women in domestic skills. The structure was renovated with money provided from the Rosenwald Fund. When the frame building burned, two Baptist churches and one Methodist church allowed the school to assemble in basements and in an annex.

In 1948, a stone building with six classrooms, a library, an office, and a cafeteria became the home of the Brevard Rosenwald School. The school stood at the latter site until its 1966 closing, once the children were allowed to attend formerly all-white schools.

The atmosphere of the school varied with leadership and personnel, some outstanding and some mediocre. A number of men served at the school for a short period of time. Mills thinks higher earnings lured them to North Carolina rather than to South Carolina. Often male teachers were ministers, who could be called away to comfort the seriously ill or to conduct a funeral. Conflicting demands of two professions resulted in absenteeism. In some classrooms, children felt encouraged, challenged, and supported. In others, students struggled because they felt that the teacher was indifferent. As in all schools, some teachers were disliked. Nevertheless, the staff sought training to improve their pedagogical skills and drilled children in basic skills of reading, writing, and arithmetic.

A dominant force effectively serving the educational needs of Rosenwald children was the combined energy of Johnstone, Mills, Hemphill, and Benjamin. During a period of more than four decades, those teachers conveyed the message that they believed in children. "I thought Mrs. Johnstone was mean because she had such high standards," Sherman Crite, Jr. said. "She was tough. It took years for me to realize she was a powerful teacher. She was really good" (interview). When Synetha Glenn Benjamin allowed "time out," girls could crochet, knit, or sew. Those influential teachers nurtured joy in learning. Other instructors, such as Hailey, Duncan, Baten, Bolden, McLaughlin, Hunter, Smith, and Coragreene Johnstone, also provided happy learning experiences for students. Julia Smith and James R. Baten fostered their love of music.

Students were trained in academics, in speech, and in music. There was a great deal of memorization and recitation, but instruction also required learners to express themselves. In 2002, at the Transylvania County Public Library, Winona Smith Whiteside recited with vigor and animation poetry that she learned in the 1930s to the delight of her audience. In December 2002, on a hospital bed recovering from a hip fracture, she recited "A Psalm of Life." Memorizing that poem may have been a chore at the time, but it has enriched her life and the lives of those with whom she shared those passages.

Classes combining grade levels were the norm, and students learned from their older peers. Recess—big recess—was a time for play and socialization. Teachers such as Hunter and Duncan organized competitive recreation. Principals Javan L. Jones and Mack Dawkins practiced with students to prepare them for competition with other schools. While playing ball or hopscotch, gathering plants and flowers, playing imaginary games about Indian spirits that haunted the Mounds, dancing around the Maypole, or jumping rope, the children formed alliances with one another that continued as lifelong friendships.

Socialization led to lifetime business, professional, and civic partnerships, as evidenced by alumni who remain active in the Transylvania Citizens Improvement Organization as well as by ministers, by public school teachers, and by industrial supervisors. The Brevard Rosenwald School was a place of learning and of celebrating one's identity. No second-class citizens lived in their community. Whether the physical facilities were the dilapidated frame structure or the temporary quarters found in church basements or the stone building, the community celebrated its glory by gathering for graduations, for operettas, for seasonal plays, or for May Day festivities. Students were allowed to speak, to sing, to act, and to strut across the stage to gather awards for regular attendance, for good citizenship, and for superior academic achievement. Community celebration prevailed over the stigma of segregation.

Unfortunately, the Rosenwald School can also be described as a place where resentment emerged—resentment that extends into the present time. Ill feeling arose from the realization that the school was inadequately financed and poorly supported. Staff, students, and parents identified deficient resources. Deep resentment resulted from the realization that new materials went to the whites, and tattered, worn-out equipment was passed on to the Rosenwald School. The lack of a high school caused bitterness. It was difficult to understand the tremendous lack of support from the white community.

Although the Rosenwald School was the site of festering resentments, it was also a place of satisfaction. School traditions involved the total black community. Events were anticipated with eager excitement, and lives were impacted in a positive way. Ordinary school days were crowned with a blaze of anticipation of special events. Even spelling bees and recess competition kindled excitement. The freedom of lunchtime was also cheerful, whether sustenance consisted of pinto beans and cornbread carried to school in a lard bucket or a scoop of peanut butter and saltines purchased at Jip Mills' store by sharing coins with a friend. Caring people, such as the cafeteria workers, the grade mothers, and the Reverend Freeman Daugherty added surprises. Heating water for hot tea or warming up soup on a pot-bellied stove lent a feeling of coziness on a wintry day. The school, enriched by traditions, was the scene of happy occasions.

The Brevard Rosenwald School was also an institution that functioned without the complete support of its governing body. Conflicting accounts exist about the role of the board of education. Staff members credited the board with providing to the best of its ability, but citizens charged that the board treated the Rosenwald community indifferently. Stories of "Jim Crow-ism" surface, but so do accounts of support by white friends.

The white community is blamed for the demise of the Rosenwald School, but the black community's lack of foresight also contributed to the school's closing. The campaign to win access to all-white schools blinded faculty and parents to the impact on the existing facility. Winning the battle for integration did not resolve resentments harbored in the recesses of hearts damaged by discrimination. Only time could heal those wounds, but in the new arena of integrated schools opportunities to excel academically, socially, athletically, and psychologically allowed new strength and growth.

How effective were the integrated schools in meeting the needs of their clientele? Many intangible factors must be considered, making it difficult to measure a school's effectiveness, but many Rosenwald graduates excelled. Students entered integrated schools with the expectation that they had to learn in order to be promoted, and parents continued to encourage their children to rise above the restrictions of poverty. Despite the supportive climate at Rosenwald, some students failed to measure up to academic expectations in their new environment. No one denies that, as is true of most schools, some of the unsuccessful joined the ranks of the unemployed or the addicted.

Graduates of both segregated and integrated Brevard schools have achieved outstanding success. Two are university administrators. One is an attorney. Many are successfully involved in religion and in education. Rosenwald alumni were equipped to make a contribution to society. Agnes Wilson transports her sister three times weekly for dialysis treatments. Audrey Hutchison cared for her mother while she was recuperating from hip replacement. Hutchison also supplies support for the daughter of Mable K. Armstrong. Reesie Madison tenderly cared for her husband until his death. The willingness of Rosenwald residents to expend energy on behalf of family members reflects the community's emphasis on being caring, compassionate citizens.

Although some former Rosenwald students are now members of the retired community, they participate in community events and continue to pursue learning. Those who are members of the working community are also involved in planning activities for clubs and other groups.

The Rosenwald experience encouraged moral and spiritual development, and involvement in church activities energized the community. Educational experiences and encouragement from their homes have enabled Rosenwald students to work, to play, and to live successfully in an integrated society.

The Brevard Rosenwald School encouraged mastery of learning and emphasized music, celebration, and tradition. Nevertheless, black citizens eventually dared to vent their bitterness against inequities and injustices in the educational system of Transylvania County. Their growing thirst for equal access to better school facilities motivated them. Because of their orientation at the Rosenwald institution, they had the conviction that they deserved the same access to better schools as white citizens. Their actions in the courtrooms during the 1950s and 1960s grew out of the self-worth instilled in them. They knew that morality should also be defined as equality.

Alumni testify that the lessons of their school days continue to influence internal monitoring during their adult years. The revelation suggests the value of positive educational experiences on the elementary level for all students—the homeless, the migrants, the legal residents, the psychologically and learning impaired, the physically challenged. Via its nurturing atmosphere, the Rosenwald School honored individual identities and was effective in the lives of students, but the influence of individuals was also crucial. The record clearly validates the important role of teachers and their never-ending influence in the lives of students. Five decades later former students recall with emotion those instructors who encouraged and supported their efforts and with equal clarity those who discouraged and hindered their growth.

Of equal importance, based on the history of the Brevard Rosenwald School, is the "triangulation" of school, home, and church. Education appears most effective when the total community values and supports it. A true partnership among home, school, and church existed in the Rosenwald community. Identity was enhanced when individuals were honored and recognized in their neighborhoods and when their accomplishments, even mishaps, were recognized and considered worthy of compassion. Alumni fondly recall their scholastic heritage and the successes of other Rosenwald students. Now school improvement teams, which include parents, students, business leaders, and educators from all levels, show an awareness of the importance of school support by an entire community.

Despite the nurturing environment, students still remember the unpleasant. Some recalled acts of injustice and indiscreet adult behavior. Though it is natural to suppress negative experiences and images, stories emerged about child abuse and neglect in the black community. Individuals outside the family circle made a difference for children via encouragement and support. Conflict existed. Bliss was not the constant state of the Brevard African American populace. Teachers were criticized and challenged, as they are in today's schools. Nor did widespread prejudice deter all whites from becoming involved in positive ways with Rosenwald "players."

Despite the struggles and hardships associated with them, students can benefit from small, community-directed, simple educational environments.

Charter schools and alternative schools may be modern attempts to recreate supportive atmospheres of the past. However, within large impersonal public schools, particularly on the secondary level, beneficial environments can exist as schools within schools. Interest groups, such as drama clubs, publication staffs, student councils, musical groups, and athletic teams, may enhance individual identities and produce feelings of self-worth. Involvement in dynamic school enterprises motivates success at all levels. Participation can bond staff, students, and parents as well as provide insulation against destructive forces of society.

At Rosenwald, traditions served as an enriching and unifying force. Today's elementary school leaders should continue to sponsor special events, such as field days, public programs, intramural athletic competition, and graduation ceremonies. At Rosenwald, sports were important to the students despite lack of finances, uniforms, equipment, and regulation-size fields. Also, expectation of performance before their classmates alleviated anxiety about public participation. Distress existed among Rosenwald students, but they learned to participate rather than to avoid the experience.

Transylvania County's black populace won its civil rights battle, but victory required perseverance and patience. Opposition tactics discouraged them, but parents persisted and claimed their children's right to the same educational facilities and opportunities as their white counterparts.

However, resentments still smolder. The Rosenwald building no longer bears the name of its benefactor. Ironically, it was renamed in honor of Eugene M. Morris, a former board of education member who consistently voted against assigning Negro graduates of the Brevard Rosenwald School to Brevard Senior High School. By changing the school's name, the dignity of past efforts to educate children at that site has been ignored. It is as though the Brevard Rosenwald School never existed. The deletion of a historical record does not equal the deletion of a memory. Rather, the deletion is an insult.

Unanimous school board action had prolonged the drudgery and the hardship of forcing African Americans to leave Transylvania County to obtain a high school education. Discrimination, as reflected in the mandate, repressed the achievements of blacks.

W.E.B. Du Bois identified the needs of black elementary schools in the South as mastery of basic subjects, adequate finances and resources, adequate time invested in schooling, and quarters that are morally and physically suited to the task of learning, as well as strong leadership, well-trained personnel, principals with executive ability, superintendents willing to invest money and effort in schools that are controlled by parents, and a population willing to support school improvements. Finances and resources were a primary need of elementary schools for Negro children, and blatant inequities existed in the Transylvania County school system.

9. CONTRIBUTIONS TO EDUCATION

As evidenced by the comparison of the 1948-49 principals' reports of Sartor and Patton, the black school's needs were not a primary concern of those who had the power to make a difference. A small item, such as a full-length mirror, was totally absent at Rosenwald, but in the nine classrooms at the all-white Pisgah Forest School, there were 10 mirrors. Access to mirrors could have enhanced the self-esteem of Rosenwald students. Another shortcoming was the lack of books in the school's library. At a time when the state was stressing the importance of improving rural school libraries, a school with fewer than the designated 500 volumes indicates disregard for learning. Resources and finances appeared minimal for the black school. The white elementary school at Pisgah Forest had more than 1,000 volumes, which were supplemented by magazines.

For seven years, Rosenwald classes assembled in churches. That arrangement, though during a time of war, was unusually long. School board minutes recorded the need to build immediately on two occasions, years apart, but no reasons for the delay were documented. A grand jury had also urged immediate construction, as cited by Nathaniel Hall (1984). However, the greatest inequity was the failure to provide a high school within the county for Rosenwald's students.

During the 1920s and 1930s, minimal efforts to provide schooling beyond the elementary level took place in the "big room" at Rosenwald. Only with concerted effort and with the decision of the courts, nationally and regionally, did the black students gain access to secondary education in their own community. A scrutiny of schools in other southern communities attests to the practice of busing Negro students beyond their communities to perpetuate schooling in all-black facilities. Transylvania County was simply practicing the philosophy, then prevalent, that separate schools were best for both races.

In the Rosenwald experience the Ninth Avenue School in Hendersonville provided an extension of the local school family because, as one source indicated, "I had my Rosenwald team there" (Alice Glaze Robinson, interview, February 25, 2000). However, a struggle was required to maintain a sense of identity because Rosenwald students felt alienated among Henderson County students. The lack of financial resources to build an extension at Rosenwald for secondary school students was a handicap.

Du Bois' comments about personnel are also an accurate assessment of a major flaw in elementary schools. During the school's more than half-century existence, outstanding educators worked there, but not every teacher employed during the school's history was qualified. Some had never attended college. Some held sub-standard certificates. Some taught only a short time until another offer lured them away. However, the prevailing memory is of the dedicated teachers who enriched the lives of their students.

Noted educator Ethel K. Mills (right) shares a laugh with friend Betty J. Reed. (Photograph by David A. Reed.)

For 18 years a woman, Ethel K. Mills, served as the interim principal. The "interim" designation, which lasted an inordinately long time, raises pertinent questions: Would an interim appointment of that length have been acceptable in a white school and for white personnel? Was it easier for the board of education to interact with a woman in that role than it would have been with a man? Were racial and gender issues involved? Was Mills kept in her position as principal because her style of leadership was non-confrontational? She espoused the view that the community rushed into the battle for desegregation. Did she possess agility in avoiding race issues? Mills handled matters in the school, the primary domain of her responsibility. However, the board of education may have employed her as interim principal to reduce their commitment to the school.

Du Bois deplored "quarters ill-suited physically and morally to the work in hand" in which Negro children were educated (1973, p. 107). The three Rosenwald environments—a frame structure, church facilities, and a stone structure—poignantly illustrate the educator's criticism. Good will, though supportive and nurturing, cannot adequately compensate for a lack of vision, equipment, and textbooks. Faculty emphasized the intellectual and psychological environment rather than the physical limitations, but they could never function as well as they could have had there been adequate resources.

Leaders at the county level were neither ethically compelled nor apparently financially able to expend "funds, thoughts, and efforts" on behalf of Transylvania County's Negro school. The inaction raises more questions: Would the board of education have allowed white children to be schooled in church basements for seven years? Would they have allowed the opening of an all-white school without providing furniture? The answers are obvious. Also, it is difficult to imagine county school administrators so carefree about one of their major responsibilities that attending public Rosenwald events was a rarity. Even more amazing is that a school burned and was completely destroyed without the superintendent being promptly notified. The process of gradual integration rates as simply another delay tactic.

Du Bois' contentions have continuing significance. Conclusions, however, must be tempered with the knowledge that Appalachian schools were poor, understaffed, and without adequate learning materials.

Nevertheless, schools for black children were poorer, grossly understaffed, and functioned with meager, outdated learning materials. Inadequate twentieth century efforts to educate Negro children implied a need for affirmative action programs and policies. Such programs and policies were long overdue. Some Negroes who graduated from high schools received financial aid to attend black colleges. However, those unable to complete or to go beyond elementary school were consumed with the hopelessness of a never-ending cycle of poverty. The statistics of African Americans incarcerated in American prisons are alarming. Deprivation hinders educational progress, whether among whites, blacks, Hispanics, Asians, or Native Americans. Equal educational standards on the elementary level are a primary place to start changing lives.

Schools were integrated, but does Brevard have integrated achievement? Have communities and schools given minority students the support essential to make higher achievement possible after years and decades and centuries of neglect? Does the need for affirmative action remain? Are needs of diverse groups being addressed in the public schools? The Brevard Rosenwald School was a microcosm, and a look at its history enlightens any discussion of these issues that adds personal and factual insight.

White indifference to the Rosenwald heritage will be assuaged in part by the erection of a historical marker at the corner of Rosenwald Lane and West Main Street in Brevard, North Carolina. A plaque on the wall of the Eugene M. Morris Education Center honoring the lifework of Ethel K. Mills, Wilkie C. Johnstone, Gertie M. Hemphill, Synetha G. Benjamin and other Rosenwald educators would alleviate some of the outrage that has lingered since the day the building ceased to be a school.

Superintendent Terry Holliday, at the request of white and black members of the community, appointed a committee to explore the possibility of erecting a historical marker. Members of the committee were Rodney Locks, Audrey Hutchison, Carl Mooney, Jr., Selena Robinson, Larry Fortenberry, Nathaniel Hall, William Robertson, James Outlaw, Barbara Conley, Amanda L. Blosser, and Betty J. Reed. Their efforts were successful, and a marker is scheduled to honor the history of the Brevard Rosenwald School.

The Rosenwald experience was a happy and productive one despite inequities and inequalities. History paints a picture of children walking eagerly to school and being joined by other children en route, climbing the hill to reach Rosenwald in all kinds of weather and being taught in an environment of respect, encouragement, discipline, and high expectations. A vital part of this picture is that the parents urged their children to learn and to respect all opportunities for an education. Whether it was earning a merit badge for Scouts or caning a chair, the acquisition of new knowledge broadened the child's educational experience.

Du Bois' insight into the basic problem of Negro education and his solutions merit applause. The problem was the ineffectiveness of the elementary schools, and the solution was simply to improve those schools. From methodology and motivation to insights and conclusion, the guiding words of Du Bois' philosophy shine as a clear light for examining educational accomplishments and aspirations, whether in the integrated suburban school of today or in the rural black school of yesterday.

Appendix A

Timeline

Era of the Old School

1897
Superintendent Judson Corn completed a school census for three colored schools in Transylvania County.

1900–1902
No colored school listed.

1904–1906
1 colored school, Boyd district.

May 31, 1909
Boyd colored 1 teacher: salary—$25
Brevard colored teachers: salary—1@$30 and 2@$25
Supt. T. C. Henderson

January 3, 1910
Reference to District 1 colored and District 2 Brevard Township colored.
J. P. Aiken had died and his unexpired term went to Alfred Benjamin.
Contract awarded to Holtzclaw to build a school for district 2 colored at a cost of $999.

June 6, 1910
Board of education orders that the old school benches at Davidson River be given to the colored district 1 School of Boyd Township.

July 1, 1912
Ordered $200 of Building Fund be appropriated to District 1 Colored to help pay for additional room.

Established school for colored children in the Chinquapin Community with gift of $100 from Brevard Colored School.

August 1, 1912
Ordered compulsory attendance in Transylvania County as per Chapter 260 of North Carolina Public School Laws of 1911.

February 19 & 20, 1915
N. C. Newbold, State Agent for Rural Negro Schools, visits the white teachers of Transylvania County.

October 8, 1915
The first Rosenwald School in North Carolina was inspected by N. C. Newbold.

April 2, 1917
Ordered R. L. Gash to be paid $50 from Building Fund for waterline to Brevard Colored School and Wilkie C. Johnstone to be paid $10 for rent of room for 5 months for Brevard Colored School.

June 3, 1917
Board of education considering bids to build another room for colored school.
Boyd district contract awarded to L.C. Orr for $500.
A copy of the contract plans indicate a 20 × 28 room with a 12 ft. ceiling, roof well braced, 8 × 10 cloakroom, 8 × 8 porch steps and a flue.

December 3, 1917
Bill from Mrs. Johnstone for $10 for four months operating the Brevard Colored School out of her house.
Bill was to be paid.

January 7, 1918
The board considered the Rosenwald Fund and put it off for further consideration.

September 21, 1919
Principal G.W. Thompson requests funds and the assignment of a Jeanes supervisor for Transylvania County.

September 30, 1919
N. C. Newbold considers the possibility of obtaining $900 from the Rosenwald Fund to use for school renovations in Transylvania County.

1919-1920
Faculty members include G.W. Thompson, Wilkie C. Johnstone, Flora Wallis, Annie Davis, Jessie B. Saville, and Lois Nelson.

Era of the Renovated Old School

January 5, 1920
Ordered accounts settled with P.E. McGuire in regard to the Newbold addition.

February 9, 1920
J.F. Mills requests Board of Education allow classes for Brevard #2 Colored to meet in private house for another month or so; request granted.

March 1, 1920
$70 provided from Building and Furniture Funds for Brevard #2 Colored with instructions for Brevard #2 to take care of note for piano.

March 26, 1920
Need for additional funds for upgrading the Colored School.
N.C. Newhold owes balance of $500 and should be contacted regarding loan for colored school from State Loan Fund.

April 5, 1920
Apply to state for $500 loan based on response of N.C. Newbold to pay for expenses incurred in adding new rooms, two cloakrooms and student and teacher desks.

May 3, 1920
Note attached to p. 189, written in pencil by P.E. McGuire providing estimate for addition of one room to colored school house: "For sum of one thousand four hundred and fifty dollars I agree to furnish all materials and labor to complete the job according to plans and specifications."

July 15, 1920
Bids for painting outside walls of Rosenwald School House.

September 8, 1920
Contract for painting, cleaning, and puttying Rosenwald awarded to Allard Allison.
Color scheme to be obtained from N.C. Newbold.
Paint ordered from General Refining Company of Cleveland, Ohio.
Board of Education was to provide paint and putty to Allard Allison.

1921-1922
Faculty members at Glade Creek were May Frazier, Aileen Mills, and Anna B. Miller. The Rosenwald School faculty included G.W. Thompson, Mrs. J.H. Johnstone, Flora W. Powell, and Annie Davis.

1922-23
In the operating budget for that year the following colored teachers are identified:

G.W. Thompson, Mrs. J.H. Johnstone, Irma Swepson, Evangeline Culler, Beatrice Reinhardt, Blanche Graham, and Mrs. A.B. Gash. Salaries range from $45 to $75. Three types of teaching certificates were held: Elementary, Grammar Grades, and Second Grade, County. One hundred and fifty eight students were served at Rosenwald, both elementary and high school, for a school term of 120 days.

1924-25
Found in ledger a list of school committees p.75 — Colored School Committees
Brevard #2 Rosenwald
Arthur Hefner
B. Benjamin
Jones Mills
J.F.W. Mills (In charge of Building)
Cleveland Hall
E.L. Simmons (In charge of Attendance)

May 5, 1925
B.C. McGuire ordered to complete Brevard #2 colored school at once.

1930–32
School Committees and Census Page
P. 99 Colored Schools
Brevard #3 Rosenwald
Arthur Hefner (Secretary)
J.F.W. Mills (Chair)
B. Benjamin

Era of Makeshift Accommodations in Churches

March 12, 1941
Rosenwald School destroyed by fire.

March 31, 1941
Proceed with plans to replace Rosenwald with semi-fireproof building.
Walls of rock or brick and central heating system.
Supt. J.B. Jones

April 4, 1945
County superintendent authorized to investigate purchase of property from Dr. English estate for Rosenwald School

May 7, 1945
The Transylvania Times records J. B. Jones comment regarding makeshift classes for

Negro students in churches is "unsatisfactory and must be remedied as soon as possible."

October 7, 1946
Request for school building bonds.
Reference to six month school term.
Need to erect new Rosenwald school building at Brevard (other schools are mentioned).

April 17, 1947
Motion to start the Rosenwald School building immediately.

June 20, 1947
Contract for constructing the Rosenwald School building awarded to R.K. Stewart & Son of High Point, North Carolina.
Amount $136,150

Era of the New Rosenwald Building

January 20, 1948
Install florescent lights in Rosenwald School and add necessary retaining walls of stone.

September 1, 1948
The Glade Creek Colored School has been closed.
The Brevard Rosenwald School has opened.

September 7, 1948
Board of Education will sell shacks used during construction at Rosenwald School.

June 20, 1949
The School Board authorizes payment of $300 to the Henderson County School Board and purchase of a new bus to transport Rosenwald students to Hendersonville to attend high school.

June 21, 1949
Negro students are to be transported to Hendersonville to attend high school at Ninth Avenue School.

May 7, 1949
Petitions approved for employment of principal and teachers at Rosenwald.

October 25, 1951
Dedication of new Ninth Avenue High School in Hendersonville, NC.

April 14, 1953
Senator Gash inquiry about the establishment of a Negro high school at Rosenwald.

April 16, 1953
The Transylvania Times reviewed a proposal by state representative Ralph Fisher to provide legislation for the construction of a Negro High School at the Rosenwald site.

August 17, 1953
Letter to Senator Gash from the Board of Education explaining why a Rosenwald High School is impossible at the present time.

Also has description of Rosenwald as containing seven rooms, including the library with only one room not in use as five are filled.

Cost for providing equal faculties for high school students would be impossible to finance.

At present time only 36 Rosenwald students are of high school age.

August 30, 1958
All county schools, including Rosenwald, have been inspected and reveal insufficient janitorial help.

Ethel Mills had received no compensation for her work for two weeks both before and after the previous school year.

The Board voted to pay her $100 for her work before and $100 for her work after the school closed.

January 8, 1960
Board of Education minutes include an inserted message to the Board of Education from Superintendent C.W. Bradburn in which he states: "Our Negro population is doing fine. I have had no word of discontent."

During this year, led by the Rev. Samuel Raper, representatives of the Negro population of Transylvania County form the Transylvania Citizens Improvement Organization (TCIO).

May 9, 1962
The Negro population asked the Board of Education for a special meeting to discuss problems related to education.

June 5, 1962
Members of the Black community petition the Board for reassignment of the Rosenwald students to Brevard Elementary School.

C.W. Bradburn is the school superintendent.

June 16, 1962
Petition denied.

June 18, 1962
Would allow eight children to attend Brevard High School and Brevard Junior High

School for August 21, 1962, School Opening — Thomas E. Rhodes, Clerk US District Court Western District of North Carolina Civil Action.

June 25, 1962
The Transylvania County Board of Education met in executive session.
Purpose was to discuss assignment of Negro children to Brevard Junior and Senior High Schools.
No decision was reached — further research was required.

July 3, 1962
Repetition Board set August 21 for hearing.

August 17, 1962
Right to educational opportunities for qualified Negroes desiring to be reassigned requested by attorney Rueben Dailey.

August 21, 1962
Hearing for parents requesting reassignment of children.
Board of Education unanimously disapproved reassignment.

November 13, 1962
Reuben J. Dailey, representing colored children desiring entrance into Transylvania County Schools, requested a meeting for the purpose of taking a deposition from the superintendent and the Board of Education.
The superintendent reported the first six weeks grades of all Negro students attending Brevard Junior High and Brevard Senior High.

March 5, 1963
Board of Education informed that a hearing was set for March 11 in Asheville, Western District Federal Court, Judge Wilson Warlick presiding to consider appeal by Negro students wishing to attend public schools in Transylvania County.

March 11, 1963
Judge Wilson Warlick ruled that the schools of Transylvania County should be completely desegregated for the 1963-64 school term.

August 1963
The football team at Brevard High School is integrated for the first time.

March 19, 1965
The 1965 Teacher Allotment Policy would be made without regard to race and expenditure classifications would not be maintained by race.

May 4, 1965
The Rosenwald Elementary Staff for the 1965-66 year was approved: Ethelwyn K. Mills, Principal, Synetha Benjamin, Mary Kilgore, Annie Hailey, James Baten.

April 20, 1965

The revised assurance of compliance agreement was approved as required by the Department of Health, Education, and Welfare in order to receive Federal funds.

September 7, 1965

Negro parents requesting children be reassigned to Brevard Elementary School were cooperative and willing to accept any reasonable assignment and allow the Board to select students for reassignment.

Compliance agreement had not yet been approved.

September 27, 1965

Mentally Retarded Organization requested space for its program.
Board contends only space to be considered is Rosenwald School.

March 1, 1966

Margaret H. Avery participates in program established by the Elementary and Secondary Act at Rosenwald.

March 9, 1966

Discussion of Title VI.
No details given.

April 5, 1966

Details for student assignment.

April 13, 1966

Motion to sign form 441B to indicate compliance with Title VI of the Civil Rights Act of 1964.

June 21, 1966

Superintendent Bradburn resigns effective June 30.
Assurance of compliance with school desegregation Title VI of Civil Rights Act of 1964.
Reference to March 1966 Federal Financial Assistance Voluntary Plan for desegregation to be submitted by July 1, 1966.

June 30, 1966

The Transylvania Times reports on the Voluntary Plan of Desegregation being adopted by the school system.
Applications must be received on or before August 24.

July 1, 1966

A Voluntary Plan of Desegregation is in place.

July 5, 1966

List of resignations include Ethelwyn Mills, Principal and 1st grade teacher, and James R. Baten, 6th grade teacher.

Synetha G. Benjamin is assigned part-time to Penrose Elementary School.

Mary B. Kilgore is assigned to Straus.

August 1966

Transylvania County Schools open with no Rosenwald School.

August 26, 1966

All resignations and transfers of faculty approved.

October 9, 1963

Board of Education surveyed former Rosenwald School and site to consider extending West Main Street to Rosenwald Lane to provide suitable access to the building, which was being converted into an education center to serve all public schools in the county.

March 6, 1967

Minutes of the meeting of Transylvania County's Board of Commissioners (p. 189, Book 8) records a request by Board of Education chairman to extend Brevard's Main Street to the Rosenwald School property to enable the Board of Education to move their office from the court house to the Rosenwald School.

Sam Helton is the School Superintendent.

April 1, 1968

Minutes of the meeting of the Board of Commissioners (p. 236, Book 8) record a meeting of the board with school superintendent Dr. R.E. Robinson and E.B. Matheson of the Board of Education to explain that the Board of Education and Wilkie C. Johnstone are trading property in the Rosenwald School area.

The trade allows the extension of Main Street to Rosenwald Lane.

December 6, 1981

The Transylvania Education Center is renamed in memory of Eugene M. Morris.

June 3, 1995

The Mayor of Brevard declares Cornelius Hunt Day.

July 1, 2000

TCIO sponsors a 40th anniversary celebration with the theme: "Rosenwald School Remembered."

July 7, 2001

TCIO sponsors an historical celebration honoring Civil Rights leaders and others. Pauline Wynn served as Mistress of Ceremonies.

December 17, 2001

The City of Brevard is awarded a Community Development Block Grant (CDBG) for the revitalization of its African American neighborhood, which has been baptized the Rosenwald Community.

March 4, 2002

The Brevard City Council designates the former Rosenwald School, the site of the Eugene M. Morris Education Center, as a local historic landmark.

Appendix B

Methodology

This book began as an attempt to probe into the history of the Brevard Rosenwald School, which had its roots in efforts to educate black children in Transylvania County. This effort required consideration of many facets of the school's history, whether contained in documents preserved as part of historical records or retained in the memories of those associated with the school. In the introduction to her study of pioneer women who lived on the Kansas frontier, Joanna L. Stratton (1981) cites the remarks of historian Arthur M. Schlesinger, Jr.:

> History is lived in the main by the unknown and forgotten. But historians perforce concentrate on the happy few who leave records, give speeches, write books, make fortunes, hold offices, win or lose battles or thrones. The historical profession is by no means insensitive to this discrepancy, nor complacent about the way the mass of humanity had been consigned forever to the shadows. Modern social historians devise brave new techniques, quantitative and other, to achieve what Emmanuel Le Roy Ladurie has called "the silent, mathematical resurrection of a total past" [p. 11].

A primary aim of this project was to resurrect the voices of the Rosenwald community to relate the true history of the school.

This study of the Rosenwald School included an analysis of school board minutes and newspaper accounts, as well as archival resources. Members of the Rosenwald community also shared their private collections of school memorabilia. I used a question protocol to interview people associated with the school. When possible, the process included taping interviews. I encouraged interviewees to share their memories and to recall both positive and negative experiences. Summaries include paraphrases of their comments. As a novice in the use of oral histories as a research technique, I consulted similar studies.

I learned to appreciate the definition of qualitative research provided by scholars Catherine Marshall and Gretchen B. Rossman, in which they refer to research as:

> ...a process of trying to gain a better understanding of the complexities of human interactions. Through systematic means, the researcher gathers information about actions and interactions, reflects on their meaning, arrives at and evaluates conclusions, and eventually puts forward an interpretation.... Real research is often confusing, messy, intensely frustrating and fundamentally nonlinear [1995, p. 15].

Since my study was centered on the human perspective, qualitative methods were required.

Building a history of the Brevard Rosenwald School involved reflective analysis. Citing University of Oregon Professor C. H. Edson, Walter R. Borg and Meredith D. Gall wrote, "There is no single definable method of historical inquiry" (1989, p. 245). Historical research is dependent on the judgment and interpretations of historians. Virtually any object or written record can be considered in historical research (Borg and Gall, 1989). As individuals struggled to recall events in the school's history, I sought other data to confirm their recollections or other stories to corroborate personal claims. Those efforts were not always successful. Developing oral histories required acknowledgement on my part that both human memory and my own interpretations could be subject to error.

By definition, oral history is the collection of any individual's spoken memories of his life, of people he has known, and events he has witnessed or in which he has participated (Hoopes, 1979, p. 7). Modern technology has robbed the present generation of written records because today's communication depends much less on writing than in the past. One strength of oral history is that it gives the ordinary citizen a role in chronicling past events. The voices of the Brevard Rosenwald School are often those of ordinary citizens, and those voices are critical to any analysis of the school's history.

Marshall and Rossman reveal four primary methods for qualitative research: "(1) participation in the setting, (2) direct observation, (3) in-depth interviewing, and (4) document review" (1995, p. 78). Because the Brevard Rosenwald School was closed in 1966, I sought in-depth, multiple interviews, and I supported my findings with document analysis. Topics related to the school were explored with more than fifty individuals at length. In addition, school board minutes, ledgers, records of deeds, report cards, graduation announcements, letters, reports and newspaper articles were analyzed. The locally produced video *A Sketch of Black Pioneers of Transylvania County* was also a resource.

Donna M. Mertens, in her 1998 *Research Methods in Education and Psychology*, states that a study begins with a set of questions designed to bring focus to the study as it deals with a particular phenomenon. Mertens also documents the important role of oral history for research dealing with powerless groups. That aspect of her treatise interested me because the group of African Americans with whom I was collaborating had elevated themselves from a level of powerlessness to one of power. As I listened to their tales of seeking an education and struggling to gain their rights, I learned that greater political and social power resulted from access to equal educational opportunities. Discoveries of that nature were a strong component of my research.

I targeted parents, teachers, staff, and students. Of those interviewed, roles sometimes overlapped. For example, after graduating from college, two individuals returned to the school as teachers, while others became parents of Rosenwald students. Agnes Lynch Wilson graduated from the Brevard Rosenwald School and then served as a substitute teacher; in addition, Wilson was working as a teacher aide financed by the Ford Foundation under a Comprehensive School Improvement Program (C.S.I.P.) grant during Rosenwald School's final year.

I made a distinct effort to include representatives from all three phases of the school's history based on its location: representatives of those who attended classes in the original building; those who were schooled when three church sites served as temporary headquarters; and former students and teachers who worked in the new building that opened in 1948. Eleven of the people in my sample attended the school in the 1920s and 1930s; eight were students who assembled in the basements and an annex of community churches. Others were students in the school housed in the new building. A few attended at two sites. I interviewed nine members of the staff, including a substitute teacher who was also a teacher aide, a graduate who served as a custodian, one teacher who became the interim principal for eighteen years, and five teachers. Some interviewees had a primary role as parents. Members of the white community were interviewed regarding the proposed Rosenwald extension to accommodate high school students. They also presented an alternative perspective about integration issues.

Ethel K. Mills began teaching at the school in 1923 and, except for a brief transfer to the Everett Farm School, remained there until its closing in 1966. Her vast experience as a teacher and as the principal of Rosenwald brought a sense of continuity to the school's history. Students, staff members, and community residents conveyed insights about the school from a variety of viewpoints.

Oral histories were supplemented with written records, including newspaper articles, school board minutes and other public documents, and the Julius Rosenwald Fund archives. However, there is a dearth of written documentation about the history of the Rosenwald School. The 1941 fire destroyed the building along with its documents, and other records were apparently lost or misplaced when total integration occurred in 1966. Students went to various states and counties to seek a high school education, and the records were often sent to other counties and states. Copies of the local newspapers for significant years are missing, both in Brevard and in Raleigh. Microfilmed copies were sometimes unreadable. Neither I nor the archivist at Fisk University succeeded in locating application forms submitted by the county superintendent requesting monies from the Rosenwald Fund, although references to those papers were found.

Interviewees lived in Brevard and in communities in the Piedmont and in coastal areas, and alumni and former faculty members ranged in age from 44 to over 100 years old. Using active listening techniques recommended by William W. Purkey and John J. Schmidt (1996), I built personally satisfying relationships with members of the black community. Comments made outside the context of the formal interview often proved invaluable. Finding history in the shared memories of those who lived it exposes a wealth of unrecorded data that exists in no other form (Allen & Montell, 1981). Those I interviewed were the experts in developing this history of the Brevard Rosenwald School. Their assistance was invaluable.

Two members of the community and I attended the Rosenwald School Conference held in Charlotte during the spring of 2001. A network of Rosenwald school enthusiasts comprises a Rosenwald Forum in North Carolina. At the Charlotte conference, school historian Dr. Thomas Hanchett was the keynote speaker, and Dr.

Peter Ascoli, grandson of Julius Rosenwald, also spoke. Granddaughters of African American educator Dr. George Edward (G. E.) Davis shared personal family recollections. Nyoni Collins of the Sankofa Center in Wake Forest, North Carolina, was the conference coordinator.

Organizational stories can provide a means to explain and to enhance the culture developed within the organization (Hansen and Kahnweiler, 1993). The stories shared by the interviewees reveal a great deal about life at the Brevard Rosenwald School. A condition which Vanessa Siddle Walker (1996) refers to as "institutional caring" existed and was brought to light by the shared memories of those interviewed. References to the school as a haven of safety confirmed the important place school played in the lives of Rosenwald students. By telling such stories, ordinary people become aware that their lives are a relevant part of history (Thompson, 1988). I was convinced that the African American citizens of Transylvania County deserved to have their history preserved.

I enlisted the assistance of others to ensure through careful scrutiny that my conclusions were reasonably accurate. Two alumni, Agnes Wilson and Nathaniel Hall, read the original document and provided comments. A writer and journalist, Howard Spanogle, provided editorial advice.

It was necessary to determine that memories were not distorted by nostalgia and to balance the collective stories of those consulted. Citing James Agee, James Hoopes quotes:

> ...history is ... an exercise of the imagination. History ... is a test of our ability imaginatively to place ourselves in the positions of other people, so that we can understand the reasons for their actions. Through research and study we learn facts about those other people.... The historical record is always incomplete. Imagination must fill in the gaps in our knowledge, though ... our imaginings must derive from facts and be consistent with them [1979, p. 3].

Always the goal was to draw truthful conclusions and to avoid censorship. Deciding which data was most useful was a concern, as was building trust with those interviewed. It was necessary to convince those consulted that my intentions were honorable and that their history was not being exploited. On a few occasions individuals shared powerful stories but requested that I not use them.

The interviewees taught me much about history, both local and otherwise. Thomas Gardin taught me about the integration of the armed forces. Nathaniel Hall was a veritable history book on the issues of slavery and the history of the community. Lois Elliott Wynn has an encyclopedic recall of the acts of kindness that were commonplace in the history of both the school and the community. I owe them a debt of gratitude.

No one interviewed remembered the construction of the original building. Gertrude Gash was living at that time, as was Bernetha Owens, but they were too young to have been impressed with community projects. There are also conflicting accounts of early efforts to educate African American children in Transylvania County, and the March 12, 1941, fire limits the study because flames destroyed the original schoolhouse and its contents. Documents were lost or destroyed during the time school personnel and students worked in makeshift environments.

I drew upon my experience as an educator with forty years of involvement in

North Carolina's public school system to evaluate the quality and extent of learning experiences provided by the Rosenwald School. I have first-hand experience with the segregated schools of western North Carolina and was teaching during the period of integration. My interest in the Brevard school was aroused by conversations with Samuel Howell and James Gardin, Brevard residents whose children attended the school. Their resentment that their children had to be bused to another county to acquire a high school education angered me. Acting on their recommendation, I began my study of the school and developed a strong personal interest in its educational saga.

Appendix C

Documents

The Black Man's Plea for Justice

Written in the early 1900s by Professor G.W. Thompson, black educator in Transylvania County, North Carolina, and retained in the papers of Dorothy Pierce Hill.

I have helped to fell the forest
I have cleared your farming lands.
And your great commercial buildings
Are the labor of my hands.

I have helped to train your children,
cooked your food and washed your clothes.
I have fed your cows and horses,
Swept your yards and scrubbed your floors.

I have been your friend and servant,
One in whom you can confide.
I have fed you when a beggar,
When others have turned you aside.

I have gone with you through battle,
Helped to settle every row.
Ruling powers of the nation,
Will you give me justice now?

I have moved away the rubbish
That which might have destroyed your health.
I have helped you in demarcations
Which support this common wealth.

I have helped to build the dwellings,
Shops, churches, stores, schools, and all
And I have helped to place the papers
And the points upon the walls.

I have helped to build the steamships,
Sailing now upon the sea,
And the pavement of your city
Is my handwork, if you please.
Now I must ask a little favor
At this time, if you will allow,
Ruling powers of the nation,
Will you give me justice now?

I seek a better education
In better Negro schools.
I am seeking no relation
Save those of the golden rule.

As ye would that men should do unto you,
Do ye unto them likewise.
For every man within his dormant [sic]
Ought to have a chance to rise.

At the shrine of this great nation
Reverently, I meekly bow.
Ruling powers of the nation,
Will you give me justice now?

I pay dear for transportation
Over all your railroad steel.
And I have been a mighty power
In this great financial field.

I have been a faithful servant
Even when a slave.
I prepared your wedding suppers
And dug your fathers' graves.

Now I ask this favor again.
At this time, if you will allow,
Ruling powers of the nation,
Will you give me justice now?

Hear me statesman,
I am pleading — to defend the black man's cause,
Will you give me the protection
That outlines your dormant laws?

Will you let my colored lawyers
Plead my case within your courts?
I am a citizen, I am loyal,
Will you recognize my vote?

I pay dear for transportation
Over all your railroad tracks
And I come up to all repairments
And I always pay my tax.

And when I don't fill blanks correctly
Will you kindly show me how?
Ruling powers of the nation,
Will you give me justice now?

From the Report Cards of Winona Smith Whiteside

Winona Smith's Report Card, 1926-27
Rosenwald School Pupil's High School Report Card
Grade 5
Teacher: Coragreene Johnstone

STUDIES	1st	2nd	3rd	4th	5th	6th	7th	8th
Reading	C	C+	C+	C+	B	C+	B-	B-
Spelling	B	B-	A-	A-	C	C+	B	C
Arithmetic	B	B+	A-	A-	A+	B	C	B+
Grammar	A-	A-	A-	A-	A-	A-	A-	B
Geography	C	A-	B-	B	B+	B-	A-	A-
History	D	C	C	B	C+	C+	B	C
Physiology		A-	B	B	B-	B+	B-	B
Deportment	B+	B+	B+	B+	B	B	B-	B
Days Absent			8	4		4		

95–100	Superior
85–95	Satisfactory
85–75	Fair
Below 75	Unsatisfactory

Winona Smith's Report Card, 1929-30
Rosenwald School Pupil's High School Report Card
Grade 8, Principal H. L. Foster

STUDIES	1st	2nd	3rd	4th	5th	6th	7th	8th
Days Present	19	20	19	19				
Days Absent	1	0	1	1				
Deportment	C+	C	C	C+	C	C	C+	C
Literature	B	B-	B-	B	B-	C	B	B
English	D	B	B+	B	B	C+	C+	B
Science	C	C+	C+	C+	C+	C	B+	B-
Civics	B	C	C-	C+	B-	B	C	D+
Arithmetic	B	A-	A	A	B+	B	A-	B

Appendix C: Documents

Home Economics	D	C+	D	B	D	C	D	C
Latin	C	C+	C	C	C	C	B	C

A+	95–100
A	90–95
B+	85–90
B	80–85
C	75–80
D	Failure

Winona Smith's Report Card, 1930-31
Rosenwald School Pupil's High School Report Card
Grade 9, Principal J. M. Harris

STUDIES	1st	2nd	3rd	4th	5th	6th	7th	8th
Days Present		17	17	18	15	16	15	14
Days Absent	3	3	2	5	4	5	6	
Times Tardy	4	3	4	4				
Deportment	B	B	B	B	B	B	B	B
English	B	B	B	B	B	B	B	B
Science	B	B	B	B	B			
History						B-	B	
Algebra	C	C+	B	B	B	C	C	B
Home Economics	C	B	B	B	B		A	
Latin [Caesar]	C	B	B	B	B	C	B	C

A+	95–100
A	90–95
B+	85–90
B	80–85
C	75–80
D	Failure

Winona Smith's Report Card, 1931-32
Rosenwald School Pupil's High School Report Card
Grade 10, Principal J. M. Harris

STUDIES	1st	2nd	3rd	4th	5th	6th	7th	8th
Deportment	C	C	C		C	C	C	C
Geography	C	B	B	B	C	C	B	B
Rhetoric	C	B	B	B	B	B	B	B
Literature	C	C	B	B	B	B	B	B
History	C	B	B	B	B	B	C	B
Latin [Caesar]	C	C						

Attitude toward school work is also monitored. The categories are: Indolent, Wastes time, Gets too much help, Work carelessly done, Gives up too easily, Shows improvement, Very commendable, and Attendance irregular.

Recitations were observed using the following: Comes poorly prepared, Can do much better, Appears not to try, Seldom does well, Inattentive, Promotion in danger, Work falling off, Grade too difficult, Shows improvement, and Very Satisfactory. Conduct includes: Restless; Inattentive, Inclined to mischief, Annoys others, Whispers too much, Rude or discourteous, Showing improvement, and Very good.

Winona Smith Whiteside continued studying at the Brevard Rosenwald School through the work designed for its high school program, but Marva Robinson Lytle was forced to travel to an adjoining county to attend high school.

From the Report Cards of Marva Robinson Lytle

Information from the report card of Ninth Avenue School, 1951-52
Hendersonville, North Carolina
Home Room Teacher: M. E. Stephens

	1	2	3	1/2	4	5	6	Year
Half Days Absent								
Times Tardy								
English								
Scholarship	B	B-	B-	B-	B-	B+	B+	B+
Cooperation	B-	B	B	B	B	B	B	B
Citizenship								
Scholarship	B+	B+	B-	B-	B+	C+	B-	B-
Cooperation	B+	B+	B+	B+	B-	B-	B-	B-
General Math								
Scholarship	C	D	D	D	C	C+	D+	C
Cooperation	B-	B-	B-	B-	C	C+	C	C
General Science								
Scholarship	C+	B	B	B-	C	B	B+	B-
Cooperation	C	C	C	C	C	B	B	B
Health and Physical Education								
Scholarship	B	B+	B+	B+	C	B	B+	B-
Cooperation	B	A-	A-	A-	C	B	B	B
Home Economics								
Scholarship	C	B-	B	B-	B	C+	B+	B+
Cooperation	C	A	A	A	A	B+	B	B

Scholarship

A	Excellent	93–100
B	Above Average	85–92
C	Average	77–84
D	Below Average	70–76
E	Failure (Passing Mark 70)	

Appendix C: Documents

No pupil who has "E" for a year average in Scholarship will be given credit for the year's work.

Cooperation
Grading includes Behavior, Effort, and Attitude. A — Above Average; B — Average; C — Below Average; D — Very Poor
Supervised Study: S — Satisfactory; U — Unsatisfactory

PROMOTED TO GRADE 10

Report Card, 1952-53

	1	2	3	1/2	4	5	6	Year
Half Days Absent								
Times Tardy								
Spanish								
Scholarship	B	B	B-	B-	B	B+	B	B
Cooperation	B+	B	B	B	B	B+	B	B
Home Economics								
Scholarship	B	B	C+	B-	B+	A-	B	B+
Cooperation	B+	B	C+	B-	B+	B+	B	B
English II								
Scholarship	B	B+	C+	C+	C	C+	C-	C+
Cooperation	B	A	C+	B	C	C+	B	B
History								
Scholarship	B	B+	C-	C+	C	B	C-	C+
Cooperation	B	A	B	B-	C	C+	C+	B
Algebra I								
Scholarship	B-	B-	C-	C+	C-	C-	D+	C-
Cooperation	B	C	C	C	C-	C+	C	C
Biology								
Scholarship	C	C	B	C+	B	A-	B	B+
Cooperation	C	C	C	C	B	B+	B	B

PROMOTED TO GRADE 11

Report Card, 1953-54

	1	2	3	1/2	4	5	6	Year
Half Days Absent								
Times Tardy								
Plane Geometry								
Scholarship	B+	C	C-	C	C+	D-	C	C-
Cooperation	A-	B	B-	B	B	C	B-	B-

Home Economics III

Scholarship	B	B	B+	B	B	C+	B-	B-
Cooperation	B+	B	B	B	B	B	B	B

English

Scholarship	C+	C+	C	C	D	C+	B	C+
Cooperation	B	B	B	B	C	C+	C+	C+

History

Scholarship	C-	C+	C	C	C+	C+	C	C
Cooperation	B	B	B	C	C+	C+	C	C+

Spanish

Scholarship	B	B	A-	A-	B	B+	B	B
Cooperation	B	B	B	B	B	B	B	B

PROMOTED TO GRADE 12

Report Card, 1954-55

	1	2	3	1/2	4	5	6	Year
Home Room								
Tardies								
Cooperation								
Absences								

Family Relationships

Scholarship	A-	B+	B	B-	B-	B-	C+	C+
Cooperation	A-	A-	A-	A-	A	A	A	A
Absences	2	3	2	7	2			

Chemistry

Scholarship	B	B	B	B	C	B	B	B
Cooperation	B	B	B	B	B	B	B	B
Absences	0							

Economics

Scholarship	B-	A-	B-	B	B	B-	B-	B-
Cooperation	A	B-	B	B	B	B	B	B
Absences					2			

English IV

Scholarship	B-	B	C	C+	B-	B	B+	B-
Cooperation	B	B	B	B	B	B	B	B
Absences					2			

World Geography

Scholarship	B	B	B	B	B	B	B	B
Cooperation	B	B	B	B	B	B	B	B
Absences	0							

GRADUATED

Although absences and tardies are designated, none were recorded until the twelfth grade. The report card was slightly altered, with a letter designation of F to replace E for failing to achieve a grade of at least 70. Behavior in the classroom was noted with the appropriate grade for all four years.

Comparing the two sets of report cards provides interesting details about policies of attendance, subjects taught, and the criteria used in grading the students.

Census for Colored Race

Census of School Children
Colored Race
Transylvania County, North Carolina
1897
Enumerator: Judson Corn

According to A. Christopher Meekins, Reference Archivist of North Carolina's State Archives, Raleigh, a census such as this one is actually a deed related to the schools and not census records, per se. His research indicated that in the 1960s inventory of county records, stipulations indicated that these records were to be filed in the schools and permanently preserved. However, all efforts to locate them proved fruitless.

The evidence provided here indicates irrefutably that schools for black children in Transylvania County existed prior to the advent of the twentieth century. Lori Pierson Jacques has a collection of papers that originated from the files of her great-grandfather, Judson Corn, who served as the Superintendent of Public Schools from 1897 to 1899. In compliance with the provisions of Section 2579 of the School Law, Corn compiled a census of all school children between the ages of six and twenty-one, and a careful estimate of the value of school property to be filed with the Register of Deeds. The school census for District No. 2 included the names of the following parents or guardians and the number of their children.

Name of Parent or Guardian	No. Children	Male	Female
R. Ponders		1	5
Brice Mills		4	3
Bill Erwin		5	4
Bart Hemphill		2	1
Jess Tomas		1	
Green Kilgore		2	1
John Cunningham		2	1
Bob Morgan		1	1
J. Loyde		1	
Tazlas Brooks		1	1
Lee Kilgore		1	
Sam Cook			1
Bob Johnson		3	1

Name	Male	Female
Andy Sharp	2	
James Mills	2	2
Loza Cunningham	1	
Ike Bailey	2	5
Jim Hall	3	
Jake Richeson	1	
Caline Erwin		1
Jake McKey		2
Tener Simmons	1	1
Mary Wallace		1
Saha Clanton	1	2
Jim Atarn	2	
J. P. Aiken	1	3
Arthur Hutchison	1	
Calins Layde	3	4
Charlie Smith	1	1
Tom Gash	1	
Rob Patton		1
Neill Miller		1
Julie Gash		1
George McKey	1	

There were 46 male students and 48 female students, for a total of 94 students. The value of the public school property including land and houses was estimated at $200.00. Only one school house was included. The document is signed by J. H. Hampton, who recorded the oath on May 31, 1897, and is signed by J.P. Aiken and W.B. Mills, Committeemen.

School Census of District No. 1
Colored Race
Transylvania County, North Carolina
1897

Name of Parent or Guardian	No. of Children Male	Female	Name of Parent or Guardian	No. of Children Male	Female
Andrew Whitesides	6	4	Lewis Ledbetter	1	3
Dean Gash		5	Henry Hutchison	2	
E. B. Clayton	1		George Orr	3	2
J. R. Kemp	4	2	Rildia Merrill	1	
Harrison McJunkins		4	Henry Walker	3	
O. S. Kemp	2	4	Anderson Mooney	1	1
Adam Hutchison	1	4	Orange Mooney	1	2
Peter Owens		3	Slena Kemp	1	1
C. W. Hemphill	2		Millard Gash	2	4
James Bostic	1	3	John Bailey		1
Cam Mills	5	2	Samuel Smith		2
James Smith	2	1	Llack Smith	1	2

Name of Parent or Guardian	No. of Children Male	Female	Name of Parent or Guardian	No. of Children Male	Female
Pink Smith	2		M. H. Hemphill	2	1
Paris Mooney	3	4	Butler Hunt	1	
Llam Hunt	1	2	George Hutchin	1	1
James Gash	3				

The list includes 53 males and 58 females, bringing the total number served to 111. The frame school building including land is valued at $75.00. The affidavit was sworn to before George C. Neill on the seventh day of June, 1897, by Committeeman J. R. Kemp.

School Census
District No. 3
Transylvania County, North Carolina
1897

Name of Parent or Guardian	No. of Children Male	Female	Name of Parent or Guardian	No. of Children Male	Female
Elias King	1	1	C.C. Sharp		2
Thomas Poor		1	Marshall Gaston	1	3
Alfred Benjamin	2	3	Arthur Hemphill	3	3
Riley Gaston		3	Jack Anderson	3	2
Mary Gaston	3	2	Sarah Kilgore	2	1
Cavsy Hopkins		1	John Gaither	1	1
Joe Allen	2	3			

With 18 males and 25 females the total school population is 43, and the frame schoolhouse, including land, is valued at $25.00. The document was sworn to before L. H. Hampton by Committeeman C.C. Sharp on June 7, 1897.

During A.F. Mitchell's tenure as Transylvania County School Superintendent, a district census summary for the Brevard Township, District No. 2, Race: Colored was completed for the School Census of 1917-18 and is today part of a private collection. According to Mitchell's census report, one frame schoolhouse with two rooms existed in the township. The number of children 18 to 21 years of age indicates a total of 18, eight males and ten females. Apparently that is an error because only one student on the list has an age greater than 18; however, no age is recorded for nine pupils. A total of 43 student names are listed. This school would be renamed Rosenwald School.

Pages 3 through 6 of the report indicates the following data:

Name of Parent or Guardian	Children
Lula Anderson	Edwin Anderson, 14; Catherine Anderson, 11; Sylvan Anderson, 9; Lockwood Anderson, 8; Lucile Anderson, 7
Ellen Fletcher	William A. Fletcher, 10; Sarah Johnson, 13
Mamie Anderson	Emma Anderson, 13; Alfred Anderson, 10; Bessie Anderson, 8

Classie Hemphill	Thelma Hemphill, 11; Jack Hemphill, 7
Mary Hemphill	Claud Hemphill, 9; Clide Hemphill, 7; Easter Hemphill, 7; Thea Hemphill (male), 16
Charlie Anderson	William Anderson, 6
Alice Ponder	Bessie Ponder, 17
W. B. Mills	Dewie Mills, 19; Eugine Mills, 17; Inez Mills, 15
Lucy Williams	R. J. Williams, 12; Authur Williams, 8
Mary Hefner	Laram Hefner (female), 6; Arthur Hefner, 6
Lula Garrett	Harvey Anderson, 12; Cora Lee Anderson, 13; Tiny Kilgore (female), 15
Corena Hutcherson	Bernetha Hutcherson, 13; Dika Hutcherson (female), 15; Clide Hutcherson (female), 17
Clara Gash	Bessie Gash, 13; Cora Gash, 12; George Gash, 8

In addition, the following males and one female are listed without indicating the names of the parents or the ages of the students: Vernon Bailey; Benjamin Russell; Manuel Irving; Jaimie Hill Johnstone; Mamie Lewey Mills; Frank Whiteside; Luther Whiteside; William Cunningham; and Isabel Whiteside.

Appendix D

Transylvania County School Superintendents 1877–2003*

1877–1885	W.P. Southern	1929–1931	S.P. Varner
1885–1887	W.H. Davis	1931–1933	J.B. Jones
1887–1888	Whit Brooks	1933–1935	G.C. Bush
1888–1890	C.M. Gallimore	1935–1957	J.B. Jones
1890–1892	F.A. Brown	1957–1966	C.W. Bradburn
1892–1896	M.L. Shipman	1966–1967	Sam Helton
1896–1897	E.S. English	1967–1969	R.E. Robinson
1897–1899	Judson Corn	1969–1986	Harry C. Corbin
1899–1903	W.L. Carmichael	1987–1995	Mickey Church
1903–1904	I.T. Newton	Interim 1995	Sonna Lyda
1904–1905	Whit Brooks	1995–1998	Richard Jones
1905–1917	T.C. Henderson	1998–2002	Terry Holliday
1917–1923	A.F. Mitchell	Interim 2002	Sonna Lyda
1923–1929	T.C. Henderson	2003–Present	Sonna Lyda

*Information provided by Betty Sherrill, Director of Transylvania County Archives, and Jenny Hunter, Executive Assistant of Transylvania County Public Schools.

Selected Bibliography

Items in this bibliography are arranged under the following subheadings: Books, Magazine Articles, Internet Sources, Theses and Dissertations, Newspaper Articles, Law Cases, Proceedings of Meetings, Interviews, Letters and Reports, Video

Books

Allen, Barbara, and Lynwood Montell. *From Memory to History. Using Oral Sources in Local Historical Research.* Nashville, TN: American Association for State and Local History, 1988.

Anderson, James D. *The Education of Blacks in the South, 1860–1935.* Chapel Hill: University of North Carolina Press, 1988.

Ashmore, Harry S. *The Negro and the Schools.* Chapel Hill: University of North Carolina Press, 1954.

Beals, Melba Pattillo. *White Is a State of Mind: A Memoir.* New York: G. P. Putnam's Sons, 1999.

Bogdan, Robert C., and Sari Knopp Biklen. *Qualitative Research for Education.* Boston: Allyn & Bacon, 1982.

Borg, Walter R., and Meredith Damien Gall. *Educational Research: An Introduction* (5th ed.). New York: Longman, 1989.

Brewer, Sue Dempsey. Sylvan Valley News 1900–1907, Brevard, NC, Genealogical and Historical Information, 1992.

———. Sylvan Valley News 1909, Brevard, NC, Genealogical and Historical Information, 1999.

———. Sylvan Valley News 1910, Brevard, NC, Genealogical and Historical Information, 2002.

Brown, Hugh Victor. *E-Qual-ity Education in North Carolina Among Negroes.* Raleigh, NC: Irving-Swain Press, Inc., 1964.

———. *A History of the Education of Negroes in North Carolina.* Raleigh, NC: Irving Spring Press, 1961.

Bullock, Henry Allen. *A History of Negro Education in the South from 1619 to the Present.* Cambridge, MA: Harvard University Press, 1967.

Davis, Cullom, Back, Kathryn, and Kay MacLean. *Oral History: From Tape to Type.* Chicago: American Library Association, 1977.

Douglass, Frederick. *Narrative of the Life of Frederick Douglass: An American Slave.* New York: Penguin Books, 1982.

Du Bois, W.E.B., edited by Herbert Aptheker. *The Education of Black People: Ten Critiques, 1906–1960.* New York: Monthly Review Press, 1973.

Embree, E., and J. Waxman. *Investment in People: The Story of the Julius Rosenwald Fund.* New York: Harper & Row, 1949.

Franklin, John Hope, and Alfred A. Moss, Jr. *From Slavery to Freedom: A History of African Americans.* New York: McGraw-Hill, 1994.

Gordon, Asa H. *Sketches of Negro Life and History in South Carolina.* (2nd ed.). Columbus: University of South Carolina Press, 1971.

Grant, Nancy L. *TVA and Black Americans: Planning for the Status Quo.* Philadelphia: Temple University Press, 1990.

Greene, Gary Franklin, and the Black History Research Committee. *A Brief History of the Black Presence in Henderson County.* Asheville, NC: Biltmore Press, 1996.

Grundy, Pamela. *Learning to Win: Sports, Education, and Social Change in Twentieth Century North Carolina.* Chapel Hill: University of North Carolina Press, 2001.

Gulliford, Andrew. *America's Country Schools.* Washington, DC: The Preservation Press, 1984.

Haley, John. *Charles N. Hunter and Race Relations in North Carolina.* Chapel Hill: University of North Carolina Press, 1987.

Hall, Nathaniel B. "The Negroes of Transylvania County 1861–1961." In Mary Jane McCrary. *Transylvania Beginnings: A History.* Easley, SC: Southern Historical Press, Inc., 1984: 153–190.

Harlan, Louis R. *Separate and Unequal: Public School Campaigns and Racism in the Southern Seaboard States, 1901–1915.* Chapel Hill: University of North Carolina Press, 1958.

Hoopes, James. *Oral History: An Introduction for Students.* Chapel Hill: University of North Carolina Press, 1979.

Inscoe, John C. *Mountain Masters: Slavery and the Sectional Crisis in Western North Carolina.* Knoxville: The University of Tennessee Press, 1996.

Kilgore, Thomas Jr., and Jini Kilgore Ross. *A Servant's Journey: The Life and Work of Thomas Kilgore.* Valley Forge, PA: Judson Press, 1998.

Leloudis, James L. *Schooling the New South: Pedagogy, Self, and Society in North Carolina, 1880–1920.* Chapel Hill: University of North Carolina Press, 1996.

Long, Thomas J., John J. Convey, and Adele R. Cheval. *Completing Dissertations in the Behavioral Sciences and Education.* San Francisco: Jossey-Bass Publishers, 1985.

Marshall, Catherine, and Gretchen B. Rossman. *Designing Qualitative Research.* (2nd ed.). Thousand Oaks, CA: SAGE Publications, Inc., 1995.

McCrary, Mary Jane. *Transylvania Beginnings: A History.* Easley, SC: Southern Historical Press, 1984.

Mertens, Donna M. *Research Methods in Education and Psychology.* Thousand Oaks, CA: SAGE Publications, 1998.

Newbold, Nathan C. *Five North Carolina Negro Educators.* Chapel Hill: University of North Carolina Press, 1939.

Office of the State Superintendent of Public Instruction. *Julius Rosenwald 1862–1932: Negro School Improvement Day Friday, March 4, 1932.* Raleigh, NC: Department of Public Instruction, 1932.

Phillips, Laura A.W., and Deborah Thompson. *Transylvania: The Architectural History of a Mountain County.* Brevard, NC: Transylvania County Joint Historic Preservation Commission, 1998.

Ploski, Harry A., and James Williams. *Reference Library of Black America.* (Vol. III). New York: Afro-American Press, 1990.

Popkewitz, T.S. "Qualitative Research: Some Thoughts About the Relation of Methodology and Social History," in Thomas S. Popkewitz, and B. Robert Tabachnick (eds.). *The Study of Schooling: Field Based Methodologies in Educational Research and Evaluation.* New York: Praeger Publishers, 1981: 155–178.

Purkey, William W., and John J. Schmidt. *Invitational Counseling: A Self-Concept Approach to Professional Practice.* Pacific Grove, CA: Brooks/Cole Publishing Company, 1996.

Sosland, Jeffrey. *A School in Every County.* Washington, DC: Economics and Science Planning, 1995.

Spivey, Donald. *Schooling for the New Slavery: Black Industrial Education, 1868–1915.* Westport, CT: Greenwood Press, 1978.

Stratton, Joanna L. *Pioneer Women: Voices from the Kansas Frontier.* New York: Simon and Schuster, 1981.

Thompson, Paul. *The Voice of the Past: Oral History.* Oxford: Oxford University Press, 1988.

Transylvania County Heritage Book Committee. *Transylvania Heritage.* Brevard, NC: Don Mills, Inc., 1995.

Transylvania County Public Schools 1954. Nashville, TN: Division of Surveys & Field Services: George Peabody College for Teachers, 1954.

Turner, William H., and Edward J. Cabbell, eds. *Blacks in Appalachia.* Lexington: The University Press of Kentucky, 1985.

Van Noppen, W. Ina, and John J. Van Noppen. *Western North Carolina Since the Civil War.* Boone, NC: Appalachian Consortium Press, 1973.

Walker, Vanessa Siddle. *Their Highest Potential: An African American School Community in the Segregated South.* Chapel Hill: University of North Carolina Press, 1996.

Williams, Juan. *Eyes on the Prize: America's Civil Rights Years 1954–1965.* New York: Penguin Books, 1987.

Woodson, C.G. *The Education of the Negro Prior to 1861.* New York: Arno Press and the New York Times, 1968.

Ziegler, Benjamin Munn, ed. *Desegregation and the Supreme Court.* Boston: D.C. Heath and Company, 1958.

Magazine Articles

Bly, Antonio T. "The Thunder During the Storm: School Desegregation in Norfolk, Virginia, 1954–1959: A Local History," *The Journal of Negro Education,* vol. 67, no. 2 (spring 1998).

Brown, Montgomery. "An Educator in the Jim Crow South," *Policy Review,* issue 80 (November/December 1996): 64.

Fox, Adrienne. "Are Parents Behind Ed Crisis?" *Investor's Business Daily* (October 27, 1987).

Gatewood, Willard B., Jr. "Eugene Clyde Brooks and Negro Education in North Carolina, 1919–1923," *The North Carolina Historical Review* (July 1961): 312–379.

Hanchett, Thomas W. "The Rosenwald Schools and Black Education in North Carolina," *The North Carolina Historical Review,* vol. 65, no. 4 (October 1988): 387–444.

Hoffman, Carl. "Selena Robinson: Steel-Willed Angel," *Appalachia*, (Appalachian Regional Commission, Washington, D.C.) vol. 30, no. 2, (May–August 1997): 36–40.

Raxter, Linda Hoxit (ed.) "James P. Aiken," *Transylvania Heritage Today*, (Alexandra's Family Tree House, Rosman, N.C.) premiere issue (summer 1999); 9–11.

Internet Sources

Alcorn, Virgie. "Rosenwald Schools," *CEFP Journal* vol. 24, no. 4 (July-August 1986): 4–5. http://130.111.64.3:86/search/aalcorn+virgie/-5,-1,0,B/frameset&aalcorn+virgie&1,1

Brody, Seymore. "Julius Rosenwald: A Prominent Philanthropist in Both War and Peace" (1996). http://www.fau.edu/library/bro55.htm

Callaway, John. "From Sears to Eternity: The Julius Rosenwald Story" (2002). http://www.networkchicago.com/chicagostories/rosenwald.htm.

Dalin, David G. "What Julius Rosenwald Knew," *Commentary* vol.105, issue 4 (April 1998). http://www.commentarymagazine.com/9804/dalin.html

Department of Public Instruction. "History of the North Carolina State Board of Education." http://www.ncpublicschools.org/state.

Eckman, John. "In Wisconsin, A Simple Idea with a Big Impact," *Newsletter Rural Policy Matters* (July 1999). http://www.ruraledu.org

Hanchett, Thomas W. "Historical Overview" (March 2, 1987). http://www.cmhpf.org/S&Rr/McClintockNewellRosen.html

Haney, James. "A Profile: Dr. James Hefner, President; Tennessee State University," (1998). http://www.tnstate.edu/jhaney/hefner.htm.

Hansen, Carol D., and William M. Kahnweiler. "Storytelling: An Instrument for Understanding the Dynamics of Corporate Relationships." *Human Relations* (December 1993). http://proquest.umi.com/pqdweb

Theses and Dissertations

Batey, M. Grant. "John Chavis: His Contribution to Education in North Carolina." Master's thesis, North Carolina College at Durham, 1954.

Emmerich, Patricia O'Toole. "The Four R's: Reading, 'Riting, 'Rithmetic, and Race Relations." Ph.D dissertation, Kansas State University, 1998.

Gavin, Alsa Franklin. "Beginnings: A History of the Founding of Baptist Churches in Transylvania County, 1795–1865." Master's thesis, Western Carolina University: Lynche's Office Supply Company, 1970.

Holcome, Ransome Ellis. "A Desegregation Study of Public Schools in North Carolina." Ph.D. dissertation, East Tennessee State University, 1985.

Liverman, Milton R. "A History of Nansemond Collegiate Institute from 1890 to 1939." Ph.D. dissertation, Virginia Polytechnic Institute and State University, 1997.

Modlin, Carolyn Carter. "The Desegregation of Southampton County, Virginia Schools, 1954–1970." Ph.D. dissertation, Virginia Polytechnic and State University, 1998.

Petit, Jodi Breckinridge. "A Community That Cared: The Study of an All Black School: E. E. Smith High, Fayetteville, North Carolina." Ph.D. dissertation, University of Kansas, 1997.

Woods, Jerry Wayne. "The Julius Rosenwald Fund Building Program: A Saga in the Growth & Development of African American Education in Selected West Tennessee Communities." Ph.D. dissertation, University of Mississippi, 1995.

Newspaper Articles

"AAA Co-Champs," *Asheville Citizen Times*, November 24, 1963, Sports, p. 1.

Albyn, Nancy. *Hendersonville Times News*, July 31, 1991, Extra.

Broom, Jarvis. "College Students Team with Rise and Shine Program," *The Transylvania Times*, December 11, 2000, p. 9a.

"Brookshire Enters NCHSAA Hall of Fame," *The Transylvania Times*, November 18, 2002, p. 6a.

Carden, Gary. "Tanneries, Buffers, and Cherry Bombs," *The Transylvania Times*, October 2, 2000, p. 3a.

Donaldson, Kelly. "Community Pride," *The Transylvania Times*, February 22, 2001, p. 1b.

Donaldson, Kelly. "After-School Fun." *The Transylvania Times*, December 4, 2000, p. 1b.

Donaldson, Kelly. "T. C. I. O. Celebration," *The Transylvania Times*, July 12, 2001, p. 1b.

"Educational Rally Day," *The Brevard News*, January 28, 1920, p. 2.

"Fabulous Drawing," *The Transylvania Times*, March 22, 1993.

"Glancing Back: New Briefs from November 13, 1952 Issue," *The Transylvania Times*, November 18, 2002.

Hall, Nathaniel. "Reflections on the Transylvania Tanning Company," *The Transylvania Times*, October 9, 2000, p. 1b.

"Help the Colored People! Colored High School Football Game" *The Transylvania Times*, November 20, 1952.

Henderson, C.W. "A Sketch of Old Pioneers and Schools," *The Transylvania Times*, June 9, 1960, p. 1.

Hildreth, Jon. "Community Support," *The Transylvania Times*, September 11, 2000, p. 1b.

"Home Buyer Program to Kick Off," *The Transylvania Times*, August 29, 2002, p. 1.

"In Transylvania County Court to Order Further Desegregation," *The Asheville Times*, March 11, 1963, p. 11.

"James Outlaw," *The Transylvania Times*, February 19, 1998, p. 2b.

Johnson, David, Jr. "Dedicate School Plant," *The Western Carolina Tribune*, October 25, 1951.

"Judge So Orders: Brevard Junior, Senior High Schools Completely Integrated," *The Transylvania Times*, March 14, 1963, p. 1.

"Local Drawing Raises $1000," *The Transylvania Times*, March 22, 1993, p. 6a.

"Mary B. Kilgore: Progress Report Is Made on Jenkins Community Center," *The Transylvania Times,* April 21, 1966,p. 4.
"MLK Day Celebrated," *The Transylvania Times,* January 23, 2003, p. 1b.
"Myers, Young Wed," *The Transylvania Times,* October 24, 2002, p. 4a.
"The Negro's Friend," *The Syvan Valley News,* May 9, 1907.
"North State Cullings," *The French Broad Hustler,* February 4, 1896, p. 1.
"Notice to School Teachers and School Committeemen in Each Voting Precinct of Transylvania County," *The Brevard News,* October 29, 1920, p. 1.
"Notice to Teachers," *The Brevard News,* January 30, 1920, p. 1.
"Notice to Teachers," *The Brevard News,* March 5, 1920, p. 1.
Penney, Ruth. "Transylvania Blacks Were Pioneers," *The Transylvania Times,* June 12, 1986, p. 1b.
Pettitt, Henry G. "Transylvania Tanning Company," *The Transylvania Times,* (November 30, 1989, p. 1b.
Phillips, Edith. "Gray's Days at the Tannery," *The Transylvania Times,* November 6, 1997, p. 1b.
"Racial Discrimination, Prejudice Still Seen as Serious Problems in N. C.," *The Transylvania Times,* January 6, 1994, p. 4B.
"Rosenwald Gears Up for Community Improvement," *The Transylvania Times,* January 13, 2003, p. 10A.
"Schools Opened Here Wednesday," *The Transylvania Times,* September 2, 1948, p. 1.
"Schools to Open on Wednesday," *The Transylvania Times,* August 26, 1948, p. 1.
Stein, Herbert. "A Model of Philanthropy," *The Wall Street Journal,* February 24, 1998, p. 22.
"TCIO 30th Anniversary," *The Transylvania Times,* December 13, 2001, p. 4a.
"TCIO to Celebrate 35th Anniversary on June 3," *The Transylvania Times,* May 25, 1995, p. 5a.
Todd, Mark. "Newfound Portrait Is a Very Special Mother's Day Gift," *The Transylvania Times,* May 6, 1993.
"Transylvania Colored Communication Council Raises $1,625," *The Transylvania Times,* November 13, 1952.
"Tribute to Hunt Scheduled," *The Transylvania Times,* June 1, 1995, p. 9a.
Voluntary Plan of Desegregation Is Adopted by School System," *The Transylvania Times,* June 30, 1966, p. 4.
Whiteside, Lewis F., Sr. "Remembering Rosenwald," *The Transylvania Times,* February 21, 2002, p. 1b.
Wills, Leigh. "Homebuyer Program to Kick Off," *The Transylvania Times,* August 29, 2002, p. 1.

Law Cases

Brown v. Board of Education, 347 W.S. 483, 74 S. Ct. 686, 691 (1954).
Brown v. Board of Education of Topeka Kansas, 349 US, 294. 75 S. Ct. 753 (1955).
Civil Rights Act of 1964, PL 88-352, 88th Congress, H. R. 7152 (July 2, 1964).
Conley et al. v. Transylvania County Board of Education et al., United States District Court, Civil Action File 2094. Copy filed with the Transylvania County Board of Education Minutes (1963).
Plessy v. Ferguson, 163 U. S. 537 (1896).

Proceedings of Meetings

Board of Commissioners Meetings of January 12, 1967 and April 1, 1968, in storage at the County Office, Brevard, NC.
Board of Education Minutes 1880–1968, and 1981, in storage at the Eugene M. Morris Education Center, Brevard, NC.
Deed Books 26, 92 and 97. Register of Deeds. In storage at the Transylvania County Courthouse, Main Street, Brevard, NC.
Ledger: Accounts of School Districts 1908-1909, 1909-1910, 1910-1911, in storage at the Eugene M. Morris Education Center, Rosenwald Lane, Brevard, NC.
Ledger: School Committees and Census Pages, 1930–32, in storage at the Eugene M. Morris Education Center, Rosenwald Lane, Brevard, North Carolina.

Interviews

Andrews, LaMuriel Brooks. February 10, 2000.
Ashley, Roberta. October 17, 2002.
Austin, Patricia. December 4, 2002.
Baten, James. October 21, 1999; March 8, 2000.
Britain, Dee. July 15, 1999.
Brookshire, Cliff. September 23, 2002.
Cantey, F. Douglas. December 18, 2002.
Cowal, Mary. November 21, 2002.
Crite, Eric. February 10, November 8, 2002.
Crite, Jonalyn Johnstone. September 5, 2002.
Crite, Sherman, Jr. November 12, 2002.
Darity, Edith Hutchison. February 23, 2000.
Dodson, Mildred Powell. June 9, July 13, 1999.
Edington, Sherry H. August 29, 2002.
Ellens, Ida Hemphill. June 18, 19, 24, 2002.
Elliott, Keith. January 20, 2003.
Foster, Wanda Johnstone. September 13, 2002.
Gardin, James. May 30, June 9, 1999; July 7, August 21, 2002.
Gardin, Robbie Outlaw. August 21, 25, 2002.
Gardin, Thomas. November 25, 2002.
Gash, Gertrude and granddaughters. June 25, 2002.
Gash, Robert T. March 9, 23, 2000.
Gordon, Frederick L. February 9, March 21, 2000.
Hailey, Annie Marie. August 21, 22, 2002.
Hall, Nathaniel. July 16, 1999; February 14, 2000.
High, Betty Hunt. February 25, 2000.
Hill, Dorothy Pierce. February 12, 13, 15, 17, March 14 2000.
Howell, Samuel. June 9, 1999.
Hunter, Paul. March 24, 2000.
Hutchison, Audrey Norman. February 10, 26, March 8, 2000.

Jamerson, Ann. December 13, 2002.
Jeter, Doris G. September 27, 2002.
Jones, Lillie Madison. November 26, 1999.
Kilgore, Thaddeus. October 16, November 1, 2002.
Lytle, Marva Robinson. February 10, 2000.
Madison, James Arthur. November 14, 2002.
Madison, Reesie Norman. February 22, 2000.
Martin, Neva Whiteside. October 31, 2002.
Miller, N. A. November 20, 2002.
Mills, Ethel Kennedy. June 6, 9, 17, July 9, October 1, December 7, 1999; February 20, March 15, 28, 2000; February 20, March 1, 2001; August 19, September 22, October 27, 2002.
Mock, Dorothy. September 2, 2002; February 23, 2003.
Norman, Myles. March 20, 2000.
Outlaw, James. February 10, 2000; December 3, 2002; January 7, 2003.
Owens, Bernetha. August 22, 25, 2002.
Owens, Daniel. February 29, March 1, 2000.
Owens, Joyce. July 8, September 26, 2002.
Owens, Michael. February 29, 2000.
Putnam, Barbara. September 29, 2002.
Raper, Samuel. July 15, 1999; July 7, 2000; September 29, October 24, November 26, 2002.
Robinson, Alice Glaze. February 24, 2000; October 25, November 11, 2002.
Robinson, Dennis. December 27, 2002.
Robinson, Selena Hall. July 16, 1999; February 14, March 9, 23, 2000; July 10, October 10, December 6, 2002.
Robinson, Willie B. August 27, 2002.
Sherrill, Betty. September 3, 2002.
Smith, Eversta B. October 22, 2002.
Smith, Julia. March 24, 2000; August 17, 2002.
Sticker, Richard. October 30, 2002.
Vaniman, Dottie. June 25, 2002.
Whiteside, Winona Smith. March 3, 5, 7, 8, 9, 11, 13, 2000.
Wilson, Agnes Lynch. February 8, March 14, 21, 2000; October 13, December 2002.
Wynn, Lois Elliott. March 24, December 17, 2002.
Wynn, William. December 17, 2002.

Letters and Reports

Allen, A.T. Biennial Report of the Superintendent of North Carolina for the Scholastic Years, 1932-33, 1933-34. Filed at the Department of Public Instruction, Raleigh, NC.
Allen, A.T. Correspondence to Max O. Gardner 1929-1933. Special Collections: Department of Public Instruction, Box 99, State Archives, Raleigh, NC.
Bradburn, C.W. letter to Transylvania County Board of Education Re update on Educational Matter, January 8, 1960. Filed with Board of Education Minutes, Eugene M. Morris Education Center, Rosenwald Lane, Brevard, NC.

Selected Bibliography

Brooks, E.C. Biennial Report of the Superintendent of North Carolina for the Scholastic Years, 1920-21, 1921-22. Filed at the Department of Public Instruction, Raleigh, NC.

Carroll, Charles F. Biennial Report of the Superintendent of Public Instruction of North Carolina, for the Scholastic Years, 1952-53, 1953-54. Filed at the Department of Public Instruction, Raleigh, NC.

Dailey, Reuben J. letter to Ralph H. Ramsey, Jr. Re Georgia Anne Conley, et al. v. Transylvania County Board of Education, November 9, 1962. Filed with Board of Education Minutes, Eugene M. Morris Education Center, Rosenwald Lane, Brevard, NC.

Erwin, Clyde A. Biennial Report of the Superintendent of Public Instruction of North Carolina for the Scholastic Years, 1944-45, 1945-46. Filed at the Department of Public Instruction, Raleigh, NC.

Erwin, Clyde A. Biennial Report of the Superintendent of Public Instruction of North Carolina for the Scholastic Years, 1948-49, 1949-50. Filed at the Department of Public Instruction, Raleigh, NC.

Joyner, James Y. Biennial Report of the Superintendent of North Carolina for the Scholastic Years, 1900-01, 1901-02. Filed at the Department of Public Instruction, Raleigh, NC.

"Reach for the Stars: Rosenwald Revitalization Strategies." Community Development Block Grant. Focus 20/20: City of Brevard, 2001.

Special Subjects File, Department of Public Instruction, Office of the Superintendent, Julius Rosenwald Fund, Box 86 and Box 87, State Archives, Raleigh, NC.

Special Subjects File, Division of Negro Education, Rosenwald Fund, Box 8, State Archives, Raleigh, NC.

Transylvania County Board of Education letter to Senator Robert T. Gash, April 17, 1953. Filed with Board of Education Minutes, Eugene M. Morris Education Center, Rosenwald Lane, Brevard, NC.

Video

Transylvania Citizens Improvement Organization, James E. Norman, producer and director. *A Sketch of Black Pioneers of Transylvania County.* February, 1994.

Index

AAUW 165
Aberdeen 23
Adams, Everett Lee 136, 169
AGFA 164
Aiken, Flora 145
Aiken, Gracie 91
Aiken, James P. "Jim" 8, 12, 44, 140, 141
Aiken, Jane Rhodes 12, 140
Aiken, Loretta (Jackie "Moms" Mabley) 139, 142
Akorn, Inc. 155
Alabama 69
Alcorn, Virgie 22
Alcovia Orr McCall Endowment 121
Alice's Educational Wonderland 150
Allen, L.T. 147
Allen School 57, 58, 105, 149
Allen School Choir 169
Allison, Allard 49
Allison, E.A. 42
Allison, Geneva 42
Allison, W.H. 42
Alternative School Program 145
America, the Beautiful 96
American Assembly of Collegiate Schools of Business 153
American Baptist Churches, USA 156
American Cancer Society 149
American Council on Education 154
An American Dilemma 121
American Red Cross 138, 139, 149
Anderson, James D. 122
Anderson, Pauline 89
Anderson, South Carolina 83

Andrews, LaMuriel Brooks 73, 76, 38, 118, 169
Appalachia 17, 19, 30
Appalachian Educational Laboratory 87
Arden, North Carolina 42
Armstrong, Bob 125, 126, 128, 129
Armstrong, Mable Kilgore 118, 139, 143, 145, 152, 178
Armstrong, Oscar 143
Ascoli, Peter 27
Asheville, North Carolina 16, 35, 57, 58, 59, 69, 82, 103, 105, 113, 124, 138, 142, 149, 155, 156
The Asheville Citizen 105, 141, 142
Asheville Showcase 54–55
The Asheville Times 108
Ashley, Roberta 121
Ashworth, Donald 175
Ashworth, Nell 175
Atlanta, Georgia 153, 155
Atlanta University 154
Austin, Patricia 52
Avery, James "Sonny" 162
Avery, Jerry 74
Avery, Margaret 94
Aycock, Charles Brantley 102

Bailey, Bernard 94
Bailey, Flora 66
Bailey, Gracie 89
Bailey, Isaac "Battling Bailey" 6
Bailey, J.B. 42
Bailey, Leonard Ossie 106
Baker, Barbara 91

INDEX

Baker, Boyce 74
Baker, David 148
Baldwin, William H., Jr. 24, 28
Ballard, Odell 89
Balsam Range 29
Baltimore, Maryland 105
Barrett & Thompson, Architects 46
Baten, James R. 64, 65, 69, 71, 73, 74, 75, 82, 83, 85, 92, 96, 98, 111, 112, 113, 118, 176
Baten Glee Club 73, 74
Beals, Patricia Pattillo 120
Bell, Joan Mills 106, 139
Benjamin, A.B. 50
Benjamin, Arnella 139
Benjamin, Avery 8
Benjamin, Belle 145
Benjamin, Floyd 91, 139, 155
Benjamin, Maxine 169
Benjamin, Sandra 91
Benjamin, Steve 94
Benjamin, Synetha Glenn Bailey 37, 39, 51, 60, 61, 64, 70, 72, 76, 89, 167, 176, 183
Benjamin, Thomas 74, 94
Bennett College 149
Bennett High School 133
Berry O'Kelley Training School 69
Best, F.S. 57
Bethel "A" Baptist Church 39, 40, 53, 107, 112, 121, 131, 145, 148, 155, 157, 158, 164–165, 167
Bethel Baptist Church 7, 8, 39, 76, 143, 155, 165
Betsill, LaRue 59
Betsill, Linda 74
Betsill, Victor 8
Bianchi, B.A. 69, 70
Bible 2, 76, 96
Biennial Report, 1952–1954 101
Bishop, George, Jr. 136
Bishop, E.E. 42
Bjerg, Dorothy Silversteen 170
Black Empowerment in Atlanta 154
Black History Month 165
Black Mountain, North Carolina 158
Black Mountain Range 29
Block Grant 162
Blocker, Karen 169
Blosser, Amanda L. 183
Blue Devils 112, 131, 132, 133
Blue Ridge Community College 57, 161, 163
Blue Ridge Community College — Transylvania Center 161
Blue Ridge Mountains 29
Board of Education (Transylvania County) 3, 25, 53, 55, 58, 65, 85, 105, 106, 107, 109, 163, 176, 178, 180, 181, 182
Board of Tax Listings (1862, Transylvania County) 29
Boiling Springs, North Carolina 57
Bolden, Mary E. 112, 167, 176
Boyd, Olivia Whiteside 106, 139
Boyd Colored School 43, 45, 46
Boyd #1 School 46
Boyd Township 46
Boys and Girls Club 161, 166
Bradburn, C.W. 106, 111, 112
Bramlett, Rad 128, 134
Branch Normal School 69
Brevard, North Carolina 1, 2, 3, 5, 6, 7, 8, 11, 14, 15, 17, 19, 21, 23, 29, 38, 42, 43, 46, 47, 54, 55, 59, 78, 80, 82, 84, 89, 95, 100, 101, 103, 105, 106, 109, 120, 121, 123, 124, 131, 132, 133, 137, 141, 142, 143, 146, 147, 150, 152, 155, 163, 164, 165, 166, 169, 170, 172, 173, 174, 179, 183
Brevard City Beautification Committee 143
Brevard City Council 110, 118, 149, 160, 165, 166
Brevard College 6, 13, 80, 90, 158, 162
Brevard Colored Industrial School 44, 45, 166
Brevard Colored School 4, 44, 45, 47, 49, 50
Brevard #2 Colored School 1, 2, 49, 140, 166
Brevard # 3 School 50
Brevard Country Club 136
Brevard-Davidson River Presbyterian Church 165
Brevard Elementary School 35, 53, 54
Brevard High School 53, 58, 80, 104, 105, 106, 107, 109, 110, 111, 112, 117, 118, 125, 127, 129, 134, 135, 136–137, 152, 153, 164, 167, 174, 180
Brevard High School Marching Band 155
Brevard Institute 47, 80
Brevard Junior High School 75, 123
Brevard Middle School 152
Brevard Music Center 6
Brevard Primary School 53
Brevard Rosenwald School 1, 2, 3,4, 7, 11, 12, 13, 14, 15, 16, 17, 18, 19, 21, 22, 25, 28, 29, 30, 31, 32, 33, 34, 35, 37, 38, 39, 40, 42, 43, 45, 48, 49, 51, 53, 54, 55, 58, 60, 70, 71, 72, 73, 77, 78, 82, 84, 85, 86, 87, 90, 92, 93, 95, 99, 101, 103. 104, 105, 106, 111, 112, 113, 117, 118, 119, 135, 136, 137, 139, 142, 147, 149, 150, 152, 153, 155, 156, 157, 159, 162, 163, 164, 166, 167, 169, 170, 172, 174, 175, 176, 177, 178, 179, 180, 183

INDEX

Brevard Senior High School *see* Brevard High School
Brevard Tannin Company 9, 42
Brevardier 135
Brewer, Sue Dempsey 41
Brittain, Dee 112
Broad Street 81
Brogden, L.C. 103
Brooks, Eugene Clyde 102
Brooks, Gloria 169
Brooks, LaMuriel *see* Andrews, LaMuriel Brooks
Brookshire, Cliff 125, 128, 129, 130, 131, 132, 133
Brower, A.S. 49, 50
Brown, Hugh V. 17
Brown, Leroy 8
Brown, Ronnie 128
Brown, Thomas J. 70
Brown v. Board of Education of Topeka Kansas see *Linda Brown v. Board of Education of Topeka Kansas*
Buchanan, Jim 128
Building and Furniture Fund 49
Bullock, Henry Allen 24
Buncombe County, NC 69, 115, 132
Burney, C.E. 61, 89, 93
Burrell, Tommy 128
Bus Stop Ministry 145

"Cabbage Patch Magic" 64
Caliex Petroleum Corporation 155
Camp, Ambro 50
Camp, Helen 74
Camp, JoAnne 91
Camp, Margarete 74
Camp, Regina 74
Camp, Robert 91
Camp Straus 162
Cantey, F. Douglas 64, 81, 158, 159
Cantrell, David 128
Carden, Gary 10
Cardoza Business High School 145
Carr, Lewis 9
Carr Lumber Company 9
Carrol, Charles F. 101
Cartledge, Louisa 164
Carver Street 6, 8, 39, 164
Caswell County, North Carolina 151, 152
Caswell County Arts Council 152
Caswell County Board of Health 152
Caswell County Human Relations Council 152
Caswell County Partnership for Children 152

Caswell County Training School 15
Caswell Messenger 151
Catholic University of America 145
CDBG (Community Development Block Grant) 2, 118, 160, 165, 166, 170
Center for Dialogue 165
Central High School (Louisville, KY) 59
Chappell, C.F. 42
Charles E. Merrill Chair 154
Charlotte, North Carolina 155, 159
The Charlotte Observer 130
Chatman, Harold 106
Chavis, John 15
Cheney State College 142
Chicago, Illinois 22, 25, 142
The Children's Center 165
Christian Women's Club 145
Church, Mickey 113
Civil Rights 4, 22, 27, 28, 31, 32, 71, 100, 108, 138, 155, 156, 162, 173, 180
Civil Rights Act of 1964 109, 173
Civil War 13, 27, 30, 40, 42
Clark, Bessie 42
Classical education 21
Clayton, Walt 83
Clemson Theater 88, 114, 115
Cleveland, Ohio 49, 142
Cleveland County, NC 57
Co-ed Theater 9, 114, 115
Coleman, Ethel 37
College Walk 155
Colliers National Weekly 25
Colored District # 1 46
Colored Domestic Science Club 163
"Colored Town" 5
Community Achievement Award 157
Community Relations Council of Brevard 147
Community Relations Council of Schenck Job Corps 149
Concord, North Carolina 58
Conley, Barbara 183
Conley, Cortney 135, 164
Conley, Georgia Anna 106
Conley, Indiana 122, 123
Conley, Justine 139, 169
Conley, Robert, Jr. 106, 128, 129, 130
Conley, Thomas 94
Connecticut 133
Cooper, M.A. 42
Corn, Judson 1, 43, 46
Cornelius Hunt Day 149
Cornelius Hunt Memorial Endowment 149, 162, 164
Cowal, Mary 121, 122, 123, 148, 165

Credle, W.F. 49, 78, 103
Crite, Brandon 169
Crite, Carolyn 155
Crite, Eric 124, 169
Crite, Marion "Mal" 172
Crite, Sherman, Jr. 8, 52, 84, 139, 148, 155, 176
Crite, Stephanie Sanders 139, 149
Crite, Terry 148
Crite, Valeria 65
Cunningham, Eliza 8

Dailey, Reuben J. 107, 108, 109
Damascus Road Anti-Racism Process 165
Darity, Edith H. 80, 82, 83, 84, 96, 106, 109, 118, 120, 139, 143, 169
Daugherty, Freeman 68, 177
Daughters of the American Revolution 99
Davenport, Kay 74
Davenport, Marie 66, 145, 159, 162
Davenport, Minnie (Cantey) 159
Davenport, Steve 91
Davidson River 142
Davidson River School 41, 46
Davis, G.E. 69, 103
Davis, the Rev. W.H. 42
Dawkins, Mack 83, 93, 177
Dawson, Mary Witmer 164
Deaver, John C. 42
Deed Book 26 (Transylvania County) 44
Dellinger, Rebecca 151
Department of Defense 165
Department of Public Instruction (NC) 23, 25, 49, 85, 101, 102, 103, 104
Depression 40
Deshauteurs, Pierre 135
Detroit, Michigan 142
Dickerson Boarding House 137
Discipline 62, 76, 77
Distinguished Christian Service Award 157
Division of Instructional Services (DPI of NC) 104
Division of Negro Education (DPI of NC) 23, 47, 102, 103, 104
Douglass, Frederick 14
Driscoll, Mike 128
Du Bois, W.E.B. (William Edward Burghardt) 19, 20, 21, 22, 28, 31, 32, 33, 60, 78, 87, 113, 122, 180, 181, 182, 183, 184
Duckworth, Charlie 81
Dudley, Lela Benjamin 8
Duncan, Robert T. 64, 65, 71, 72, 91, 96, 112, 167, 176, 177
Duncan, Robert T., Jr. 91
Dunham Music Company 55

DuPont 158
Durham, North Carolina 155, 158

Easley, Governor Michael F. 160
East Forsyth High School 131
Eastern Star 152
Ecusta Paper Corporation 54, 107, 126, 148, 162
Edington, Sherry 64
Edwards, Dickie 128
Ellens, Ida Hemphill 66, 93, 94, 164, 166
Elliott, Brenda 57, 173
Elliott, Cail 106, 139
Elliott, Grady, Jr. 91
Elliott, Grady, Sr. 8, 127, 148, 162
Elliott, Keith 106, 110, 127, 128, 129, 130, 131, 132, 133, 134, 139
Elliott, Trilby Erwin 66, 145
Emory University 15
England 145
English, William 136
Erwin, Archie 139
Erwin, Charles 116
Erwin, Clyde A. 101, 102
Erwin, Kay 74
Erwin, Marshall 76, 139, 162
Erwin, Sara "Mary" *see* Smith, Sara Mary Erwin
Ethel K. Mills Citizenship Award 167
Ethics Committee of Transylvania County 158
Eugene M. Morris Education Center 4, 37, 118, 119, 161, 162, 183
Everett, Randall W. 43
Everett Farm 12
Everett Farm School 35, 43, 50

Farquhar, Robroy 169
Ferguson, G.H. 102, 103
Ferguson, John H. 31
Ferguson, Tommy 106, 128, 130
First Baptist Church 141
First United Methodist Church 165
Fisher, Lloyd 128, 130
Fisher, Ralph 57, 105
Fisk University 3, 20, 60, 78, 142
Flat Rock Playhouse 169
Florida 32
The Florida Sun Review 110, 153
Formulation 153
Fortenberry, Larry 162, 164, 165, 183
Foster, Howard 79
4C Club 143
4-H Advisory Council 165
Franklin, North Carolina 34

INDEX   227

Franklin Park 170
Franks, Rodney 128
French Broad 5, 6
French Broad Baptist Church 43, 166
The French Broad Hustler 11, 141
French Broad River 50
Friendship Baptist Church (New York) 156
Friendship Baptist Church (Winston-Salem) 156
Frog Bottom 5, 6
Fuller, Vivian 154

Gallimore, C.M. 42
Gallimore, Van 42
Galloway, N.W. 42
Garden Club 145
Gardian Angel Award 157
Gardin, Doris *see* Jeter, Doris Gardin
Gardin, James, Sr. 3, 56, 84
Gardin, James Edward, Jr. 106
Gardin, Laura 169
Gardin, Robbie Outlaw 66, 76, 80, 99, 174
Gardin, Ruby 174
Gardin, Thomas 6, 8, 10, 56, 165, 173
Gardin, Vernon 139
Gardin, Will 169
Garren, John 128, 134
Garrett, Adeline 44
Garrett, Barbara 139
Garrett, Robert A. 44
Gary, Kays 130
Gash, Annie 43
Gash, Dwight 106
Gash, Eural 43
Gash, Gertrude 5, 43, 60
Gash, Jerry 94
Gash, Joy 169
Gash, Linda *see* Locks, Linda Gash
Gash, Pritchard 50
Gash, R.L. 42
Gash, Randall 68, 79
Gash, Robert T. 57
General Education Board 103
General Refining Company 49
George Peabody College for Teachers 26
Georgia 7
Georgia Hill 7
Germany 25
The Gettysburg Address 64
Gillespie, George 42
Glade Creek 5, 6, 58, 76, 84, 121
Glade Creek Baptist Church 166
Glade Creek (Colored) School 5, 35, 43, 47, 49, 50, 51
Glaze, Edna Mae 91, 145

Glaze, Nelson 91
Glaze, Pinkie 150
Glaze, Quillie 150
Glenn, Synetha F. *see* Benjamin, Synetha
Gloster, Hugh M. 154
Gloucester Lumber Company 9
Goose Hollow 7, 93
Gordon, Alfreida 74
Gordon, Althea 139
Gordon, Frederick L., Jr. 60, 64, 67, 68, 76, 81, 91, 96, 98, 106, 111, 118, 139, 157
Gordon, Frederick L., Sr. 157
Gordon, Tyrone 148
Gordon, Vincent 74
Gordon, Vinie 107, 157
Gordon, Will 88
Gray, Luther 10
Greasy Corner 6, 7, 93, 166
Great Emancipator 25
Great Migration 25
Great Smokies 29
Green Bethel High School 57
The Green Fly Cafeteria 68
Greene County 23
Greeneville, Tennessee 132, 133
Greensboro, North Carolina 101, 154
Greensboro Opera Company 155
Griffin, Judy 162
Griffin, Norman N., Jr. 106
Grimke, John Foucherєau 14
Guilford County Public Schools 75, 150
Gunn Memorial Library 151

Habitat for Humanity 145, 149
Hailey, Annie Marie Hutchison 8, 39, 64, 68, 73, 89, 90, 142, 176
Hall, Bernard 145
Hall, Dennis Cleveland 140
Hall, Etta Aiken 8
Hall, Jimell 162
Hall, Mamie 169
Hall, Nathaniel 6, 11, 38, 42, 43, 52, 58, 61, 69, 73, 77, 78, 83, 88, 89, 90, 92, 95, 97, 105, 139, 145, 146, 162, 175, 181, 183
Hall, Winston 145
Hamilton, E.B. 42
Hamilton, Larry 128
Hampton Institute 27
Hanchett, Thomas 79
Hardin, Charles 106
Harlan, John 31
Harris, Carolyn 169
Harris, Dottie Hill 23, 123, 139
Harris, Fannye Biddy 108, 114, 116, 121, 162
Harris, J.M. 79

Harris, Julia 145
Harris, Larry "Bubba" 88, 162
Harris, Margaret 74
Harry S Truman's Presidential Committee on Civil Rights 173
Harvard University 154
Hayes, J. Frances 9
Hefner, Arthur, Jr. 154
Hefner, Arthur, Sr. 50
Hefner, James Arthur 139, 153
Heirs of Truth 153
Helping Johnny to Read 145
Hemphill, Charles W. 136
Hemphill, Ethel Ann 169
Hemphill, Gertrude "Gertie" Miles 43, 51, 60, 63, 64, 72, 94, 98, 167, 176, 183
Hemphill, John 169
Hemphill, Lillian 91
Hemphill, Michelle 169
Hemphill, Nellie 95
Hemphill, Paul 94, 148
Hemphill, Rosie *see* Robinson, Rosie H.
Hemphill, Rosie Mae 66
Hemphill, Spurgeon 43, 51
Hemphill, Zeb 175
Henderson, Rosetta Madison 139
Henderson, T.C. 45, 47
Henderson County, North Carolina 43, 55, 105, 107, 109, 116, 181
Henderson Institute 83
Hendersonville, North Carolina 3, 16, 40, 55, 56, 58, 74, 84, 107, 108, 117, 129, 153, 154, 155, 181
Hendersonville Board of Education (School Board) 147
Hendersonville High School 81
Henley, William Ernest 71
Herrin, Ben 42, 63
Herschell, Thomas 137
High, Betty Jean Hunt 8, 40, 68, 95, 109, 110, 114, 139, 169
High Point Enterprise 149
Hill, Beverly 139
Hill, Dorothy Pierce 8, 38, 52, 54, 58, 61, 73, 80, 82, 84, 88, 90, 97, 115, 116, 117
Hill, Dottie *see* Harris, Dottie Hill
Hill, Robert Emory 91, 116, 136
Hill, Sandra 136
Hill, Walter 136
Hill Street School 103, 142
Hill's Parlor 8
Hillview Children's Services Center 161
Hirsch, Emil Rabbi 25
Holliday, Terry K. 118–119, 183
Holtzclaw, R.W. 45

Holtzclaw, T.C. 45
Howell, Cornelia 122, 123, 162
Howell, Herman 106
Howell, Keith 7, 99, 148
Howell, Lewis 106
Howell, Raymond 94
Howell, Samuel 3, 56, 112
Howell, Samuel, Jr. 99, 106
Howell, Willie 106
Huff, Buddy 128
Huffman, Steve 149
Hughey, L.H. 128
Hunt, Agnes 63, 145
Hunt, Charles 74, 110, 123
Hunt, Cornelius, Jr. 110
Hunt, Cornelius, Sr. 59, 89, 107, 109, 110, 131, 139, 147, 148, 149, 162, 170
Hunt, Margaret 110
Hunt, Norma 169
Hunt, Patricia 91
Hunt, William "Bill" 94, 110
Hunter, Paul 65, 69, 75, 76, 93, 96, 112, 167, 176, 177
Hunter, Wayne 128, 130
Hutchison, Audrey 84, 85, 89, 90, 92, 117–118, 139, 143, 178, 183
Hutchison, Ed 8
Hutchison, Edith Roberta *see* Darity, Edith H.
Hutchison, Frenchie 169
Hutchison, Harlan 169
Hutchison, Helen Jean 106
Hutchison, Henry 91
Hutchison, James 50
Hutchison, Ophelia 8
Hutchison, Richard 91
Hutchison, Robert L. 106, 139
Hutchison, Victoria 145
Hutchison, William Henry 8

Ida B. Wells Institute 154
Indian Mounds 44, 177
Industrial education 21, 24, 28, 104
Inscoe, John C. 30
Integration 2, 17, 22, 29, 34, 41, 51, 57, 66, 87, 99, 104, 105, 106, 109, 111, 112, 113, 117, 119, 120, 121, 124, 125, 132, 134, 146, 157, 162, 166, 174, 178, 183
"Invictus" 71

Jackson, Benny 74
Jackson, Bill 143
Jackson, Michael 74
Jackson State University 153
Jamerson, Ann 138

INDEX

James A. Hefner Award 154
Jeanes, Anna T. 24
Jeanes' Supervisor for Transylvania County 48
Jeter, Doris Gardin 60, 91
Jeter, Llellyn 145
Jim Crow 24, 32, 178
John Thrash Farm 12
Johnson, Henry, Jr. 91
Johnson, Jim 128
Johnson, Ollie 128, 134
Johnstone, Coragreene 61, 71, 96, 137, 142, 176
Johnstone, Dr. J.H. 44, 47
Johnstone, James 8, 74
Johnstone, Ruth 162
Johnstone, Vickie 65
Johnstone, Wendell 148
Johnstone, Wilkie C. (Mrs. J.H.) 37, 39, 47, 51, 53, 60, 61, 64, 69, 70, 76, 84, 95, 137, 138, 145, 176, 183
Johnstone School 166
Jolly Twelve 143
Jones, Cedric 153
Jones, Ella Whitmire 65, 74, 139, 162
Jones, J.B. 52, 53, 55, 57, 62, 67, 79
Jones, Javan L. 37, 62, 83, 90, 95, 137, 177
Jones, Lillie Madison 66, 71, 75, 76, 81, 83, 91, 96, 105, 112, 114, 139, 149
Jones, Mary Agnes 63
Jones, Thomas H. 14
Jones, Winnie Belle 89, 90
Joyner, James Y. 46, 103

Kelley, Evon 8, 162
Kelly, Drusilla 74
Kemp, Homer 97
Kennedy, James Thomas 34, 35
Kennedy, John F. 132
Kids in Camp 165
Kilgore, Elizabeth Garrett 143
Kilgore, Eugenia 155
Kilgore, John 143
Kilgore, Leander A."Lee" 44
Kilgore, Mary B. 64, 65, 94, 162, 169
Kilgore, Melissia 89
Kilgore, Pam 65
Kilgore, Richard 169
Kilgore, Robert 91, 95
Kilgore, Rockefeller 136, 162
Kilgore, Sonya 65
Kilgore, Thaddeus 139
Kilgore, Thomas, Jr. 59, 71, 95, 96, 105, 137, 138, 139, 155, 157
Kilgore, Thomas, Sr. 156

Kilgore, Thomas "Tommy" 74, 155
Killian, Annie Bell 8
Killian, Edward 8
Killian, Jim 43
Killian, Maude 90
King, Martin Luther, Jr. 8, 157
King Cotton Hotel 131
Kings Mountain, North Carolina 47, 59
Kingsport, Tennessee 133, 158
Kitchen, Brock 128
The Kitchen Mechanic 143
Knox, Luretha Young 139
Knoxville, Tennessee 44
Kornegay, A.H. 55
Ku Klux Klan 122, 123, 125, 172

"The Land of Counterpane" 64
Land of the Sky Regional Council 147, 149, 160
Lake Lure, North Carolina 137
Leakesville, North Carolina 131
Leloudis, James L. 23
Leopard, George 128
Lewis, Frankie M. 158
"Lift Every Voice and Sing" 73, 90, 162
Lincoln, Abraham 25
Lincoln Academy 47, 59
Linda Brown v. Board of Education of Topeka, Kansas (1953 and 1954) 17, 100, 101, 104, 105, 106
The Link 87
Little Rock, Arkansas 120
"Little Sally Walker" 64
Livingstone College 93, 150, 152
Lloyd, Charles 8
Locks, Linda Gash 74, 123, 162, 165
Locks, Rodney 162, 164, 165, 166, 183
Loeb, Art 126
Louisiana 152
Louisville, Kentucky 59
Lutheran Church of the Good Shepherd 165
Lyday, A.E. (Dr.) 42
Lyday, Randal 125
Lyday, William (Dr.) 42
Lynch, Arthur 139
Lynch, Reginald "Reggie" 125, 128, 130, 134
Lynch, Vincent 94
Lytle, Marva 8, 139
Lytle, Penny 139

M2K Middle School Mentoring Program 155
Mable Armstrong Award in Scouting 122
Mabley, Jackie "Moms" 142
MacFie, Spencer 128

Mackey, Annie Belle 61, 162
Mackey, Cleo 8, 51
Mackey, Gayle 82
Mackey, Mrs. S.M. 42
Macon County 34
Madison, Eloise 110
Madison, Gary 106, 111, 139
Madison, James A., Jr. 139, 152, 153
Madison, James A., Sr. 110, 111
Madison, Reesie Norman 38, 52, 61, 83, 90, 92, 98, 109, 110, 122, 139, 143, 145, 162, 178
Madison, Rosetta *see* Henderson, Rosetta Madison
Madison, Timmy 169
Main Street 81, 140, 142, 155, 183
Marable, John 129
Martin, Neva Whiteside 98, 106, 139, 152
Mary C. Jenkins Community Center 84, 122, 131, 143, 149, 161, 162, 165, 169
Maryland 105, 133
Mass Choir 145
Massachusetts Institute of Technology (MIT) 27
Matching funds 26, 27
Matheson, E.B. 106
May Day 97, 98, 177
McCall, Alcovia Orr 108, 114
McCall, Homer 57
McCants, Linda 139
McGuire, C.C. 49
McGuire, Joe 123
McGuire, P.E. 47, 49
McLaughlin, William 72, 176
Medford, E.M. 57
Metcalf, Don 128, 134
Metcalf, Mike 128, 134
Metcalf, Roger 128
Method, North Carolina 69
Michael, J.H. 35, 69, 70, 115
Miller, N.A. 124, 125, 126, 127, 129, 131, 133, 167, 175
Mills, Althea 65, 74
Mills, Callie 8, 145
Mills, Edith 145
Mills, Ethel Kennedy 3, 4, 23, 34, 35, 37, 39, 43, 51, 52, 54, 55, 60, 62, 66, 67, 69, 70, 72, 73, 75, 76, 77, 78, 80, 81, 83, 92, 93, 94, 97, 98, 99, 112, 113, 114, 118, 120, 124, 138, 145, 150, 153, 166, 167, 176, 182, 183
Mills, Frances 169
Mills, Fred 8, 51, 80, 92, 114, 126, 175
Mills, J.F.W. "Mr. Jip" 8, 44, 50, 56, 84, 155, 177
Mills, Joan *see* Bell, Joan Mills

Mills, Johnsie Lee 66, 107, 139, 145, 162
Mills, Jones 44
Mills, Ora 66
Mills, Philip 11
Mills, Vernon 6
Mills, William 139, 169
Mills, William "Po Bill" 136
Mills Avenue 6, 7
Mills Chapel A.M.E. Zion 39
Miner, J.J. 45
Miner Teachers College 145
Mississippi 136, 153
Mitchell, A.F. 48, 49, 50
Mock, Dorothy 149, 162
Mooney, Carl, Jr. 74, 123, 139, 183
Mooney, Catherine 145
Mooney, Cyrus 96
Mooney, Gwyn 65, 139
Mooney, Mary Alice Wilkes 158
Mooney, Shelia 139
Moore, Gregory 74
Moore, Dr. H.M. 89
Moore, Haywood 94
Moore, LaTonya 169
Moore, Ora 94
Moore, Rhonda 169
Moore County 23
Mooresville, North Carolina 150
Morehouse College 153, 154, 155, 157
Morgan, Harry 57, 106
Morris, Eugene M. 106, 113, 118, 180
Moss, Charles 139, 148
Moss, Eddie, Jr. 136, 148
Moss, Marjorie 162, 164
Moss, Wendell 135
Mt. Mitchell 29
Mountain Lily Lodge #117 155
Mountain Masters: Slavery and the Sectional Crisis in Western North Carolina 30
Mountain MicroEnterprise Fund 161
Mucklerene, Judy 74
Munich, Germany 145
Myers Dining Hall 162
Myrdal, Gunnar 121

NAACP 11, 20, 100, 132, 152, 156
Nantahala Range 29
Narrative of the Life of Frederick Douglass 14
Nashville, Tennessee 20, 49, 154
National Association of Social and Behavioral Scientists 154
National Congress of Colored Parents and Teachers 92
The National Observer 130

Negro National Anthem 73, 90
The Negroes of Transylvania County: 1861–1961 42, 145
Neighbors in Ministry (NIM) 155, 158, 164, 165
Nelson Mandela Humanitarian Award 157
New Bethel Baptist Church 156
New Orleans, Louisiana 31, 82
New York City, NY 25, 155
New York Life Insurance Company 155
Newbold, N.C. 1, 23, 47, 48, 49, 103, 120
Newfound Range 29
Nicholson, R.L. 42
Ninth Avenue High School (formerly Ninth Avenue Union School) 40, 55, 56, 63, 74, 81, 84, 94, 105, 107, 109, 110, 116, 117, 129, 152, 153, 154, 155, 158, 181
Norfolk, Virginia 101
Norman, Alma 169
Norman, Betty Jean 106
Norman, Gwyn 65
Norman, Jacob 162
Norman, Keith 74
Norman, Michelle 169
Norman, Robert 139
Norman, Ronald 169
Norman, Rosetta 91, 139
Norman, Rudy 169
Norman, Rufus 148
Norman, Stevie 148
Norman, Virginia 74
North Carolina 16, 23, 24, 26, 29, 32, 100, 101, 102, 103, 129, 133, 167, 173, 174, 176
North Carolina A & T University 149, 153, 154
North Carolina Advancement School 85
North Carolina Baptist Foundation 121
North Carolina Central University 155–156
North Carolina College (Central College) 158
North Carolina College (Durham) 155
North Carolina Constitutional Convention of 1868 40, 41
North Carolina High School Athletic Association's Hall of Fame 129
North Carolina State Archives 23, 47, 49

Oakdale Avenue 6
Olin Corporation 148, 158
Oliver Cromwell Elementary School (Baltimore, MD) 105
Open Bible Church of God 162
Operation Unity 157
Operational Budgets, 1919–1945 49

Orlando, Florida 110, 153
Ormond, Ben F. 151
Orr, Gurley 50
Orr, L.C. 46
Orr, Walter 42
Osborne, W.K. 42
Outlaw, Bridget 155
Outlaw, Clifford 139, 169
Outlaw, James 54, 76, 79, 81, 114, 139, 155, 183
Outlaw, Sidney 155
Owen, Jesse C. 12
Owens, Bernetha Mills 12, 37, 93, 145
Owens, Carol 123
Owens, Cathy 123
Owens, Daniel 40, 56, 57, 93
Owens, Dora 12
Owens, George Eliot, Jr. 56, 84
Owens, Joyce 123, 124, 174
Owens, Nancy 91
Owens, Pete 12
Owens, Michael 73, 77, 80, 90, 92, 93, 117, 139
Oxford University 143

Palmer Method 97
Parent-Teacher Association (PTA) 55, 82, 84, 88, 92, 118, 145
Parker, Kenneth 128
Parton, George 141, 142
Parton, Mark Aiken 141, 142
Pasadena Research Laboratories 155
Patton, Annie May 86, 181
Patton, Ed 42
Patton, F.H. 42
Patton, J.J. 42
Patton, J.S. 42
Patton, T.E., Jr. 42
Patton, T.T. 41, 42
Payton, Benjamin 154
Peabody, George 23
Peace Corps 139
Pearsall Plan 173
Peddy, Roberta O. 69, 70
Peekskill, New York 75
Peevy, Don 128
Penney, Ruth 140
Penson, Frank Earl 91
Peterson, John 128, 134, 149
Phi Kappa Phi 153
Philadelphia, PA 90
Phillips, I.Z. 41, 42
Pickens, South Carolina 125
Pierce, Dorothy *see* Hill, Dorothy Pierce
Pierce, Mattie 8

232 INDEX

Pine Bluff, Arkansas 69
Pinnacle 5, 6
Pisgah Forest 9, 164, 174
Pisgah Forest Elementary School 53, 86, 87, 181
Pisgah Forest Ranger Station 3
Pisgah Range 29
Pittillo, Dillard 11
Plessy, Homer A. 31
Plessy v. Ferguson (1896) 11, 32, 100, 104
Poe, Edgar Allan 71
Pomp and Circumstance 91
Poor, Ed 42
Prayer Pilgrimage for Freedom 156
President's Committee on Civil Rights (Harry S Truman) 173
Price, David 175
Price, Homer 7
Princeton University 15, 154
Probart Street 6, 52
Progressive National Baptist Association 156
Proverbs 75
Pruden, Emily 47, 84
"A Psalm of Life" 176
Public Policy for the Black Community: Strategies & Perspectives 154

Raleigh, North Carolina 3, 23, 40, 46, 102, 105
Ramsey, John 147
Ramsey, Ralph 107
Ramsey, Tom 106
Raper, Samuel A. 107, 108, 109, 111, 112, 121, 131, 148, 162, 175
"The Raven" 71
Recess 64, 75, 96, 97, 177
Red Cross 138, 139
Reed, Betty J. 182, 183
Reese, Larry 128
Reidsville, North Carolina 132, 152
The Revelation of Saint Orgne the Damned 20
Revitalization 162, 163, 164, 165, 166, 167, 170
Revitalization Advisory Committee 160
Revitalization Block Grant 165
Rice, Thomas "Daddy" 32
Riley, Lessie B. 145
Rise and Shine Program 145, 165
Rising Star Baptist Church 156
Roberts, Dickie 128, 134
Robertson, William 183
Robinson, Alice Glaze 40, 67, 72, 73, 76, 77, 93, 95, 98, 114, 117, 137, 139, 150, 151–152
Robinson, Alvis Louise 106
Robinson, Dennis 136, 173

Robinson, Greg 74
Robinson, Gwyn 65
Robinson, Judy Shea 106
Robinson, Mamie Etta 106
Robinson, Maxine 169
Robinson, Nellie H. 164
Robinson, Ollie 74
Robinson, Richard A. 106
Robinson, Rita 91
Robinson, Rosie H. 74
Robinson, Selena Hall 11, 12, 17, 37, 38, 52, 61, 69, 73, 77, 78, 89, 95, 97, 105, 106, 107, 113, 121, 139, 140, 146, 147, 162, 170, 183
Robinson, Walter 162
Robinson, Wilkie 83, 122, 138, 145, 162
Rockefeller, John D., Jr. 24
Rockingham County 152
Rockingham County's Title I Reading Program 152
Rosemond, Bessie 11
Rosemond, John L. "Johnny" 136, 169
Rosenwald, Julius 1, 15, 19, 20, 22, 24, 25, 26, 27, 28, 31, 32, 33, 78, 100, 118, 120, 167, 170, 171, 173
Rosenwald Community 118–119
Rosenwald Fund 1, 4, 22, 23, 24, 25, 32, 47, 48, 49, 50, 170, 176
Rosenwald Lane 4, 7, 183
Rosenwald Revitalization Project 7
Rosman, North Carolina 12, 83
Rosman Elementary School 53, 57
Rosman High School 57, 89
Rosman Research Station 165
Rosman Tanning Extract Company 9
Rotary Club 113
Rout, Helen Kilgore 163, 166
Royal Pines 137
Rural School and Community Trust Policy Program 87
Rutherford County 41

Sachs, Paul 28
Sacred Heart Catholic Church 165
SAFE 158, 165
Safety Patrol 94
St. John's Episcopal Church 142
St. Philip's Episcopal Church 122, 165
Saleeby, Charles 128, 134
Salem College 152
Sales, Robbie 128
Saluda, NC 80
San Clemente, California 155
Sanders, Bruce 74
Sanders, Buddy 94
Sanders, Jennifer 169

INDEX 233

Sanders, Stanley 11
Sanders, Stephanie 169
Sandler, Edna 139
Sansosti, Glenda 160
Sartor, J.P. (John Pulaska) 39, 51, 52, 61, 76, 77, 85, 86, 93, 181
Schenck Job Corps Center 121, 147, 155
Scholarship Loan Fund for Prospective Teachers 104
School Committee/Committeemen 50, 54, 55, 61, 87, 89, 90
A School in Every County 25
School Law (North Carolina) of 1869 41
Scouts/Scouting 65
Scruggs, Maggie Gardin 122, 162
Scruggs, Paul 128, 130, 131
Sears Roebuck and Company 1, 15, 25
Second Baptist Church of Los Angeles 156
Segregation 1, 2, 6, 9, 16, 24, 31, 32, 42, 60, 87, 100, 104, 106, 138, 162, 166, 172, 173, 174, 175, 177
A Servant's Journey 95, 137
Sessoms, Nathaniel 62, 116
Shady Grove School 42
Sharing House 122, 145
Sharp, Condrey 8, 164
Sharp, Ed 99
Sharp, Henry 11
Sharp, Susie 93
Shaw Divinity School 157
Shelby, North Carolina 107, 108, 153
Shell Oil Company 155
Shepard, I.M. 42
Shiflet, Pete 143
Shipman, E.O. 42
Shook, Danny 128, 130
Shuford, C.A. 42
Shuford, Fred 11
Silversteen, Mrs. J.S. (Elizabeth) 90, 99
Silversteen, Joseph Simpson 9
Silversteen Memorial Park 170
Sinai Congregation of Chicago 25
Sing Sing 142
Siniard, Ray 128
Skerett, Rickey 128
Slater, John 24
Slowe, Martha M. 163
Smith, Ada 66
Smith, Charlie 50
Smith, Clara Elizabeth 106
Smith, Ella Bernice 91
Smith, Evelyn 162
Smith, Eversta Bailey 6, 7, 37, 83
Smith, Harriet 142
Smith, James 169

Smith, Julia 63, 64, 65, 66, 73, 75, 77, 82, 95, 145, 176
Smith, Kemp 97
Smith, Laura 169
Smith, Lewis 50
Smith, Maggie Jane 106
Smith, Nyoka 169
Smith, Richard 94, 148
Smith, Robert G. III 106
Smith, Robert Gudger 12
Smith, Sara Mary Erwin 12
Smith, Sylvia 169
Smith, Tommy 74
Smith, W.H. 42
Solow, Robert M. 27
Some Facts about the Education of Negroes in North Carolina: 1921-1960 102
Sosland, Jeffrey 25
Soul Food Restaurant 166
South Carolina 14, 32, 58, 112, 133, 176
Southern Baptist Association Convention 152, 157
Spanogle, Juanita 166
Spartanburg, South Carolina 48, 88
Spartanburg County, South Carolina 48
Spaulding, C.C. 102
Spelling bees 37
Spelman College 142
Sports Illustrated 132
Springfield, Illinois 25
Stanford University 38
Stein, Herbert 27, 28
Stennis, John C. 101
Stephens-Lee High School 59, 138, 155
Stephens Lee High School Orchestra 169
Stevenson, Robert Louis 64
Stowe, Harriet Beecher 40
Straus, Harry H. 54
Straus Park 148
Stricker, Richard 143
Suber, David 122
Swepson, Irma (Irma S. Mills) 70
Sylvan Valley Festival 169
The Sylvan Valley News 41, 44, 114, 141, 163

Talledega College 142
Talley, W.H. 42
The Tams 136, 169
El Tango 137
Task Force for Better Schools 158
Taylor, Charles 132
T.C. Roberson High School 130
TCIO (Transylvania Citizens Improvement Organization) 71, 106, 107, 108, 109, 122, 145, 147, 148, 149, 162, 163, 164, 165, 177

234 INDEX

Tennessee State University 153
Terrell, Bob 142
Terrell, Ethel 68
They've Been Neglected Too Long 145
Thomas, Hershell 137
Thomas Kilgore, Jr. Center 157
Thompson, G.W. 1, 4, 37, 47
Tifton, Georgia 123, 174
Timothy (Second Epistle) 76
Todd, Mark 164
Townsend, Perry 42
Toxaway Tanning Company 9
Tradition 6, 60, 62, 67, 71, 75, 76, 77, 82, 87, 89, 91, 95, 96, 98, 99, 105
Training 35, 63, 68, 69, 71, 75, 176
Transylvania Beginnings: A History 145
Transylvania Community Hospital 121, 162
Transylvania County, North Carolina 3, 4, 5, 8, 9, 11, 12, 13, 17, 19, 22, 23, 24, 25, 29, 30, 32, 41, 42, 44, 46, 47, 48, 51, 56, 57, 59, 77, 78, 83, 87, 100, 101, 104, 105, 106, 108, 109, 111, 113, 114, 117, 118, 119, 120, 124, 138, 140, 146, 147, 148, 149, 155, 161, 163, 164, 166, 173, 175, 179, 180, 181, 182
Transylvania County Board of Education (School Board) 16, 113, 115, 117, 119
Transylvania County Citizens Concerned for Children 158
Transylvania County Education Association 149
Transylvania County Historical Society 147
Transylvania County Human Relations Council 155
Transylvania County Public Library 172, 176
Transylvania County's Human Relations Council 147
Transylvania Dispute Settlement Center 165
Transylvania Heritage Today 141
Transylvania Tanning Company (also Transylvania Tanning and Extract Company) 6, 9, 10, 68, 92
The Transylvania Times 7, 8, 10, 35, 105, 109, 140, 143, 147, 164, 169
Transylvania Trust 9
Trent, Ricky 128
Truman, Harry S 173
Tryon, North Carolina 37
Turner, Henrietta 145
Tuskegee Institute 23, 25, 69, 70, 153
Tuttle, the Rev. R.G. 42

Unakas 29
United Kingdom 165
United States Air Force 153, 155
United States Army 6, 145, 158
United States District Court, Western District of North Carolina 101, 106, 108
United States Forest Service's National Volunteer Award 147
United States Supreme Court 17, 31, 100, 104, 105, 106, 113, 173
United Way 143, 149, 155
University of Colorado–Boulder 154
University of London 143
University of Michigan 69, 142
University of North Carolina 23, 159
University of North Carolina–Greensboro 155
University of Rhode Island–Kingston 152
University of Southern California 157
University of Wisconsin–Madison 154
Up from Slavery 28
Uplift Club 143, 145

Vaniman, Dottie 52
Varner, S.E., Jr. 117
Vietnam War 153
Virginia Tech 149

Wake Forest University 132
Walker, Raymond 91
Walker, Vanessa Siddle 15, 17
Walker-Wilson, Greg 161
Wall Street Journal 27
Walnut Cove, North Carolina 156
Warlick, Judge Wilson 107, 108, 109
Warren, Earl 100
Warren, Lindsey 126
Washington, Booker T. 23, 28, 122
Washington, D.C. 58, 133, 136, 145, 156
Waynesboro, Georgia 158
W.E.B. Du Bois Award 154
Western Carolina Community Action, Inc. 161
Western Carolina University 3, 129, 157
Western North Carolina Community Action (WCCA) 146, 158
Wheat Fields of Harvest 153
White, David 161
Whiteplains, New York 142
Whiteside, Cecilia 74, 98
Whiteside, Evon 152
Whiteside, Julius 8
Whiteside, LeRoy 8
Whiteside, Lewis F. 8, 66, 91, 139, 152
Whiteside, Neva *see* Martin, Neva Whiteside
Whiteside, Olivia *see* Boyd, Olivia Whiteside

INDEX

Whiteside, Roy 8
Whiteside, Samuel 8
Whiteside, Winona Smith 8, 38, 71, 79, 89, 90, 105, 139, 142, 176
Whiteside Café 8
Whitmire, Charles 136, 139
Whitmire, Ella *see* Jones, Ella Whitmire
Whitmire, James "Tank" 128, 129, 130, 133
Whitmire, Johnny Mack 91
Whitmire, W.F. 42
Wilkes, Craig 106
Wilkes, Kenneth 106
Wilkes, Shirley 169
William, Michael R. 154
William E. Harman Awards 27
Wilmington, North Carolina 14, 63, 95
Wilson, A.H. 155
Wilson, Agnes Lynch 7, 63, 67, 76, 81, 84, 85, 88, 92, 95, 98, 106, 114, 117, 139, 169, 178
Wilson, G.L. (Mrs.) 42
Wilson, G.W. 42
Wilson, Thomas 42
Wilson, Jefferson 42
Winston-Salem, North Carolina 3, 69, 85, 131, 151
Winston-Salem State College 63, 69
Winston-Salem State Teachers College 69, 70, 156, 157
Winston-Salem State University 69
Wisconsin 87
"Without Vision, the People Perish" 162
WLOS TV 124

Woodruff, South Carolina 155
Woods, Tom 137, 138
Woolworth's 155
World Peace Camp 149
World War I 24, 138
World War II 38, 40, 114, 138, 139, 145
Wortham, Mrs. (Teacher) 63
WPNF Radio Station 117
Writers' Guild of America 155
Wynn, Brad 169
Wynn, Charlie 94
Wynn, Clark 74
Wynn, Josephine 162, 169
Wynn, Lindsey 106
Wynn, Lois Elliott 57, 64, 93, 97, 139, 169
Wynn, Lynette 65
Wynn, Reper 106
Wynn, Steve 106
Wynn, Steve Willis 106
Wynn, Ulysses 162, 163
Wynn, William, Jr. 158

Yanceyville, North Carolina 72, 77, 93, 150, 151
Young, Bruce 74
Young, Greg 161
Young, Morris 94, 139
Young, Nadine 65
Young, Robert L. 94

Zachary, J.F. 57
Zebulon, North Carolina 109
Zeta Phi Beta Sorority 152

www.ingramcontent.com/pod-product-compliance
Ingram Content Group UK Ltd.
Pitfield, Milton Keynes, MK11 3LW, UK
UKHW041941140426
5217IPUK00014B/600